About the Author

Pierre Berton, well-known and well-loved Canadian author, journalist, and media personality, hailed from Whitehorse, Yukon. During his career, he wrote fifty books for adults and twenty-two for children, popularizing Canadian history and culture and reflecting on his life and times. With more than thirty literary awards and a dozen honorary degrees to his credit, Berton was also a Companion of the Order of Canada.

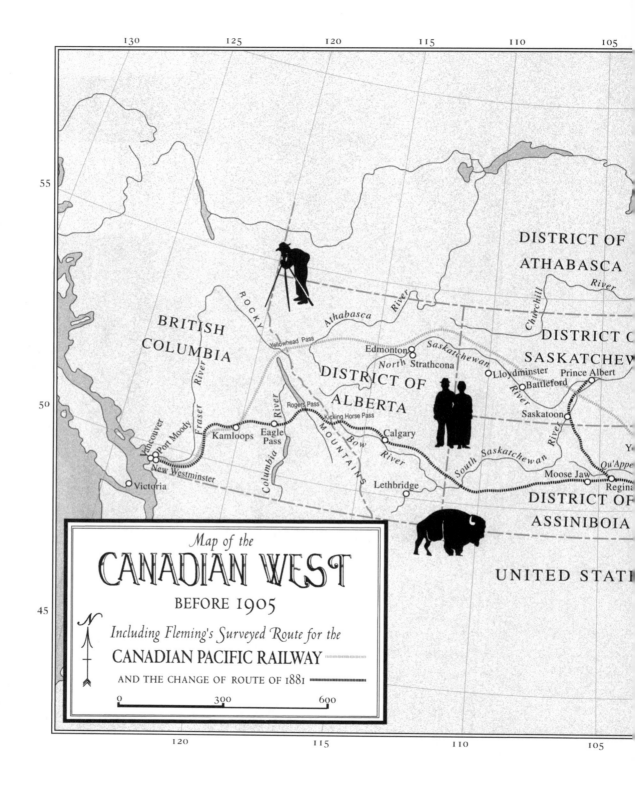

130   125   120   115   110   105

55

DISTRICT OF
ATHABASCA

River

50

BRITISH
COLUMBIA

ROCKY

Athabasca   *River*

Yellowhead Pass

Churchill

DISTRICT O
SASKATCHEW

Edmonton
North   Strathcona
Saskatchewan

Lloydminster   Prince Albert
Battleford

DISTRICT OF
ALBERTA

Fraser River

Columbia River

Rogers Pass

Kicking Horse Pass

MOUNTAINS

Vancouver
Port Moody
Kamloops
Eagle
Pass

New Westminster

Victoria

Calgary

Bow River

Lethbridge

Saskatoon

South Saskatchewan River

Moose Jaw
Qu'Appe
Y
Regin

DISTRICT OF
ASSINIBOIA

UNITED STATI

45

Map of the
CANADIAN WEST
BEFORE 1905

Including Fleming's Surveyed Route for the
CANADIAN PACIFIC RAILWAY

AND THE CHANGE OF ROUTE OF 1881

N

0   300   600

120   115   110   105

95 90 85 80 75

55

DISTRICT

Nelson River

OF

KEEWATIN

Lake
Winnipeg

50

ONTARIO

MANITOBA

Lake
Manitoba

Winnipeg River

Winnipeg   Selkirk   Julius
                        Muskeg

English

Birch lake
(Desolation Camp)

Brandon   Rat Portage   River   Prince Arthur's Landing   Port Munro   Magpie

Portage   Red River   St. Boniface   Hawk Lake   Wabigoon   Red   Nepigon   Dog
la Prairie   Lake of   Rock   Lake

                                          the Woods   Rainy   Winston's   Jackfish
                                                      Lake   Dock   Bay

                                          Fort Frances   Maligne River   Fort William   Sudbury   North Bay

                                                                          Thunder   Lake   Superior   Lake
                                                                          Bay   Nipissing

                                                                                          Sault Ste.
                                                                                          Marie

45

Lake   Huron

Lake   Michigan

100 95 90 85

Cover and interior design by John Luckhurst
Cover image courtesy Provincial Archives of Alberta (B6014)
Map by Brian Smith
Copyedited by Ann Sullivan
Proofread by Lesley Reynolds
Scans by ABL Imaging

The publisher gratefully acknowledges the support of
The Canada Council for the Arts and the Department of Canadian Heritage.

THE CANADA COUNCIL | LE CONSEIL DES ARTS
FOR THE ARTS | DU CANADA
SINCE 1957 | DEPUIS 1957

We acknowledge the financial support of the Government of Canada through the
Book Publishing Industry Development Program (BPIDP) for our publishing activities.

Printed in Canada by Friesens

05 06 07 08 09 / 5 4 3 2 1

First published in the United States in 2006 by
Fitzhenry & Whiteside
121 Harvard Avenue, Suite 2
Allston, MA 02134

Library and Archives Canada Cataloguing in Publication

Berton, Pierre, 1920-2004.
    Pierre Berton's Canada moves west / Pierre Berton.
(Pierre Berton's history for young Canadians)

Includes index.

Collection of 5 previously published works: The railway pathfinders,
The men in sheepskin coats, A Prairie nightmare, Steel across the plains,
and Steel across the sheild.

ISBN 1-894856-74-0

1. Canada, Western--History--Juvenile literature. I. Title.
II. Title: Canada moves West. III. Series: Berton, Pierre,
1920-2004. Pierre
Berton's history for young Canadians.

FC3206.B48 2005   j971.2   C2005-903437-8

FIFTH HOUSE LTD.
A Fitzhenry & Whiteside Company
1511, 1800-4 St. SW
Calgary, Alberta T2S 2S5

1-800-387-9776
www.fitzhenry.ca

Canada Moves West
An Omnibus

Pierre Berton

FIFTH
HOUSE

CONTENTS

Foreword *by Arthur Slade*

You may have heard that Canadian history is boring. Nothing interesting has ever happened in this sleepy, slow country. Ever. It's just one big yawn after another for hundreds and hundreds of years. But if you said that to the Canadian soldiers who took Vimy Ridge in the First World War, the Mounties who rode across the prairies after the Cypress Hills Massacre, or Nellie McClung and the Famous Five as they fought for women's rights, you'd get a big laugh.

The late, great, Pierre Berton would have given you more than a laugh—he'd have given you an earful. He was a remarkable historian and a brilliant storyteller. He may be gone now, but thankfully he has left us his writing. The five books collected here in *Canada Moves West* bring history to life in vivid, exciting, sometimes gross, sometimes amazing, ways.

Wherever you are in Canada, take a look out the window. There are jet trails in the sky, train tracks stitched across the ground, and paved highways jammed with cars. Now, close your eyes and imagine this vast land without any of those things. No cities west of Winnipeg; no roads or electricity; just wild, mostly unpopulated wilderness. Who would dare to build a railway across it?

The first great obstacle to the railway was the Canadian Shield—1,600 kilometers (994 miles) of rock, muskeg, and swamps that could swallow locomotives in one gulp. Then came the flat, treeless prairies. It would be much easier to lay tracks there, as long as you were willing to put up with floods, snow storms, and burning heat. The final task would be to blast a path through the majestic and imposing Rockies to British Columbia.

Berton tells us how our national railway was completed, giving us fabulous details and "explosively" interesting historical tidbits. Did you know that in order to get the railways through the Canadian Shield the builders had to blast the rock with nitroglycerin, a yellow liquid that was so volatile it could only be carried on a man's back? And if that man tripped, well there wouldn't be much left of him or anyone who happened to be nearby. The "navvies," the rail workers, used to love drinking Forty-Rod, a whisky so strong that if you drank one glass you could only walk forty yards before you'd collapse into a stupor. There were "spikers," guys who could drive a spike home in two blows. Or men like Big Jack, who would pick up a nine-metre (30-foot) rail that weighed 254 kilograms (560 pounds) and toss it around like a feather. It was a hard life, but exciting. They were building something brand new: the backbone of a country.

Through Berton we don't just learn the stories of the big players—the prime ministers, railroad tycoons, and generals—we also learn about the lives of ordinary folk who did the grunt work required to build a nation. We travel along with Robert Rylatt in the summer of 1871. Rylatt, a retired soldier, was hired to take charge of the pack train of supplies for a survey party trying to find a way through the Rockies for the new national railway. He freezes; he starves; a man drowns in the river only a few feet away from him; he has to defend himself from a co-worker with a hatchet; he loses his dog in an icy river; and, while he's gone, his wife dies. Did I mention he also gets scurvy?

Then there are dreamers like Louis Riel, who led the Métis in a rebellion against the Canadian government. And there are charlatans like Isaac Barr, who guided thousands of British colonists to a promised colony that turned out to be just a few tents. And there are hard, intelligent businessmen like William Cornelius Van Horne, the CPR's general manager in 1882, who made sure the tracks were built across the prairies in one season. No one believed it could be done, but he did it.

Berton details some of the oddest things. Can you imagine being Wes Speers, a colonization agent, standing on the open prairie waiting for the Doukhobors to arrive? Two thousand men, women, and children appear, marching south to the Promised Land in late October. Overtaken by religious fervor, they throw away their hats, cloaks, and shoes and walk barefoot until their feet are frozen and bleeding. It was perhaps one of the strangest sights ever to be seen on the prairies. If you'd been Wes Speers what would you have done?

There are plenty of other characters, including whisky peddlers, navvies, swindlers, bankers, idiots, and farmers. Settlers travelled across the Atlantic Ocean from England, Ireland, Scotland, and the European continent. Some were rich, while others spent their last dimes for a ticket and were packed into the holds of old, rusted ships, hanging on as the storms tossed them about. When they arrived, they layed track, cut a farm out of nothing, nailed together houses and created the communities that helped build this land of ours. It was a hard life, but they were brave. Many died. Canada wouldn't be what it is today without their sacrifice.

Everything written in these books is real. From the building of the railroad to the opening of the prairies to the cannons firing in the Riel Rebellion—it's all here just waiting to leap out at you. The stories are *so* real that it's as though Berton is leading us down the surveyor's mountain paths, helping us swing the hammer on the rails, or cut the sod along with the pioneers. Canadian history is alive and well, thanks in large part to Pierre Berton. Read on and find out for yourself.

Walter Moberly and the CPR
Geological Survey Party in Victoria,
British Columbia, July 1871.
(COURTESY BRITISH COLUMBIA ARCHIVES, A-01484)

THE RAILWAY PATHFINDERS

CONTENTS

The Ties That Bind

THE STORY OF THE BUILDING OF THE PACIFIC RAILWAY ACROSS THE GNARLED ROCKS OF THE CANADIAN SHIELD, ACROSS THE WAVING BUFFALO GRASS OF THE CENTRAL PLAINS, AND THROUGH THE PASSES OF THREE MOUNTAIN RANGES IN BRITISH COLUMBIA, IS ONE OF THE GREAT EPICS IN CANADIAN HISTORY.

The railway held us together in the days before automobiles, buses, airplanes or broadcasting. Before it was built, Canada was not a transcontinental country. One thousand miles (1,600 km) of rock and muskeg separated Ottawa and Toronto from the West. The prairies were the preserve of the Hudson's Bay Company, and of the Indians and Métis. There weren't even bridges across the great rivers because the Hudson's Bay Company didn't want settlers to invade their private territory.

Beyond the plains stood a wall of cloud-tossed peaks—no fewer than three great mountain ramparts, the Rockies, the Selkirks, and the Coastal Mountains.

Vancouver did not exist. Neither did Revelstoke, Banff, Calgary, Moose Jaw, Regina, or Brandon. They were created by the railway—and so were scores of other towns and villages that sprang up when the line of steel was driven.

We built the West at the same time we built the railway, and so the saga of its construction—and a romantic and adventurous saga it is—is central to our knowledge of Canadian history. Every nation has such an epic—the *voortrek* of the Boers in what is now South Africa, the Long March of the Chinese under Mao Zedong (1934–35), the American Civil War (1861–65), the French Revolution (1789–93), the Spanish Armada (1588). Ours is the only country in which the great epic is the building of a railway.

It's important to remember that the railway builders of the nineteenth century were operating blindly. No one knew where the western terminus would be. No one knew whether or not there were passes in the mountains through which the steel could thread its way. No one realized that there were swamps so vast that they could, and would, swallow an entire locomotive at a single gulp. No one realized the depth of the chasms in the mountains that would require the tallest wooden trestle bridges in the world.

In those days there was no mechanical earthmoving equipment—no bulldozers, for instance—only horse-drawn scrapers. The railroad builders would have to tear their way through massive obstacles using the most primitive of methods.

Yet they did it, joining Canada from sea to sea and shaping a nation in the process. Today we drive from point to point along the Trans-Canada Highway that follows the railway route. We cross the Rogers Pass in the Selkirks by private car. But none of this easy sightseeing would have been possible if the railway builders hadn't done the spadework (literally in many cases) that made it all come true.

CHAPTER ONE

Walter Moberly Finds a Pass

IN THE SPRING OF 1871, A BEARDED CANADIAN SURVEYOR AND ENGINEER NAMED WALTER MOBERLY WAS WORKING IN SALT LAKE CITY, THE CAPITAL OF UTAH, WHEN THE STUNNING NEWS CAME THAT CANADA HAD MADE AN AGREEMENT WITH HIS NATIVE BRITISH COLUMBIA. THE PACT WAS HISTORIC. BRITISH COLUMBIA WOULD JOIN CONFEDERATION AND BECOME PART OF CANADA IF A RAILWAY COULD BE BUILT FROM CENTRAL CANADA TO THE PACIFIC OCEAN. THAT LINE OF STEEL WOULD HELP TIE THE FORMER BRITISH COLONY TO THE NEW NATION.

The story of the building of the Canadian Pacific Railway is long and dramatic. But nothing in that story is more dramatic than the stories of the men who found the route for the line. Nobody can build a railway unless they know where it's going and how it's going to get there. Surveyors for the Pacific Railway were assigned the task of finding the easiest and best route—first across the Canadian Shield (in what is now northern Ontario), then the prairies, and finally through the mountain walls that lie between the prairies and British Columbia. Walter Moberly was one of these men.

No life was harsher than that suffered by members of the Canadian Pacific Survey crews. None was less rewarding. Underpaid and overworked, they rarely saw their families. It was not often possible for mail to reach them. They slept in slime and snowdrifts, suffered from sunstroke, frostbite, scurvy, and fatigue. They often fought with one another, as happens when weary men are thrown together for long, lonely periods of isolation. And yet the surveyors kept on, year after year.

They explored great sections of Canada. The first engineers scaled mountains that had never before been climbed. They crossed lakes that had never known a white man's paddle. They forded rivers that weren't on any map. Each one walked with a uniform stride, developed through years of habit, measuring the distances as they went, checking the altitudes and examining the land with a practised gaze.

Always in their mind's eye they saw the finished line of steel—curves, grades, valley crossings, bridges and trestles, tunnels, cuts, and fills. From 1871 to 1877 they explored forty-six thousand miles (74,000 km) of Canada.

Twelve thousand of these miles (19,300 km) were then charted, foot by foot, by scores of survey parties. Axemen, following the original blazes on the trees left by the first pathfinders, hacked the lines clear of brush. Men known as chainmen—after the long surveyor's chain that measured distances—followed, dividing the line into hundred-foot (30-m) sections, each marked by a stake. Behind the chainmen came the transit men, who figured out the angle of each bend and tried to estimate those distances that a chain couldn't measure.

Behind the transits, the rodmen and levellers worked, figuring out the altitudes, and marking them every half-mile (0.8 km).

And by 1877, there were twenty-five thousand of these benchmarks, as they were called, and more than six hundred thousand stakes scattered across the West, from the Canadian Shield to the Pacific. By then the lives of thirty-eight men had been taken by drowning, forest fire, exposure, illness, and shipwreck.

They were a strange breed—hard-drinking, quarrelsome, jealous of each other sometimes, tough, and often strange, even weird. The members of each survey party wanted *their* route to be the one chosen for the Pacific Railway. But since the surveyors ended up discovering at least seven routes through the mountains of British Columbia, only one could be successful. Every surveyor fought to have *his* route accepted as official. That led to arguments, and sometimes fisticuffs.

Walter Moberly was sure that he knew the best—indeed the only— route through the mountains. That is why he went immediately to Ottawa, to push his case before John A. Macdonald, the prime minister.

Every surveyor tends to fall in love with the new country he explores. Moberly had fallen in love with a notch in the Gold Range (now the Monashee Mountains). This was Eagle Pass, which he had discovered and named back in the summer of 1865 after watching a flight of eagles winging their way through the mountains.

Moberly knew that eagles generally follow a stream, or make for an opening in the wall of granite. And so he followed the route of the birds and discovered the pass he was seeking.

For many years Moberly would tell the romantic story of how he finally left his companions after a sleepless night and made his way down into the valley of the Eagle River. There he hacked out a blaze on a tree, and wrote the announcement: "This is the Pass for the Overland Railway." And, as it turned out many years later, he was right.

Now, in the fall of 1871, with a pact made with British Columbia and survey gangs being assembled, Moberly hightailed it for Ottawa. His rival, Alfred Waddington, was already trying to start a railway company, and Moberly hated Waddington. In fact, he hated anyone who tried to promote any railway route to the Pacific other than the one he had discovered through Eagle Pass.

Waddington was a fanatic on the subject of the Pacific coast's Bute Inlet as an endpoint for the railway. He had explored it. But Moberly was just as fanatical on the subject of Eagle Pass. In Moberly's view, the railway should run through Eagle Pass and down the Fraser River into Burrard Inlet, the present site of Vancouver—south of Bute Inlet. He considered Burrard *his* inlet. He had trudged along its shores before any white man settled there. Now he meant to present his case to the prime minister himself.

Walter Moberly had gone to school in Barrie, Ontario, with a tawny-haired girl named Suzanne Agnes Bernard. Now she was Lady Macdonald, wife of the prime minister. And of course, when Moberly turned up in Ottawa, that spring of 1871, she invited her former schoolmate to lunch at Earnscliffe, the prime minister's turreted residence on the Ottawa River.

Here, the weather-beaten surveyor, with his long, ragged beard and burning eyes, pressed his vision of the railway on Macdonald. With supreme confidence he insisted he could tell the prime minister exactly where to locate the line from the prairies to the seacoast. He went even further. "You can commence construction of the line six weeks after I get back to British Columbia," he said firmly.

That, as things turned out, was more than impossible. But surveyors were not only a hardy breed, they were also an optimistic breed. And Moberly had to add a postscript to what he said. "Of course, I don't know how many millions you have," he announced, "but it's going to cost you money to get through those canyons." The prime minister was impressed.

Moberly was a fighter who came from a family of fighters. He was half Polish—his mother's father had been in command of the Russian artillery at the famous Battle of Borodino, which effectively stopped Napoleon, the French emperor, in his march towards Moscow.

Moberly's father was a captain in the Royal Navy. As a young engineer, Moberly had worked on the Northern Railway between Toronto and Collingwood, excited by tales of the frontier. The Fraser gold rush of 1848 took him west. And there, in 1859, he helped lay out the city of New Westminster near the Burrard Inlet.

It was Moberly who had also located, surveyed, and built part of the historic corduroy road from Yale on the Fraser River north to the Cariboo gold fields, over which thousands of would-be prospectors trudged, or rattled in carriages, or rode on horseback to reach the fabled treasure.

He had as many lives as a cat. Once, while on horseback in the Athabaska country, he was swept into a river and carried two hundred feet (60m) downstream. He seized an overhanging tree, hauled himself from the saddle, and climbed to safety.

But he was a better surveyor than businessman. The road left him in debt. It took him eight years to pay off what he owed. And like so many surveyors of that time he was also in politics. But he resigned his seat in the legislature to take the post of assistant surveyor general for British Columbia. It was in that role that he discovered the Eagle Pass in the Gold Range.

Now he was returning to British Columbia with the prime minister's blessing. He would be district engineer in charge of the region between Shuswap Lake, to the west of the Gold Range, and the eastern foothills of the Rockies. Moberly was about to turn forty. He was as flexible as a willow and as tough as tempered steel. He was probably the best axeman in the country—and every surveyor had to be an axeman to fight his way through the jungles of the British Columbia rain forest.

Moberly never seemed to tire. He had a passion for dancing, and when he emerged from the wilderness, he would dance the night out in Victoria. He loved to drink, and he loved to sing, but as one friend said, "No amount of relaxation and conviviality would impair his staying power when he plunged into the wilds again."

He had as many lives as a cat. Once, while on horseback in the Athabaska country, he was swept into a river and carried two hundred feet (60 m) downstream. He seized an overhanging tree, hauled himself from the saddle, and climbed to safety.

On a cold January day he fell through the ice of Shuswap Lake and very nearly drowned, for the surface was so rotten it broke under his hands. Almost exhausted from his struggle in the icy water, he managed somehow to pull the snowshoes from his feet and, with one in each hand, he spread out his arms on the ice and climbed to safety. Another time on the Columbia River he gave chase in a spruce bark canoe to a bear. He cornered the animal against the riverbank, put an old military pistol against its ear, and shot it dead, seizing it by its hind legs before it sank—all at very great risk, not to mention the terror and the fear of his companions in the frail craft.

He was, in short, a "character." He was vain, stubborn, and very independent. He wouldn't work with anybody he didn't agree with. That was a problem, because Moberly disagreed with anyone who thought there was any railway route to the Pacific other than the one that he had in his mind. He'd been thinking about the railway longer than most of his colleagues— ever since his explorations in 1858. And now, thirteen years later, he set out to confirm his findings.

He began on July 20, 1871, the very day the new province entered Confederation. His favourite mountain area was bounded by the Eagle Pass of the Gold Range and the Howse Pass in the Rockies, just north of the now famous Kicking Horse. This was the area in which he was to take charge.

Between these two mountain chains, the Gold Range to the west and the Rockies to the east, lay an island of frightening peaks—the apparently unclimbable Selkirks. It was in the hairpin-shaped trench around this barrier that the Columbia River flowed, first northwest, then southeast again, until it passed within a few miles of its source. Moberly believed that the railway should cut through the Rockies by the Howse Pass. It would then coil around the Selkirks by following the Columbia valley. After that it would make its way through the Gold Range by "his" Eagle Pass. That would lead to Kamloops and the canyons of the Fraser.

He spent the next eight months in the mountains and trenches of British Columbia. He travelled down the olive-green Columbia with a crazy flotilla of leaky boats, burned-out logs, and bark canoes, patched with old rags and bacon grease.

He trudged up and down the sides of mountains, hanging on to the reins of his pack horses, always with a faithful company of Indians, for whom he showed greater respect than he did for the white man. He said that the Indian, "when made to feel that confidence and trust is reposed in him, will work in all kinds of weather, and should supplies run short, on little or no food, without a murmur; not so the generality of white men."

Like so many of his colleagues, who were forced to fend for themselves in the wilderness and survive, he was a difficult and prickly man. He was also a very good surveyor, which makes his personal tragedy all the more bitter. For, as we shall see, Walter Moberly, the man who first found a pass for the railway, was doomed to disappointment.

CHAPTER TWO

Life on a Survey Gang

To understand a surveyor's life, it is fascinating to examine the story of one ordinary surveyor. For Moberly, certainly, life could be disappointing, but it was also stimulating. But for the men under him — the axemen, the packers, the chainmen, the levellers, the rodmen — it could be pitiless. Fortunately, we have the record of one such man who left a diary behind him. His name was Robert M. Rylatt. He was a former sergeant with the Royal Engineers. Moberly hired him to take charge of the pack train of supplies for Party "S" to survey the Howse Pass in the Rockies that summer of 1871.

Rylatt had a distinguished career as a soldier. He won three medals fighting the Turkish Army on the Danube in Eastern Europe and later in the Crimean War (1853–56). He came to Canada as part of an engineering party under Colonel R. C. Moody, the man who laid out New Westminster, the first capital of the new colony of British Columbia. But for all of his few years in Canada, he was facing tragedy. His wife had become a hopeless invalid, and Rylatt desperately needed money. And so, with some misgivings, he signed on with Walter Moberly for the ordeal of his life.

The job would take him away from his wife for almost two years. His description of that "painful hour of parting" is heart-rending. Rising from her pillow, his wife, Jane, cried out, "Oh, Bob, I shall never see you again."

Rylatt hastened off, "fearing each step to hear her cries." On the steamboat that took him away, he wrote, "I felt as if I had ruthlessly abandoned her, as every stroke of the paddles bore me further from her."

But that was the life of a surveyor in the days of the Canadian Pacific

Survey. Long periods of isolation and long periods of hunger were their lot. But had Rylatt known what lay ahead he would never have signed a contract with the Canadian Pacific Railway.

Once he began there was no way he could quit. He was actually a prisoner in the mountains, walled off by a five-hundred-mile (800-km) barrier of granite peaks and impassable forests, which few men would dare to penetrate by themselves. He thought the job would take a year. He left New Westminster in July of 1871. He didn't get back until June of 1873.

So here he was, a member of Survey Party "S." His immediate boss was E. C. Gillette, an American engineer with a good reputation whom Moberly had known for years. Under Gillette were four surveyors and sixteen men—mainly axemen hired to chop their way through the difficult forests—together with eight Mexican and Indian packers, who carried the biggest loads, and one man, a hunter, who brought in fresh meat. The forty-five pack animals also carried close to seven tons (6.4 tonnes) of food and equipment.

In order to reach the Rocky Mountains, this cumbersome party, loaded down with goods and supplies, had to struggle over hills littered with loose boulders, and make their way through mud holes so deep that the horses were mired to their bellies.

Rylatt was in charge of the pack train. And so, over and over again, he had to go through the tiring business of unloading each horse, hauling him out of the mud, and reloading him. Some couldn't be saved. As he wrote:

"How worried would be any member of the Humane society, could he see the treatment animals in a Pack Train receive, where the animals themselves are only a secondary consideration, the open sores on their backs, from hard and incessant packing, angry and running with humour, over which the Packer, too often, if not closely watched, without waiting throws the heavy *apparajos* or Pack saddle, and as the cinch [*he spells it 'sinch'*] is tightened … the poor beast groans, rears and plunges and not unfrequently sinks down under the pain, only to be whipped again into position."

The axemen moved ahead of the horses. It was their job to hack their way through the massive network of fallen cedars and to cut tunnels in a green tangle as thick as any Borneo jungle. After that they laid down patches of corduroy—literally a wooden roadway made of logs—for the animals to cross.

The men pushed straight across the Selkirk Mountains into the Kootenay country. They didn't reach the upper Columbia until late September. They headed down this roaring river on rafts and in small canoes, watching with growing alarm as it swelled in size with every mile. On the third day, the raft on which Rylatt was travelling hit a submerged log in the rapids and was sucked under. The five men on the raft leaped for the shore. One fell short, the current pulled him under with the raft, and he was never seen again.

At the mouth of the Blaeberry River, which flows down from the summit of Howse Pass to join the Columbia, the axemen were faced with a daunting task. It was their job to chop a pathway to the top, through forests that had not been trodden since the pass had been discovered a dozen years before. The autumn winds had reduced the country to a muck so thick that one mule couldn't be pulled out of it. Rylatt was forced to shoot him in his swampy prison.

And yet there were moments of great beauty and mystery. And here among the silent peaks Rylatt was moved. On his first Sunday in the mountains he found himself alone—the others were working five miles (8 km) farther up the pass. This was his first experience in the wilderness and he made the most of it.

He watched the sun drop down behind the glaciers on the mountaintops. The day's dying light tipped the snows with a gold that turned to red, while in the shadowed gorges the ice could be seen in long streaks of filmy blue. Rylatt watched as the glow left the peaks and the gloom filled up the valleys. He continued to watch as velvet night followed ghostly twilight. And he saw the pale rays of the northern lights compete with the stars to cast softening halos of light on those everlasting snowfields.

Then suddenly he began to shiver. A sense of terrible loneliness overcame him. It was the silence—the uncanny overpowering silence of the Canadian wilderness. Not a leaf stirred, no insect hummed, not even the noise of the water in the creek far away broke the silence. Rylatt listened for a sound, but he didn't hear even the rustle of a falling leaf. He made a fire. It wasn't that he wanted just to keep warm, he wanted to hear *something*—

the crackling of the wood—to break the loneliness. It occurred to him that no one who had not experienced what he was going through would ever understand what it was like to be truly alone.

He wrote in his diary: "Your sense of being alone in the heart of the city, or even in a village, or within easy distance of fellow beings … gives you no claim to use the term 'alone'. You may have the feeling peculiar to being alone—that is all. Listen sometime when you think you are alone … can you hear a footfall; a door slam in the distance; a carriage go by? Or the rumble of one …? Can you hear a dog bark? Have you a cricket on the hearth or even the ticking of a clock …?"

Now he realized for the first time that the tiniest of sounds could give a feeling of relief—"the sense of knowing your species are at no great distance." But here, in the solitude of the Rockies, there was only the terrible silence.

His sense of isolation was increased by the onset of winter. The mail did not come. Now Gillette and his men began chopping their pathway to the top of the pass. By the time the trail was opened on October 26, the snow was already falling.

The next day, with eight inches (20 cm) blanketing the mountains, Walter Moberly and the surveyors gathered at the summit of the Howse Pass, ready at last to start work. But the instruments were so full of water they were useless, while the slopes were so slippery with wet snow that no man could maintain a footing.

The next day another foot (30 cm) of snow fell. Now the engineers realized that nothing more could be done. The party settled down for a long winter at the foot of the pass about one hundred miles (160 km) north of the present site of Banff. It would be May before the mountain trails would be passable again. For those sections that ran through the canyons it would be much later.

It wouldn't really be safe to travel with loaded pack horses before June. Even then the mountain torrents could be crossed only with difficulty, being swollen with melting snow from above. And so the twenty-nine members of the party, including (as it turned out) two ex-convicts, were faced with each other's company for six or seven months.

Every man in that party worried about getting his mail and getting his wages. Because of bungling it would be months before they saw a pay-cheque. A civil servant in Victoria—a political appointee—had kept the money, banked it, and taken the interest for himself. And the mail wasn't forwarded. It lay around for months in various post offices, because no plans had been made to handle it. To get it, one of the packers set off in late November for Wild Horse Creek, a five-hundred-mile (800-km) journey on snowshoes.

He brought some letters back, but none for Rylatt, who was sick with worry over his wife's condition. That night he scribbled in his diary, "Poor wife, are you dead or alive? Have the two deposits of money I sent reached you? It may easily be understood in my case, how hard it is to receive no word, no sign, and altogether I am very miserable."

The only link with civilization was Walter Moberly himself. He left camp on December 4, heading for New Westminster. En route he planned to trek across the high barrier of the Selkirk Mountains, hoping to find a pass for the railway somewhere in that wilderness of jagged peaks. He took one man with him, a Frenchman named Verdier who had just learned that his wife had eloped, leaving their five children alone. Rylatt sent a note with some money to his own wife with Verdier, knowing there would be no further word from her until the following May or June.

New Westminster, the nearest pinpoint of civilization, was four hundred miles (640 km) away, but Moberly travelled it as casually as if he were setting off on a pleasant Sunday hike. He went straight over the tops of the glaciers that cover the Selkirks, hoping to find a gap in that mountain wall through which the railway might go. On New Year's Day, 1872, he was all alone in an abandoned trapper's hut. He wrote in his diary, "I think it ... one of the most wretched and dreary places I ever saw ... this was the most wretched New Year's Day I ever spent."

In spite of his long trek across the Selkirk Mountains, Walter Moberly did not find what he was seeking. When he reached Victoria he reported to his boss, Sandford Fleming in Ottawa, that there was no practical pass through that long rampart of chiselled peaks. He would have to find some other way of getting the railway through British Columbia to the coast.

CHAPTER THREE

"The Jolly C.P.S."

BY 1872, SANDFORD FLEMING, MOBERLY'S BOSS, HAD DISPATCHED TWENTY-ONE SURVEY PARTIES — A TOTAL OF EIGHT HUNDRED MEN — ACROSS THE COUNTRY TO LAY OUT THE ROUTE OF THE PACIFIC RAILWAY.

The engineer-in-chief was a huge man with a vast beard and an awesome reputation. At the age of forty-five he still had half his life ahead of him in which to complete the Intercolonial Railway in the Maritimes, plan the Canadian Pacific, devise a workable system of Standard Time, promote the Pacific cable, act as ambassador to Hawaii, publish a book of short prayers, become chancellor of Queen's University in Kingston, Ont., girdle the globe, and cross Canada by foot, snowshoe, dog team, horseback, dugout canoe, and, finally, by rail.

He was a dedicated amateur, whose interests ranged from a study of early steamboats to colour blindness. He was a competent artist, a better than average chess player, an amateur lawyer, a graceful public speaker, a prolific diarist and author who, at his death, had some 150 articles, reports, books, and pamphlets to his credit. It was Fleming who, back in 1862, had come up with the first credible plan for a Pacific railway. Now it was his task to put that plan into practice.

It would not be easy.

A very special kind of man was needed, and, as Fleming reported after his first season, it was impossible to find enough of them.

"Many of those we were obliged to take," he wrote, "were unequal to the very arduous labour they had to undergo," causing a very considerable delay and difficulty in pushing the work.

Fleming was soon reporting that it was impossible to hire the kind of men he needed for the survey. In 1871, for example, two crews in northern

Ontario simply gave up the ghost. One party had had enough by the late summer; the second, learning they would be required to stay out all winter, "suffered a few days of cold and snow, and then promptly trooped into Fort Garry" near present-day Winnipeg. There weren't enough good men to do the job and Fleming and his staff had to employ incompetents.

The wonder was that anyone worked on the surveys at all. In spite of the difficulty of getting men each year, there was little job security—even for the most experienced engineers. Crews were dropped at the end of the summer, and left without any winter work, and not rehired again until the following spring.

They led a lonely, remote existence—cut off from news of family, friends, or the world at large, in a land where the Native rites and customs were as foreign as those of an Oriental kingdom. One surveyor, Henry Cambie (a street in Vancouver is now named for him), found that out. Exploring the east branch of the Homathco River in central British Columbia, Cambie came upon a band of Indians who were so far away from civilization that many of the women had never seen a beard "and would not believe that mine really grew on my chin."

Another surveyor named Jason Allard, who worked for Moberly, made the mistake of accepting an invitation to visit an Indian lodge. He made the second mistake of sitting on a bear rug next to a good-looking Indian woman. He realized too late that this was the same as an offer of marriage. The only way he could get out of it was to trade her back to her father for a handsome finger ring.

And yet they went out, year after year—men who for the most part were tough, intelligent, and uncomplaining. They drank heavily. And when they drank they sang their theme song—the song of the Canadian Pacific Survey:

Far away from those we love dearest,
Who long and wish for home,
The thought of whom each lone heart cheereth,
As 'mid these North-west wilds we roam,
Yet still each one performs his duty
And gaily sings:

Tra, la, la, la, la, la, la, la, la, la, la
Hurra! The jolly C.P.S.!
They're at home upon Superior's shore,
Hurra! we'll drink to them success,
And a safe return once more.

But it was often a nightmare just to reach that "home upon Superior's shore." Charles Aeneas Shaw, who was with the survey for the whole of its existence, remembered his own initiation in November of 1872. Shaw, then eighteen years old, was hired as a packer by a party trying to locate a line west from Prince Arthur's Landing (now Thunder Bay, Ontario).

The trick was to try to reach the landing before winter sealed off the lake. The survey party tried first in a tiny little steamer, the *Mary Ward*. The boat hit a reef in a howling blizzard, and three of the men drowned. The rest returned to Toronto and picked up new kits and then set off again.

They made their way overland to Duluth in the United States. There they offered to pay as much as $2,500 for a tugboat to take them up the lake. But conditions were so desperate no seasoned skipper would attempt the crossing. However, the party bought a small fishing boat and in mid-December started rowing and sailing to their destination.

Imagine the situation! The temperature sank to 52 degrees below zero (−47ºC)—so cold that each crewman had to chip from the blades of his oars a ball of ice the size of a man's head. They crept along the shoreline, sleeping in the snow at night, living on frozen pork and hardtack, and even surviving a full-force gale. On New Year's Day the lake froze and they abandoned the boat. They built toboggans out of strips sawn from frozen birch logs, and then hiked with their supplies the last fifty miles to Prince Arthur's Landing.

Such hardships were commonplace. One man, J. H. E. Secretan, was reduced to eating rose haws washed down with swamp water during a survey near Lake Nepigon in 1871. That same year—the year in which Robert Rylatt was toiling in the Rockies—seven members of a survey supply party were lost near Jackfish River in northern Ontario, as a result of a forest fire so hot the very soil was burned away. Only one body was found. Of the remainder there was no trace, except for six holes scratched out in a nearby swamp and apparently left behind when the smoke grew too thick.

It was difficult to get supplies to these isolated men, and that resulted in costly delays and bitter arguments. Henry Carre, in charge of a party working out of Lac des Isles in the Thunder Bay area, found himself in a country through which no white man had ever travelled. He couldn't finish his survey because his supplies couldn't reach him, and he had to turn back. Otherwise, he said, "I verily believe the whole party would have been starved to death."

Another surveyor, working near Long Lake north of Superior that same year, had to take his party off surveying to pick blueberries to save their lives. The group had had nothing to eat for a week.

One survey party, working north of Wabigoon west of Prince Arthur's Landing, were caught by the winter without toboggans, tents, clothing, or boots. Their leader, William Kirkpatrick, a resourceful man, made forty pairs of snowshoes and thirty toboggans with his own hands. Then he sewed up a tent out of canvas and borrowed another made of skins from the Indians so his people wouldn't freeze to death.

In the winter of 1871 in the Thompson River country of central BC, forty miles (64 km) out of Kamloops, one survey party lost almost all of its pack animals. Eighty-six died from cold, hunger, or overwork.

There was an even worse work expedition in 1875. The leader of that party, E. W. Jarvis, was given the job of examining the Smoky River Pass in the northern Rockies. He set off in January with two companions, six Indians, and twenty dogs.

The stories he and his comrades have left behind present an uncanny series of spectacles—almost like a sequence in a modern motion picture:

- the eerie figure of Alec McDonald in charge of the dog trains, knocking on the door of the shack in 49 below zero (−45°C) weather, sheathed in ice from head to toe.
- the spectacle of the lead dog who made a feeble effort to rise, gave one final flick of his tail, and rolled over dead. His legs were frozen stiff to the shoulders.
- the weird noises heard one night by the entire party—the distinct but ghostly sound of a tree being felled two hundred yards (183 m) away, without any signs of snowshoes or axemanship to be seen the following morning.

The Jarvis party travelled light, with two blankets for each man and a single piece of light cotton sheeting for a tent. They moved through a land that had never been explored. A good deal of the time they had no idea where they were.

They camped out in temperatures that had dropped to 53 below (–47ºC). They fell through thin ice and had to climb out soaked to the skin, with their snowshoes still tied to their feet. They stumbled down deep canyons and found the way blocked by frozen waterfalls two hundred feet (61 m) high.

One day they experienced a sudden change of temperature. It went from 42 below (-41ºC) to 40 above (4ºC). This brought on a strange weariness—as if they were suddenly plunged into the tropics.

One morning, while mushing down a frozen river, they turned a corner and saw an abyss yawning before them. The entire party was perched on an ice ledge of a frozen waterfall 210 feet (64 m) high. And the ledge itself was no more than two feet (0.6 m) thick!

One night they camped below a blue glacier when, without warning, great chunks of it gave way. Above them they could see masses of ice and rock chasing one another and leaping from point to point "as if playing some weird, gigantic game." One chunk of limestone, ten feet (3 m) thick, scudded past them, tearing a tunnel through the trees before it plunged into the river.

By March the dogs were dying. Even the Indians were in a mournful state of despair, declaring they would never see their homes again and weeping bitterly. Jarvis was very thin and very white and very quiet. They had reached the Smoky Pass but Jarvis was doubtful about going farther. His assistant, C. F. Hannington, said however that he would rather starve than turn back. And now it began to look as if he would.

"I have been thinking of 'the dearest spot on earth to me,'" Hannington wrote in his journal, "—of our Mother and Father and all my brothers and sisters and friends—of the happy days at home—of all the good deeds I have left undone and all the bad ones committed. If ever our bones will be discovered, when and by whom. If our friends will mourn long for us or do as is often done, forget us as soon as possible. In short, I have been looking death in the face …"

Meanwhile, Jarvis felt a curious kind of numbness taking hold of his limbs. They pushed forward on their snowshoes looking like men marking time in slow motion. And yet they made it.

Hannington had lost thirty-three pounds (15 kg); Jarvis was down to a bony 125 (57 kg). When they were finally given food in Edmonton, in what is now Alberta, they fell sick and began to vomit, but still they kept on across the blizzard-swept prairies until they reached Fort Garry. They had spent 116 days on the trail, and had travelled 1,887 miles (3,037 km). Nine hundred and thirty-two of those miles (1,500 km) were covered on snowshoes. When the dogs died they carried on with all of their goods on their backs.

Why did they do it? Why did any of them do it? They certainly didn't do it for profit. There was little enough of that. Nor did they do it for adventure—there was too much of that.

The answer seems clear from what they wrote and what they did. Each man did it for glory. Each man was driven by the slender, but always present hope, that someday his name would be recognized and placed on the map, on a mountain peak, or a river, or an inlet, or—glory of glories—would go into the history books as the one who had bested all others and located the route for the great railway.

CHAPTER FOUR

Moberly Disobeys Orders

EVEN THOUGH WALTER MOBERLY HADN'T FOUND A WAY THROUGH THE HIGH SELKIRK MOUNTAINS, HE WAS CONVINCED THAT HE HAD FOUND THE RIGHT PASS THROUGH THE ROCKIES. THE HOWSE PASS WAS HIS PASS; HE HAD FOUND IT, HE HAD SURVEYED IT, HE OWNED IT. HE WAS ABSOLUTELY SURE THAT THIS WAS THE ONLY ROUTE THE RAILWAY COULD TAKE. AFTER THAT IT WOULD HAVE TO GET AROUND THE SELKIRKS BY FOLLOWING THE BIG BEND OF THE COLUMBIA RIVER, AND THEN WORK ITS WAY THROUGH THE GOLD RANGE BY THE EAGLE PASS, WHICH HE HAD ALSO DISCOVERED.

In spite of the fact that Sandford Fleming had twenty-one teams of surveyors out searching for different routes, Walter Moberly was convinced that his route was the only one that would work. He was so sure of himself that without anybody's permission he started to locate an actual line for the railway through the Howse Pass.

Moberly figured he would get the permission later and that Fleming, his boss, would back him. But all that Fleming wanted and agreed to was known as a simple "trial line" through the pass. That simply meant a series of blazes on trees to find out if it were at all practical for a railway.

Moberly was planning something far more ambitious—and without permission! He wanted a detailed *location* survey. That is the kind that engineers make only when finally, through exploration and trial lines, they have firmly decided on the route.

Moberly hadn't done that. He'd walked through the pass, but made only a brief investigation of a route from the summit to the Columbia River. All the same, that spring of 1872, he set about hiring extra men, taking on trains of pack animals, and buying thousands of dollars' worth of supplies, great quantities of which he planned to cache at Eagle Pass. He figured it would take two seasons to locate the line. He and his men were prepared to stay out all winter.

And then just four hours before he and his party were scheduled to leave Victoria, the British Columbia capital on Vancouver Island, for the interior, he received a staggering blow. A telegram arrived, literally at the eleventh hour, since the boat was scheduled to leave at three in the morning. It was from Fleming announcing that another pass had officially been adopted for the route of the Canadian Pacific Railway.

Fleming's pass, far to the north, was the Yellowhead Pass two hundred miles (320 km) west of present-day Edmonton. The chief surveyor ordered Moberly to abandon the Howse Pass and to move his survey parties north. He would go by way of the Athabasca Pass, and then take charge of a survey through the Yellowhead. All Moberly's dreams dissolved at that moment. "His" route was not to be *the* route, after all.

He rushed to Portland, Oregon, where he had to buy his way out of the costly contracts he'd signed. Unfortunately, most of the supplies that he ordered had already been dispatched to the remote mountain areas where they could never be used. Seven thousand dollars' worth were abandoned forever at the Eagle Pass.

Another problem raised its head. Moberly would need to hire pack trains to move men and supplies from the original position, north to the Athabaska country where Fleming wanted him. But it was late in the season. Most pack trains were engaged far in advance, when it was cheap to rent pack animals. Moberly realized that if the packers knew his problem, they would hike up the prices. So he'd have to get around the packers who were heading for the Howse Pass, race on ahead of them, intercept them, and then reorder the horses for the Yellowhead survey before the owners caught on to the change of plans.

Off he went. First he headed through Oregon by stagecoach, which broke down. And then by steamboat, which sank. He continued on through the state of Washington on horseback, and re-entered British Columbia in the Kootenay country. There he successfully intercepted the packers and hired them all, together with four hundred horses. Hacking a trail through the jungle-like growth as he went, he finally reached the Columbia River.

On May 15, he reached his party at the Howse Pass, told them the route had been abandoned and the party must move north to the Athabaska country, and to the despised Yellowhead Pass. Fleming, who was travelling across Canada along the proposed future line of the railway, had agreed to meet him there. But it was heavy going for Moberly. The pack trail had literally to be carved, foot by foot, out of the tangle of falling cedars that barred the way up through the cavernous valleys of the Columbia, the Thompson, and the Albreda Rivers.

He finally reached the Yellowhead in early September. One day, just west of Jasper House, he came upon fresh tracks, which the Indians told him were those of "men of the East." A short time later he ran into the Reverend Doctor James Grant, who was the principal of Queen's University and Fleming's companion on his trans-Canada trek. Grant carried a long stick in his hand and was "driving some worn-out and very dilapidated pack animals."

The meeting that followed must have been disagreeable to both Moberly and Fleming. Grant didn't mention it in his book about the trip. He simply wrote that Moberly's was the first face they had seen since leaving the prairies. To meet him, Grant said, was "like reopening communication with the world … how welcome he was, we need not say!" Fleming thought differently.

That evening everybody had a glass of punch and a cigar on Fleming. They drank toasts to the Queen and to the country. Moberly put Grant in a good humour because he had some oatmeal, and so the minister could finally enjoy a Sunday breakfast of porridge for the first time in many days. Fleming decided to wait until the Sunday service was over before confronting Moberly. The twenty-one men from both sides of the mountains—English, Scots, Irish, and Indians—representing every one of the six Canadian provinces, joined in the hymn singing. Grant preached a sermon. Then, finally, Moberly made his report to his chief.

This must have been a painful interview. Fleming was aghast at the slow progress made, and even more by Moberly's reckless spending on useless supplies, tons of which had been left forever at Eagle Pass. "It seemed to me as if some country store had been bought out when I first saw the account," he later recalled. Imagine: four hundred pack horses! Why so many? The engineer couldn't understand it. He decided to fire Moberly but then realized he couldn't afford to do that. Somebody had to take charge at the Yellowhead and push the surveys forward. Moberly was the only one with enough experience.

Moberly was disgusted with Fleming and not about to take a verbal spanking from him. In abandoning his pet line, he thought Fleming had been positively "unpatriotic." To use any other pass than his, was, in his own mind, little short of treason.

He was prepared to leave the service, but he couldn't because of the men and animals he had left to winter at the Howse Pass. He knew that they relied on him to see them safely through. After Fleming and his party had left, Moberly began to worry over the slow progress of the survey under his command. Bad luck seemed to dog his footsteps. The parties were taking a long time to arrive. In fact, with Moberly out of the way, they had simply sat down to wait out the winter.

CHAPTER FIVE

The Ordeal of Robert Rylatt

BY THE END OF 1871 ROBERT RYLATT HAD COME TO THE END OF HIS TETHER. HE FELT HE HAD REACHED THE VERY BOTTOM. MOBERLY HAD GONE ON HIS WILD GOOSE CHASE ACROSS THE SELKIRKS. THEN ONE DAY RYLATT CUT HIS THUMB AND OPENED A SMALL ROLL OF BANDAGE MATERIAL HIS WIFE HAD STOWED IN HIS KIT. IT BROUGHT BACK SAD MEMORIES.

"When I saw scraps of oiled silk, fingers of old gloves, and the softest of lint, how tenderly I felt towards her, but when a slip of paper came to light, on which were the words 'God bless you, Bob' it made me feel wretched …"

On Christmas Day the thermometer dropped to 34 below zero (−37ºC). The following day the mercury froze solid. Although Christmas dinner was served piping hot, the food was frozen to the plates before the men could consume it.

By New Year's Eve 1871—the same evening that saw Moberly alone in a cabin in the Selkirks—Rylatt felt he had reached rock bottom. He and four others sat in their cabin seeing the old year out, trying to keep warm. Though a rousing fire had been lit, each man had to change position constantly so that the side of his body away from the heat did not become numbed with cold.

They talked of their wives and other adventures they had had, but there was no mirth. When they looked at their watches and saw that it was the New Year, they crept into their blankets. It was quite a time before Rylatt slept, for his brain was haunted by past memories. It was the first time he had not spent the New Year with his wife.

Four more months of this prison-like existence lay ahead. Personal angers had been bubbling beneath the surface, and now began to burst out. Rylatt and the chief surveyor, Gillette, had been speaking to each other only when necessary. In one argument Gillette had thrown a grouse bone in Rylatt's face. Rylatt had replied with a cup of hot coffee. At that point Gillette had threatened to shoot him.

By February Rylatt had a deadly hatred for his boss. He was convinced Gillette was going crazy. Gillette felt the same way about Rylatt.

Rylatt wrote in his diary: "That man, Gillette, is not only a fool but an unmanly cur, deserving the sympathy of none, and the power that pitched forth such a being into even our rough society, and placed him pro tem at the head of it, ought to be blackballed." Gillette threatened to drill a hole in Rylatt with his pistol.

The absolute lack of activity soured the tempers of the party. Rylatt, in March, noted in his diary: "The roughs of the party are in open mutiny. Growling at their food, cursing me for being out of sugar; all this I care little for … but my pent up feelings found vent today, and the leader of the roughs will carry my mark to his grave. I have been through somewhat an exciting scene and don't care to have it repeated."

This is what had happened: seven of the most mutinous members of the party had gathered at the cookhouse door, planning to rush it and seize the food and sugar they wrongly believed Rylatt was secretly hoarding.

In the argument that followed, Rylatt was threatened by the ringleader, an Australian ex-convict named Roberts. Then Rylatt snatched up a hatchet, and when Roberts made a move towards him, he chopped off three of his fingers.

That drove off the mob, but they came back in an hour armed with axes. Rylatt held them off with his rifle, and stayed on guard until they quieted down.

As the sun grew warmer in April, and the river ice showed signs of breaking up, much of this ill humour disappeared. At last, in May, some mail arrived. But still Rylatt had no word of his wife. The man who had agreed to carry letters from Wild Horse Creek to Hope on the Fraser the previous fall had perished in the snows. His body was not discovered until the spring. The mailbag lay beside it.

Rylatt was frantic with anxiety. "I cannot understand why no line has reached me from my wife," he wrote. "Is she dead? … the suspense is terrible … surely someone of our many acquaintances would have let me know

… Generally people are ready to signal bad news. My chum Jack had bad news; his house being burned down. His wife it would appear was enjoying herself at a Ball … he lost everything …"

On May 6 Rylatt had got it into his head that his wife wasn't dead but had gone out of her mind, and this thought haunted him.

And then on May 15 Walter Moberly arrived with the startling news that the Howse Pass route had been abandoned. All their work had been useless. Moberly ordered the party to quit its headquarters on the Columbia, and move north. He knew it would be touch and go. The high Athabasca Pass was many miles away, and they would have to get to it before the blizzards blocked it and cut them off from the work at the Yellowhead.

But Rylatt had some good news at last. Moberly had a letter from Rylatt's wife. He had been carrying it around so long, the cover had been worn away. Rylatt got it on May 15, 1872. It was dated October 9, 1871.

Moberly dealt swiftly with the mutineers and with Gillette, whom he blamed for the troubles. Four of the malcontents were dismissed. Gillette was suspended. A new man, Ashdowne Green, was put in charge of the party.

As Rylatt wrote, "I cannot forget the look of hatred on Roberts's face as, upon my leaving in the boat, he held up to my sight his mutilated hand and exclaimed: 'You see this; it will help me to remember you!'"

Gillette tried to carry out his threat to shoot Rylatt. But as his hand reached for the pistol in his belt, Rylatt knocked him down with a heavy blow, and another member of the party restrained his arms.

Guided by Chief Kinbasket of the Kootenay Indians, "a daring little shrivelled up old fellow," the party started on the long journey north. They were forced to break a trail for their pack horses as they moved through dense clouds of mosquitoes. Rylatt had smothered his face with mosquito muslin, and smeared his hands with bacon grease. But nothing kept them off. The heat only melted the grease and sent it under his clothing.

Then, in mid-August, a grizzly bear attacked Chief Kinbasket, who barely had time to raise his axe and aim a blow before the weapon was dashed aside. In a moment he was in the embrace of the monster. The huge forepaws gripped and the immense claws tore into his back. The bear held the Indian up and fastening the chief's shoulder in his jaws raised one of his hind feet, tore a gash, commencing at the abdomen and cutting through to the bowels—fairly stripping the flesh and muscles from one of his sides.

They didn't find Chief Kinbasket until the following morning. Miraculously he was still alive and, more miraculously, he survived. But the party had lost its trailblazer.

In late September they reached the boat encampment at the big bend of the Columbia River. Now the route took a right angle towards the Rockies and the foot of the Athabasca Pass. But it seemed impossible to reach the Yellowhead before the winter set in.

The party hesitated. And there, in the shadow of the glowering peaks, with the brooding forests hanging over them, and the moon glistening on the great rustling river, they indulged in a weird caper. On September 22 they held a grand ball.

"Think of it," Rylatt wrote in his diary, "a dance—and an enjoyable dance at that."

The best whistler in the party became "the orchestra." He knew all the latest dance tunes—"Little Brown Jug," "The Man on the Flying Trapeze," "Shoo-Fly Don't Bother Me." As Rylatt wrote, "He puckered his mouth, beat loud time on an empty soap box with a stick, and the graceful forms began to whirl." The dancers were deadly serious. Several were assigned the role of a lady partner, and later allowed to change about.

Rylatt described his assistant, Dick White, dancing with one such "lady," a great six-footer, hairy-faced, and with a fist like a sledge, pants tucked into his boots still covered with river mud, "while Dick, with eyeglasses adjusted, held the huge hand gingerly by the tips of his fingers, then circling the waist of this delicate creature with the gentleness due to modesty and the fair sex, his lovely partner occasionally letting out a yell of hilarity would roll the quid of tobacco to his other cheek of his sweet face, discharging the juice beneath the feet of the dancers."

The dancing grew wilder as the full moon shed its light on the scene. When the whistler gave out, the dancers themselves shouted the tunes aloud. The entire crew seemed to have forgotten where they were. In their minds they saw themselves in some vast ballroom far from the dripping forests, the swamps, and the dead trees.

"They were now in the last dance, and appeared to have gone mad, and when at last the orchestra stopped, and Dick White doffed his cap with the indispensable flourish, and the moon shone on his bald scalp as he offered his arm to the fair one at his side, preparatory to leading her to a seat on the log, I fairly screamed with laughter, and then, to see that modest young lady suddenly throw out one of her number eleven boots, and her sledgehammer arm, and place Dick in an instant on his back and to observe the lady dancing a jig around him, yelling at the same time that made the distant hills echo, was glorious fun."

In this way Rylatt and his friends by temporary madness saved themselves from a larger insanity.

The next day Rylatt got three letters from his wife. The last was written by a neighbour because she was too ill to hold a pen. "Oh, Bob, come home," she wrote, "I can't bear it!" But he couldn't go home. He had a two-year contract with Moberly, and Moberly wouldn't release him. As the fall rains began, pouring down in such sheets that they couldn't prepare a hot meal, the party moved north again.

The whole valley was like a lake. Rylatt's clothing was drenched every night. He took it off, wrung it out, and then went to bed in soaking wet blankets. The following morning he put on his wet clothing again, shivering all over, his teeth chattering, as he realized how difficult it was going to be to make breakfast. Warm breakfasts were impossible. All they got were flapjacks covered with bacon grease and a muddy coffee made from beans placed in a piece of canvas and bruised between two rocks.

Now, with winter setting in and their goods and supplies far behind, they found themselves in the heart of the Rockies, 6,500 feet (1,980 m) above sea level, fifty miles (80 km) from their wintering place, "where no trail exists, nor ever has existed."

The country was totally unexplored. Every mile was a horror. There were swamps to be crossed, heavy timber to be hacked through, and dense undergrowth to be chopped off so the animals could make it.

For weeks there was no scrap of news. But then on October 19 the pack train arrived and Rylatt was handed a slip of paper on which was scribbled the message he'd been dreading:

"Dear Rylatt—the papers state your wife has passed beyond the stream of time. Don't be cut up, dear old fellow."

There were no details. Three days later, brooding in his tent, Rylatt was startled by a strange cry. His faithful dog, Nip, who had shared all his hardships, his blankets, and his food, had broken through the shore ice and was struggling vainly in the river. Rylatt tried to save him but failed. "Oh, God," he cried in his distress, "must everything be taken from me?"

And so the winter passed. By April Rylatt was nearly dead of scurvy, a disease caused primarily by the lack of dietary vitamin C. His mouth was in a dreadful state, the gums black, the teeth loose. In fact the gums swelled so badly at times they almost covered his teeth. It was impossible for him to chew anything, and he had to bolt his food without chewing. His legs had become black below the knee. His breath was sour and he was troubled with a dry cough. "I feel like an old man," he wrote.

Finally he talked Moberly into allowing him to quit the service and go home. And so, on the evening of May 13, 1873, he said his goodbyes. It was a bittersweet leave-taking. Suddenly he felt a pang of regret at having to turn his back on his comrades. They crowded around him with warm handshakes and clumsy words of farewell. The cook made some doughnuts especially for the occasion. These men had been together for two years, and they had come to know one another as men only can under conditions of hardship and stress.

Rylatt set off with one companion, a burly Scot named Henry Baird. They took three horses and headed south towards Kamloops, through unknown country. They trudged through soaking moss, "so deep an animal could be buried overhead and suffocate." They swam and reswam the ice-cold rivers, pack horses and all. They crawled on their hands and knees across fallen timber. They stamped out a trail through the crust of melting snow. They foundered in the rapids of the treacherous rivers and they slashed away at the underbrush, whipping their animals unmercifully as they struggled on in search of feed for them.

A month went by. They were still on the trail. Their provisions were lost, their matches were almost gone, their sugar was used up, and all they had between them and starvation was a single sack of flour. Kamloops was still 150 miles (240 km) away.

At this point they came upon a meadow where the horses could graze. And so they made a fire, dried their clothing, and cooked some pancakes.

Then they stretched out before the blaze—the closest thing to comfort they'd known for many weeks.

And here these two exhausted, weather-beaten men fell to thinking about the future Canadian Pacific Railway. In their mind's eye they could see a train of cars sweeping along the flat, over the fierce streams, puffing and snorting at the mountains, and shrieking wildly, as some beast of the forest, scared at the new puffing monster, scurried off.

They talked about the passengers looking with weary eyes, hoping for the end of the route. They could almost see these travellers settling back in their corners in the parlour car, yawning, and complaining of tiredness, and dozing.

Then their thoughts turned to the dining car. And these two hungry men began to describe the kind of dinner that might be served on such a train in the future: "Hot joints, mealy potatoes, pies, cheese, etc., and wine to be had for the paying for."

The fantasy grew. They began to think about the imaginary passengers, and the imaginary train. They pretended these passengers were looking out the train gazing on *them*, and remarking, "Those two fellows yonder seem to have it pretty much to themselves, as they toast their skins … and are doubtless happier and more at freedom than we …"

Finally the train of imagination rolled on beyond the forested horizon. Rylatt and Baird roused themselves, and counted their matches. They realized there would not be many more hot meals. They still had a long way to go, but the end of that long sentence in the Canadian Pacific Survey was at last in sight.

They cooked some more flapjacks on what was left of the fire—they would eat them cold on the following day. They saved what little tea and tobacco was left for an emergency. Then, wearily, they picked up their loads, gathered their grazing horses, and with that strange vision of the future still fresh in their minds, set off once again into reality.

CHAPTER SIX

"That Old Devil" Marcus Smith

BY THE FALL OF 1872, SANDFORD FLEMING HAD LOST ALL CONFIDENCE IN WALTER MOBERLY. HE SENT AN INDIAN RUNNER TO THE MOBERLY PARTY, WITH A MESSAGE ORDERING MOBERLY BACK TO KAMLOOPS. HE SAID HE HAD CHANGED HIS MIND ABOUT THE SURVEYS OF THE LINE. MOBERLY WAS TO PLACE THE SUPPLIES AND PACK ANIMALS IN THE CHARGE OF ANOTHER MAN.

Fleming believed this raw tactic would force Moberly to quit the service. But Moberly stubbornly decided to ignore the order and press on with a survey of the Yellowhead, come hell or blizzard. He felt "the instructions conveyed in the letter were too childish to be followed." He carried on the work anyway, according to his own best judgment and would only obey orders "when I could see they were sensible, but not otherwise." Moberly said he went into the service "for business, not to be made a fool of."

Fleming tried again after the New Year, 1873. He sent another message by a Métis runner, telling Moberly that a new man, Marcus Smith, had taken over. Smith, who had been in charge of a party exploring the Homathco River in 1872 while Moberly was at Howse, would now be in charge of *all* surveys in British Columbia. He would, in short, be Moberly's boss. This did not sit well with Moberly.

He did some work for Smith, who wanted to find out if there was a pass that could be used up the North Thompson River. Moberly reported "an impenetrable wall of rock, snow and ice." Then, finally, he did quit.

Moberly left for Ottawa, where he had a chilly meeting with Fleming. He hung around the capital waiting for the engineer-in-chief to sign his expense accounts. Fleming turned down the first one and then had a second auditor go over Moberly's bill again. Finally he passed the expenses, but Moberly had waited so long that he was forced to borrow money to pay for his room and board.

Moberly left British Columbia and moved to Winnipeg, where he got a job building the city's first sewers. For the rest of his life he complained bitterly about the way Fleming had treated him. Eventually, the railway *would* go south, but not through Moberly's favourite pass—the Howse. The railway builders discarded it—as they discarded the Yellowhead—in favour of the Kicking Horse.

There was one triumph, however, of which Walter Moberly could not be cheated. Twenty years after he discovered the Eagle Pass, the last spike of the Canadian Pacific Railway would be driven at Craigellachie. It was a significant spot, though not everybody realized it. For it was there that Moberly had stood and, in that mystical moment, had chalked on a blazed tree his prophecy that the overland railway would have to come this way.

Marcus Smith, the surveyor who replaced Moberly, was undoubtedly the most controversial figure the Canadian Pacific Survey produced. No two men seemed to agree about him. Moberly liked him. Another called him "a wonderful man to my mind." A third mentioned "the fire and sparkle of Marcus Smith's genius." But somebody else said he was "a very crabbed and impatient man, though withal very kind of heart."

Some of those who worked under him used harsher terms. Rylatt, when he was at a low point on the Columbia, wrote in a fury that "Smith was a hard, unjust, and arbitrary wretch." In the summer of 1872, a young surveyor named Edgar Fawcett, toiling in the Homathco country, called him "an old devil" and wrote in his diary, "I did not come here to be blackguarded by Mr. Smith for forty-five dollars a month." And when Smith announced he was leaving the party and moving on, another member wrote in his diary that it was "the best news we have heard since we left Victoria."

Smith was a pretty good hater himself. He called one man "a Yankee sneak," and another "a little toady." The man who replaced Sandford Fleming, Collingwood Schreiber, was "mean and unfair," in Smith's mind. Another was "a thorough fraud," and a third "a crazy conceited fellow."

Smith was suspicious of all politicians. He thought that Alexander Mackenzie, the prime minister who followed John A. Macdonald, was dishonest. He suspected the Governor General, Lord Dufferin, of speculating in railway lands. As for Macdonald himself, he would "sacrifice anything or anybody to smooth down difficulties."

This gives you a pretty good idea of the tensions that existed among men who are driven hard in the far corners of the country. But Smith was special. Like Moberly who wanted the Howse Pass, and Fleming who wanted the Yellowhead Pass, Smith had his own route to the Pacific and he bitterly opposed anybody who dared to disagree.

Smith's route led through the Pine Pass, which is well to the north of the Yellowhead, and then southwest through Fort George, in the heart of British Columbia, across the Chilcotin plains to the headwaters of the Homathco River and thence down that turbulent river to its mouth at Bute Inlet on the Pacific.

Smith quarrelled with anyone who favoured any other line. He fought with Fleming because Fleming wanted to go through the Yellowhead and down the Fraser River to Burrard Inlet (the present site of Vancouver). He fought with his colleague, Henry Cambie, because Cambie wanted to take the railroad through to Port Simpson on the Pacific Ocean well to the north. He also fought with Alexander Mackenzie, who was both prime minister and minister of public works. In fact, he even refused to speak to him because Mackenzie dared to argue with him.

He used every trick he knew to force the government to accept his Pine Pass-Bute Inlet route. He wrote to members of parliament. He sent secret surveys into the north. He arranged for letters and articles to appear in the newspapers. He bombarded everybody with his views.

He was darkly suspicious of conspiracies. He believed his reports were being suppressed out of jealousy. He blamed Fleming for that. Fleming, a mild man, bore it all calmly.

But Fleming did his best to get rid of Smith. In fact, he thought at one point that he had fired him. But Smith stuck around. Fleming then acted as if Smith didn't exist. But Smith was a born survivor. And he wasn't fired.

Smith was entranced by the long fiord of Bute Inlet, which led to the turbulent Homathco. "A scene of gloomy grandeur, probably not met with in any other part of the world," he called it. It was, in short, love at first sight as it had been with Moberly and the Howse Pass.

Most surveyors' diaries are pretty blunt. A tired man, squatting at the edge of a riverbank, scribbling with a stub of pencil and greasy notebook, doesn't generally wax poetic; but Smith did. He had a habit of noting curious things around him—the character of Indian communities, for instance, or the spectacle of a young Native girl throwing off her clothes and bathing in the river. Sometimes he was positively lyrical about his favourite region:

"Scene awfully grand—the river rushing and foaming in a narrow chain between walls of rock, a frowning cliff overhanging all, and the snow-capped mountains piercing clouds and hidden by curtains of glaciers glittering blue and cold in the sunlight." That isn't the way most surveyors wrote.

Later on he wrote for an official government report an equally poetic description of the Chilcotin meadows—"the silence of the plains only broken by the silent tread of the Indian or the sad wail of the solitary loon." Of his favourite canyon, the Homathco, he wrote, "The awful grandeur of the mountains, the roar of the waters, and the constant sense of danger kept the nerves strong and the mind active."

His description of the "charming" mile-wide valleys of the Chilcotin and Chilanko Rivers sounded like that of a lovelorn suitor composing a tribute to his girlfriend. Smith wrote of bottom lands, ripe and mellow with bunch growth, with clear streams winding through them in graceful curves, of the pale, greyish-green of the grasses "in agreeable harmony with the dark foliage of the spruce," and of the "picturesque irregularity of the evergreens … the whole forming a scene of pristine beauty rarely to be met with." Compared to the routine language of some of his colleagues, Smith's seemed almost sensual.

He had just turned fifty-six—a stubby man with a barrel chest, as tough as leather and bristly as a warthog. His hooded eyes, drooping moustache, and grizzled beard gave him an almost sour look. Born in the English county of Northumberland, he'd been a land surveyor all his life, first in England and Wales, then in South Africa, and since 1850 in Canada.

Like so many of the other surveyors—men accustomed to fending for themselves in severe climates—he was totally self-confident and more than a little proud.

"I have no claim for genius," he wrote at the close of his career (he lived to be eighty-nine), "but a strong love of my profession, and an aptitude and energy of carrying out great works, and a determination for honesty and accuracy for which I have so far carried out, that in long practice there has never been a dollar lost to any of my employers from any blunder of mine."

He was a hard drinker. In the so-called dry areas, he carried a keg of "lime juice" which really contained whisky. He wasn't an easy man to work with, for he didn't allow incompetence or fatigue or indeed any kind of human frailty. One of his employees, Edgar Fawcett, was toiling up a steep, rocky hill in June 1872 when a huge boulder bounced down the slope and struck him a blow that knocked him out. Smith was infuriated. He said he couldn't have children working for him. "That boy who could not keep out of the way of stones would have to be sent home," he said.

He was distressed by anything that delayed the survey. He expected his men to be as tough as he was. As George Hargreaves, one of the levellers in his party, wrote in his diary in June of 1872, "Sunday morning and no one sorry for it except perhaps old Smith, who I think would like to keep every-one at work night and day and then growl and snap at anyone who came near or happened to speak to him."

Three days later he wrote that "Old Smith came to camp about 7:30 and boiled over, accusing us of putting obstacles in his way and saying he would carry through the survey if he had to send five thousand miles for men."

Six days later: "Had a row with Old Smith for not bringing the levels through before stopping work … Says he, 'what did you mean by saying you was through, you must be an idiot.'"

Two days after that: "It appears Smith had a big row with two or three of the men and also with Bristow, the Transit. Called him a Gd-dmd fool and Idiot, who said he would not have such language used to him, that he would go home to Canada if he continued to use it, and also told Smith he was stopping the work by carrying on so. Smith told him to go back to his instrument or he would give him the Gd damdist daming ever he had dam'd …"

Young Fawcett's diary also reveals his feelings about Smith: "It was most awful the way that old devil swore and went on generally," he wrote a week after the incident with the boulder. "He swore at me for the most ordinary things and kept us from dinner until half-past two."

Smith certainly made no distinctions. He barked equally at transit men, levellers, axemen, and Indian packers with a fine democracy. But the Indians weren't going to take any of Smith's insults. They simply unloaded their canoes and prepared to head off into the wilderness.

Smith called in Hargreaves and asked him who had authorized the Indians to leave. Hargreaves replied the Indians didn't require any authorization to do anything.

That remark seemed to astonish Smith. "He said we must talk about that," Hargreaves wrote, "only while he was talking about it, they were going, which put him in a flutter rather."

Smith asked what the Indians wanted. The Indians replied they didn't want to work for him. Hargreaves stopped a mass walkout by apologizing on Smith's behalf and agreeing to pay the Indians in cash at the time of every trip.

But if Smith was hard on the others, he was also hard on himself. When he was sixty years of age, he travelled for one thousand miles (1,600 km) through the Lake Superior country by canoe, all in a single summer, making two hundred portages that varied from a few yards to four miles (6.4 km).

But if Smith was hard on the others, he was also hard on himself. When he was sixty years of age, he travelled for one thousand miles (1,600 km) through the Lake Superior country by canoe, all in a single summer, making two hundred portages that varied from a few yards to four miles (6.4 km).

Young chainmen and their rodmen who worked for him must have seen him as a superman, although a satanic one. At the end of each day they were so thoroughly exhausted they were prepared to throw in the sponge. Some of their diary excerpts from the Bute Inlet survey of 1872, when Smith was driving his men without mercy, give an idea of how hard the job was:

"So tired I could hardly drag myself along. After one of the hardest, hottest and longest days I had ever experienced in my life, we arrived at 'w' camp. I was so far done in I could not get up and sat down to rest."

"Yesterday I really thought I should have to give in I felt so the loss of having eaten nothing all day but a bit of bread and fat pork in 12 hours. If this is surveying, I have had my bellyful of it."

"I am heartily sick of the whole business and feel like turning tail."

" … legs and feet all benumbed and aching fearfully. I felt like giving up and leaving it many times but knowing it had to be done sometime, and if we left it today would have to go again tomorrow, managed to get through …"

It must have galled these younger men that the demonic Smith, a man twice their age, was driving hard late into the evening, scaling the rocks and forging through the icy waters with enough breath left in his barrel chest to fling curses upon the stragglers. Actually, his own diary reveals he was as exhausted as any. He "felt terribly used up," he wrote on July 9, 1872—a phrase that keeps recurring on those cramped pages. But he would not give up. That night, used up or not, he had to work out the calculations of his travels across the mountains.

Four days after that, when he finally boarded the boat to Victoria, to the immense relief of his men, he was close to collapse. "Fatigue set in after a month of excessive labour and anxiety, and I lay and dozed the hours away, totally unfit for anything."

Yet, sick or not, Smith was back in the same country a month later. He was tortured by pains and cramps in his hip and his left leg. By August 11 he was so ill he couldn't get out of bed until noon. But he did get up. He threw a saddle on his horse and headed off across a swamp—a swamp so bad that he had to leave it and make his way up the side of a hill, still on horseback.

After that detour, he plunged into another swamp. This time the horse was caught in the mud. Smith tried to spur it on, but the saddle slipped off and he tumbled in. He was too weak to put the saddle back on his horse, and yet he managed to crawl all the way to the head of the lake, where he found two Indians who looked after him.

He was still at it in the same country in the summer of 1875. By then he was in his sixtieth year. He confided to a friend that he had "less heart for that journey than any I have undertaken. I am far from well and very weak, and the mountain torrents are very high."

When Smith wrote that letter, he was planning to force his way from the Chilcotin plains through the Cascade Mountains by way of the Homathco Pass and down to Bute Inlet. He set off on foot with five Lillooet Indians and a Chilcotin guide, struggling for two and a half days along the dripping cliffs of the canyons. It often took him several hours to move a few yards, because the party had to climb as high as fifteen hundred feet (457 m), and climb down again to get around the spurs of rocks that jutted from the face of the canyon wall.

At one point, Smith found he couldn't bridge a torrent. Six of the largest trees, which they had thrown across the chasm, had been swept away like so many chips. He and his men were forced to detour by way of a glacier, fifteen miles (24 km) long, whose sharp ridges they crossed on their hands and knees. That was not the kind of summer excursion that any doctor would prescribe for a sick man in his sixtieth year.

En route to the coast, Smith discovered that the bridges that had been built for him had been swept away by the mountain torrents. It took him and his men seven hours to build a fly bridge over the Grand Canyon of the Homathco. He said it "looked like a fishing rod and line hanging over the torrent, the butt end resting on the ground and loaded with boulders." He tested it himself, creeping out over it, then dropping heavily to the rocks below. It took him six hours, scrambling over tangled creepers, huge deadfalls, and masses of detached rocks, to reach camp.

Smith's love-hate relationship with this strangely haunting land of grim canyons and smiling meadows had, to borrow his own phrase, used him up. Would all his work be in vain? Survey parties were crawling over the rumpled face of British Columbia and probing the ragged fiords of the coastline, seeking the best method of reaching the Pacific by railway. Sandford Fleming was considering no fewer than eleven different routes, leading down the mountain spine to salt water. Only two led through Smith's country.

What if another route should be chosen? What if all those ghastly days in the numbing bogs and among the brooding crags should end in defeat? But Marcus Smith was not a man to contemplate defeat. And he had not yet begun to fight.

CHAPTER SEVEN

The Battle of the Routes

THEY CALLED IT THE "BATTLE OF THE ROUTES." EVERYBODY, IT SEEMED—
POLITICIANS AS WELL AS SURVEYORS—HAD THEIR OWN FAVOURITE ROUTE. AND
EACH HAD HIS OWN REASONS WHY "HIS" ROUTE THROUGH THE MOUNTAINS AND
DOWN TO THE SEACOAST SHOULD BE CHOSEN. ALL THE ROUTES LED OUT OF
FORT SASKATCHEWAN NOT FAR FROM FORT EDMONTON. BUT FROM
EDMONTON THERE WERE SEVEN POSSIBLE WAYS FOR THE RAILWAY TO REACH
THE OCEAN.

As far as British Columbia was concerned, there were only two routes
that really mattered. One was the ancient trail used by the fur traders and
explorers through the Yellowhead Pass and down the Fraser canyon to
Burrard Inlet. If chosen, it could guarantee the prosperity of the interior
cities—Kamloops, Yale, and New Westminster—and all the valley points
between. This was the route for which mainland BC was prepared to fight.

The other route would probably lead from the Yellowhead through the
Cariboo country and the Chilcotin plains to Marcus Smith's favourite river,
the Homathco, and then on to Bute Inlet. At that point it would leap the
straits to Nanaimo, and thence to Victoria. It would guarantee the prosperity of the dying Cariboo gold region, and also of Vancouver Island. And so,
the city of Victoria on Vancouver Island, and New Westminster on the
mainland, together with the interior towns, fought the Battle of the Routes.

By 1877 the battle had reached the stage of a pamphlet war—the tried-
and-true technique of those days. Print and paper were cheap. Pamphlets
could be issued as swiftly as a newspaper. Supporters of burning causes
fought each other with words as in earlier times they had duelled with
swords. So in the Battle of the Routes the opponents attacked each other
with blizzards of paper.

By 1877, Fleming, who favoured the Yellowhead Pass, was unable to make up his mind on the best way to the Pacific. By 1875 there was general understanding that Bute Inlet would be the terminus. But in 1876, Fleming decided, a bit late, that he ought to ask the Royal Navy its opinion of the various harbours along the coast. The overwhelming opinion, to his surprise, was in favour of Burrard Inlet, not Bute.

Fleming was walking a difficult line. He knew that whichever route was chosen he would be attacked by the supporters of the other one. But he had an alternative idea. He pointed out that the harbour at the mouth of the Skeena River, near present-day Prince Rupert, was five hundred miles (800 km) closer to the Orient than the other two. The Navy dismissed that as "totally unfit for the Ocean Terminus." But Fleming refused to rule it out.

Then in 1876, Fleming's doctor ordered a complete rest. The Battle of the Routes had unnerved him. Marcus Smith took over temporarily in his place. For nineteen months between the spring of 1876 and 1878, he was in charge.

Of course, Smith wouldn't give up Bute Inlet, which he had surveyed with such enthusiasm. Actually the route that he chose was totally impractical. There wasn't room to build a city as a terminus for the railway in the narrow confines of the inlet. Also the rails would have to cross the ocean to Vancouver Island, leaping by causeway from island to island—no fewer than seven islands—at an enormous cost and some danger, since the waters were treacherous.

But Marcus Smith was adamant. In his view the railway would not only go through Bute Inlet, it would cross the Rockies—not at Sandford Fleming's favourite pass, the Yellowhead, but by the Pine Pass, five hundred miles (800 km) to the north. He decided to send a survey party to the Pine River country on a completely confidential trip. And he went out to British Columbia himself, to return full of enthusiasm for the Peace River country.

He speeded up his behind-the-scenes work to get his route approved. He told his assistant, Joseph Hunter, to leak some information to the press about his Pine Pass explorations, but to make sure it wasn't official. Then he told Hunter to allow himself to be pumped by reporters into praising the country he had explored. Meanwhile, Smith issued an anonymous press release, which began, "Not withstanding that the matter has been kept very quiet, it has leaked out that the explorations of the acting Engineer-in-Chief Marcus Smith, from the East, and Mr. Hunter, from the West, last summer have been most successful." The press release praised the Pine Pass/Bute Inlet route.

Smith saw dark plots and sinister motives everywhere. He lived in a cloak-and-dagger world of the mind, in which he imagined himself desperately fighting off, at great personal and financial risk, the dark forces of treason and corruption. For he believed so strongly in his own route that it did not occur to him that anybody could advocate another route without being crooked.

Meanwhile, he was up against the new prime minister, Alexander Mackenzie, who favoured the Burrard route. In order to get his way, the prime minister actually had to get around his own acting engineer-in-chief.

Smith saw dark plots and sinister motives everywhere. He lived in a cloak-and-dagger world of the mind, in which he imagined himself desperately fighting off, at great personal and financial risk, the dark forces of treason and corruption.

There were many reasons why Mackenzie wanted to go by way of Burrard Inlet. One was the navy report, which favoured it. Another was the strong urging of several mainland members of parliament. The Governor General himself had been out west and thought the Burrard Inlet route was the best. New surveys by Henry Cambie, ordered by Mackenzie himself (without Smith's knowledge), had also suggested the Burrard route. And finally, there was Smith's bullheadedness. He had got the prime minister's back up. By March 1878, Mackenzie had ceased to consult him or even speak to him.

Meanwhile, Smith continued to press for the Bute Inlet route. He suggested another year's delay to settle the final location of the line. That presented the prime minister with a problem. He could scarcely settle on Burrard Inlet in the face of the direct and public opposition of his acting chief engineer. The islanders in Victoria would pounce on that, and cry foul. He had only one choice. Without telling Marcus Smith, he sent for Sandford Fleming, who found his sick leave in England interrupted.

Fleming found his department in an uproar. Smith had stated in public that some of his people were working secretly with railway contractors—a charge designed to anger the members of that proud service. An unholy row followed. Smith told Fleming he no longer had confidence in him. He said Fleming must no longer consider him, Smith, a member of the department. As Fleming later put it, "he did not receive his dismissal, but he was as good as dismissed and I was not at liberty to consult him any longer, inasmuch as he was no longer a public officer."

Obviously he expected Smith to quit, as he had expected Moberly to quit, but Smith hung on—as he had once hung on to the slippery crags of the Homathco canyon. Meanwhile, Fleming was finally convinced that if engineering decisions alone were to govern the selection of a route, and if that selection couldn't be postponed further, then the Bute Inlet route should be rejected, and the Burrard Inlet route selected.

And that was that. On July 12, 1878, the government settled officially on the Fraser River/Burrard Inlet route, and prepared to call for tenders for the building of the railway through the Fraser River.

This meant that a new city—Vancouver—would spring up on Burrard Inlet. But that was several years in the future. Before that happened, Fleming's favourite route through the Yellowhead Pass would also be rejected by the new company organized to build the Canadian Pacific Railway.

The railway would not go through the Pine Pass, or the Yellowhead Pass, or the Howse Pass, or any of the other passes that had been located through the mountains by dedicated men, working under impossible conditions. In the end the railway would be taken far to the south, through the Kicking Horse Pass, the closest to the American border. That meant that other men would have to run survey lines through the three ranges of mountains that blocked the way to the seacoast. These would not be members of the Canadian Pacific Survey; they would be new surveyors working for a private company. But that is another story.

INDEX

Galician immigrants in Quebec City, circa 1911.
(COURTESY LIBRARY AND ARCHIVES CANADA, PA-010401)

THE MEN IN SHEEPSKIN COATS

CONTENTS

OVERVIEW

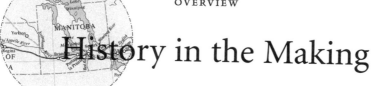

History in the Making

EVERYONE WHO LIVES IN THIS COUNTRY IS AN IMMIGRANT—OR A DESCENDANT OF IMMIGRANTS. THIS INCLUDES THE ABORIGINAL PEOPLES, THOSE NATIVE CANADIANS WHOSE ANCESTORS CROSSED THE LAND BRIDGE BETWEEN SIBERIA AND ALASKA THOUSANDS OF YEARS AGO. FOR THERE WAS A TIME WHEN ASIA, AFRICA, AND EUROPE WERE POPULATED, BUT NO HUMAN BEINGS ROAMED THIS CONTINENT.

Few immigrants to Canada have had an easy time. Neither the land nor the people has welcomed newcomers. The land may seem beautiful to us, but it was harsh and forbidding to those who had to contend with a savage terrain just emerging from the Ice Age. The French and English who invaded the new country after the fifteenth century had to contend, in their turn, with those who had come before. So it was then; so it is today.

We do not welcome strangers to Canada, whether they be Asians, Ukrainians, or even English. There was a time in this country when signs were posted in store windows announcing: "NO ENGLISH NEED APPLY." In our own time we have seen this kind of unthinking attitude applied to Sikhs, Pakistanis, Chinese, Japanese, and Italians. Every one of us, then, springs from a strange culture much misunderstood by those who came before. Every one of us is the descendant of immigrants who were themselves looked on with suspicion and even hatred. That process continues to this day, as wave after wave of new strangers reaches our shores.

Why, one wonders, do they come at all? The answer, in most cases, is that they have had to. The people you will meet in this book had little choice, if they were to free themselves of the poverty and hopelessness of their own land. And that still applies today. We are, in many respects, a nation of refugees—from war, from dictatorship, from overcrowding, from want.

But there is another side to the coin. Those who made the difficult choice to leave hearth and home to seek a new life in a new world were also the most daring members of their communities. It requires an enormous act of courage and will to say goodbye forever to friends and family, as the immigrants from Eastern Europe did at the turn of the century. They were, as this book makes clear, a steadfast, enterprising, and hardy group of people; most immigrants are. The very nature of their decision makes them so.

They were never a liability, as many suggested at the time. They were an asset, as we now know, for they brought something of their own culture with them and thus enriched the culture of the new land they themselves helped to build. The story has no ending, for they are still arriving on our shores, these strange new people, helping to enrich us all, as the men and women in sheepskin coats did a century ago.

CHAPTER ONE

Josef Oleskow's Dream

THIS IS THE STORY OF ONE OF THE GREATEST MASS MOVEMENTS IN HISTORY—
THE FILLING UP OF AN EMPTY LAND, A THOUSAND MILES (1,600 KM) BROAD,
WITH MORE THAN ONE MILLION PEOPLE IN LESS THAN ONE GENERATION. IT IS
THE STORY OF THE OPENING OF THE CANADIAN WEST, FROM WINNIPEG TO THE
ROCKY MOUNTAINS, IN THE YEARS BETWEEN 1896 AND 1914. IT IS THE STORY
OF THE CREATION OF A STATE WITHIN A STATE, AND THE TRANSFORMATION OF
A NATION.

It begins, of course, with the Canadian Pacific Railway—but that is
another tale. British Columbia was promised a national railway in return
for joining Confederation. The famous line was completed in 1885 as a
result of that promise. But depression struck, and in spite of the fact that
the railway was supposed to bring people out to the empty Northwest,
scarcely anybody came. For ten years, the land remained almost as empty as
it had been in the days when the Hudson's Bay Company was in control.

But there was treasure in the West—not gold but rich, black soil,
scoured off the old rocks of the Canadian Shield by the moving glaciers of
the last ice age, and pushed by a bulldozer action onto the land we call the
prairies. This vast acreage of topsoil, perfect for grain growers, would help
make Canada the breadbasket of the world.

But this was also dry country. Little rain fell. The winters were cold. The
kind of wheat that had been grown in the southern parts of the world
would not flourish in Canada. Furthermore, men were needed—and
women too—to harvest the grain. In the Russian Ukraine, there were men
and women aplenty, most of them hungry and badly nourished, some of
whom had their eyes on the plains of Canada, and many who dreamed of a
better world across the sea.

So let us meet one of these dreamers. His name was Josef Oleskow, a

Slavic professor of agriculture from Eastern Europe, and in the hot summer of 1895 he made his way by train on a journey of discovery to the Canadian West.

Anyone who saw him would know he was a stranger to the country. His hair, dark and thick, was not parted, but combed straight back, European style. His moustache didn't droop over his lips in the North American way, but turned sharply upward, into two fierce points. He was dressed formally and neatly—dark suit, high starched collar, thick tie.

He was a handsome man of thirty-five years, with dark, intelligent eyes and regular features, and he was enchanted by the New World. The people, he thought, were so clean and, equally important, so independent. Here, there were no lords, no peasants. Here, everyone was a master!

And officials did not act as they did back home. They were workers just like everybody else. They had no special privileges. Their offices were operated like stores. Why, you could walk in without even bowing! And the man behind the desk—even a cabinet minister—would probably keep his hat on.

But the *waste*! For two days, Dr. Oleskow's train plunged through the blackened forests of the Canadian Shield. These vast stretches of burned timber were a painful sight to him—a cemetery of dead trees. Apparently nobody had bothered to put out the flames that were ruining the land. Back in his native Ruthenia, then a part of the Ukraine in the Carpathian Mountains, wood was the most precious of all commodities. People hoarded it. But here the professor saw Canadians destroying their heritage. Why, he discovered, when they cleared the land they actually tossed the stumps into the nearest ravine!

The train left the blackened desert of the Shield and burst into the prairies. Here were other wonders. The Canadians, the professor realized, had an axe with a curved handle that fitted the shape of the hand. It was strange to him. He tested it and wondered why his own countrymen had failed to improve the design of their own farm implements, in spite of several centuries of toil.

Then as the train passed through the grainfields of Manitoba, he saw that nobody was using a sickle or a scythe. Machines, not men, were harvesting the wheat. If a man didn't own a machine, he could always rent one from a neighbour.

At Portage la Prairie he watched these marvellous machines follow one another in a staggered row across the wide fields, and marvelled at the horses that drew them. These were not the skinny, miserable nags of his native Carpathian mountains, but big, husky animals with real leather harnesses.

And yet the land was so empty! The only city of any consequence was Winnipeg. From Portage the plains rolled westward without a fence, the soil undisturbed by a plough. The waist-high buffalo grass was broken only by a thin network of trails that were really nothing but ruts. The occasional river valley was bordered by cottonwood and wolf willow. Indians in brightly coloured blankets squatted in groups on the station platforms. Mountains of buffalo bones lined the track in the far west.

But where were the farms? Strung out along the railway the professor found a series of tiny settlements—mere clusters of frame buildings lining wooden sidewalks. Regina, the capital of what was then called the North West Territories, the so-called Queen City of the Plains, had fewer than two thousand people, huddled in wooden shacks that straggled for two miles (3.2 km) across a plain that was as flat as a kitchen table.

Saskatoon scarcely existed—just a railway station and a few houses. Calgary was a glorified cowtown of four thousand. Edmonton was little more than a trading post. These were primitive settlements. Calgary's dusty streets stank of horse manure. And Regina stank, too, from the hotel slops that drenched the main street. In Edmonton you could hear the piercing squeal of the ungreased Red River carts drawn along Portage Avenue by oxen and ponies. In the smaller villages, cows, pigs, and chickens wandered loose.

These little islands of civilization were lost in the great sweep of the prairies—wave after wave of grassland, rolling west towards the foothills, so that the country, from the Red River to the Rockies, looked like a prehistoric ocean that had somehow been frozen. But, as Dr. Oleskow noted, the earth everywhere was rich and black. His own countrymen were starved for land. He realized that this empty country could be their salvation.

He went as far west as Edmonton. A handful of his fellow countrymen had preceded him, and he was astonished by their new prosperity. Vasyl Tasiv had come out in 1892 with only $40. Now he owned a house in Winnipeg, two cows, and had $120 in the bank. Yurko Paish had managed to send $120 home—a small fortune. Dmytro Widynovich had arrived with $40 in 1893 and already had been able to save $400, an enormous sum at a time when an all-wool suit could be purchased for four dollars, and a three-course meal in a restaurant cost no more than twenty-five cents.

It was easy to borrow money. In a town of twenty houses there were three banks, all eager to lend it. You could buy a machine on time. The problem, the professor saw, was not how to borrow money, but how to stop from borrowing too much and going into debt. This was an optimistic country. People talked only of success. Nobody thought of failure.

And yet he was a bit embarrassed by his countrymen. They seemed to him to be dressed in rags. They didn't appear to bathe and that offended him. He was convinced that newcomers must not look and act like serfs! They would have to wear suits that would cover their bare chests. They must get rid of hooks and ribbons in favour of real buttons. They would have to scrub themselves regularly. They must learn to use a knife and fork. And above all, they would have to get rid of the stigma of slavery. They had to learn to lift their heads and look squarely into the eyes of others—instead of peering up from under their brows like dogs.

The professor, of course, was looking for perfection, or at least *his* idea of perfection. It was his dream to turn these Ruthenian peasants into instant Canadian farmers, using Canadian farming techniques, wearing Canadian clothes, and speaking Canadian English. This was a magic vision. The professor would not be the only one who would hold it.

He was shocked during a visit to one farm of Ruthenian colonists. Why, the children seemed to be clothed in filthy cast-offs! As for the women—they didn't even bother to wear blouses.

"For heaven's sake," he cried. "How could you let yourselves go like this?"

To which one woman gave a perfectly sensible answer. She said, "And why not? There is no one to dress for."

But then it must be remembered that Dr. Oleskow had never been a peasant. In his dark suit, he was more out of place than his countrymen. He was a scholar with a doctorate in botany, chemistry, and geology. He was a member of the faculty of the teachers' college in Lemberg—in that section of the old Austro-Hungarian Empire then known as Ruthenia. He was paid $600 a year—an enormous sum for those times and those places.

He wanted to better the conditions of the peasantry, partly by improving the mineral and chemical content of the soil, but also by reducing the population through emigration.

But he didn't want his countrymen to set off for the jungles of Brazil, as so many had. That was the wrong place to go. His whole idea was to redirect the flow to the Canadian prairies. And secondly, he wanted to prevent the Ruthenian emigrants from being cheated by crooked agents working for the major shipping companies.

Brazil was offering some goodies—free travel, free land, financial help. The peasants in Ruthenia actually believed the Brazilian propaganda, which suggested they could lie at their ease, while monkeys came down from the trees to do all the work. In fact, those who reached Brazil were treated little better than slaves.

The steamboat agents were a real problem. They were paid extra money for every ticket they sold. They fooled each emigrant in a dozen ways. They charged huge sums to exchange money, took huge fees for fake medical examinations, and bribed the petty officials to ignore their swindles. That explains why these Slavic peasants often arrived in Canada without any money at all.

Dr. Oleskow wanted to change all that. There were too many people in Ruthenia, and as a result wages were very low. There were, in fact, two *million* people too many. But the exploitation of the unschooled emigrants had to be stopped, and that is why the Ruthenian Population Society had sent Dr. Oleskow to Canada.

Dr. Oleskow went to the federal government in Ottawa and announced that he was prepared to quit his university post and help control all emigration from Ruthenia and its provinces of Galicia and Bukovina (both part of the modern Ukraine). He didn't want to be paid; he would do it as a labour of love. He wanted to plan a well-organized movement, separate from the steamship companies and their agents. He wanted to choose his people carefully—farmers who had some money and who could be protected from exploitation. These people would be the best stock that Eastern Europe could offer.

Alas, Josef Oleskow was a man ahead of his time. The government was interested, but cautious. It had already had its share of crackpot idealists.

The civil servants knew that Oleskow was not a crackpot, but they were worried about setting a precedent.

Then, in 1896, the government changed. The Conservatives were defeated and the Liberals, under Sir Wilfrid Laurier, came into power. An active new minister, Clifford Sifton, took over the Department of Immigration. But unfortunately, Oleskow's scheme did not meet with any enthusiasm from the Austrian government. And the land-owning nobility, who controlled that government, wanted to keep the labour force high and the wages low. Any loss of population would affect them.

Oleskow grew dejected. Thousands read his pamphlets describing the wonders of the Canadian West and planned to leave. But it was the shipping agents who profited. They slipped into the villages disguised as peddlers and signed up anybody they could, promising the moon and cheating their victims.

Oleskow's plan was never adopted. Instead, in 1900, Clifford Sifton decided that almost anyone who had the means to get to Canada would be let in. By that time Oleskow's little trickle of new arrivals had become a tidal wave. For better or worse, his report on the West, in the pamphlet that thousands read, had started a chain reaction.

By 1903, the Galicians, as they were then called (we know them as Poles and Ukrainians today), were strung out by the tens of thousands along the northern rim of the prairies. Josef Oleskow went back to his home and became the director of a teachers' college. But he was gravely ill. On October 18, 1903, the man who helped start it all, but who would soon be forgotten, was dead at the age of forty-three.

CHAPTER TWO

Clifford Sifton's Campaign

MORE THAN ANYBODY ELSE, ONE MAN IS IDENTIFIED WITH THE GREAT TIDAL
WAVE OF EASTERN EUROPEANS WHO POURED INTO THE CANADIAN PRAIRIES IN
THE YEARS BEFORE THE FIRST WORLD WAR. HE WAS A POWERFUL POLITICIAN
NAMED CLIFFORD SIFTON, WHOSE STRENGTHS AND FLAWS WERE AS IMPRESSIVE
AS HIS STRAPPING SIX-FOOT (1.8-M) FIGURE.

Sifton's name will always be connected with a series of dramatic
images—the grimy immigrant ships crammed with strange, dark-featured
farmers; the colonist cars, crowded with kerchiefed women and men in
coats of rough sheepskin; the hovels grubbed out of tough prairie sod; the
covered wagons lumbering across the border from the United States; the
babel of tongues in Winnipeg's immigration hall; the bell tents of the
English colonists whitening the plains of Saskatoon; the gaggle of barefoot-
ed Doukhobor fanatics tramping down the frosted roads of Saskatchewan.

Sifton held the post of Minister of the Interior in Wilfrid Laurier's cabinet. His goal was clear. He intended to fill up the West with practical farmers—and nobody else. He didn't want city people, clerks, shopkeepers, or
artisans. He didn't want southern Mediterranean people, such as Italians or
Spanish. He certainly didn't want Jews, for he claimed (quite wrongly, as the
State of Israel was to demonstrate) that Jews didn't make good farmers.

He was convinced that the northern races were the ones who were best
for the Canadian West. Scots, Scandinavians, Germans, and British would
make excellent citizens. He even thought the northern English would be
better than the southern English. He actually paid a higher price to those
steamship agents who got people to emigrate from northern England. And
the northern Slavs—Poles, Ukrainians, and all others identified in those
early days as "Galicians"—were welcomed.

Canada was more realistic and also more cautious than the United States, which had welcomed the masses of Europe to its shores, confident in the belief that, once established, they couldn't help but flourish as Americans. Canada wanted only those who wouldn't cost the taxpayers any money.

The Americans saw their country as a home for the downtrodden. Canada really didn't want the downtrodden because they couldn't contribute to the wealth of the nation.

It could be said that, while most emigrants set off for the United States in *search* of something vaguely called the American Dream, the ones who came to Canada were escaping from something that might be called the European nightmare. The Americans offered liberty. The Canadians offered something more practical: free land.

Everybody who arrived in the Northwest was entitled to choose a quarter section—160 acres (65 hectares) of public land. All he had to do was pay a $10 registration fee. He would have to live on that land and do a certain amount of work on it for three years. If he could stick it out, the land was his.

But before Canada could convince anybody to take up land, some facts about this strange and unknown realm at the top of North America would have to be broadcast.

First, they had to get rid of the image of the West as a snow-covered desert. In Ireland a respected journal was warning people to stay away from Canada because, it said, Manitoba was "a kind of Siberia." One of Sifton's first moves was to prevent anybody publishing the Manitoba temperatures, but he gave that up because it might prove even more alarming.

However, snow was never mentioned in the pamphlets that his department issued. "Cold" was another taboo word. The weather was described as "bracing" and "invigorating." One pamphlet, in fact, said it was so mild that the "soft maple" could grow five feet (1.5 m) in a single season! And if the prospective immigrants confused the Manitoba maple, a weed tree, with the eastern hardwood—Canada's symbol—well, that was too bad.

In his anti-cold campaign, Sifton had the enthusiastic support of the CPR's colourful chairman, William Cornelius Van Horne, who never lost an opportunity to suggest that the prairies were close to being subtropical. He once made a speech in Europe in which he announced that the coldest weather he'd ever known was in Rome and Florence. "I pine for Winnipeg to thaw me," he said. "The atmosphere in the far West intoxicates you, it is so very invigorating"—and he said it with a straight face!

But there were better lures than the weather. Canada was advertised not only as a free country, but also an orderly one. No one needed to carry a gun in the Canadian West. The Mounted Police were establishing an international reputation in the Yukon and they would see to that.

Also, the land was free. In addition to your free quarter section, you could usually pick up an adjoining quarter section for a song. Anybody willing to work in the West could make money. The titles of the government pamphlets told the story: *The Wondrous West; Canada, Land of Opportunity; Prosperity Follows Settlement.*

In the first year—1896—Sifton's department sent out sixty-five thousand pamphlets. By 1900 the number had reached one million. The best known appeared just after he left office. In thirty-three pages of large type, *The Last and Best West* played on the American myth that praised the farmer as the finest type of citizen. It echoed the legend that the most successful men "have as a rule been those whose youth was spent on a farm."

Sifton took direct charge of this propaganda. One very successful pamphlet was made up of a series of letters taken from thousands collected by the department from farmers praising the West. The pamphlets were optimistic, but they never indulged in exaggeration.

What kind of man was Sifton? Certainly he had the reputation of being an iron man, who "never gets tired, works like a horse, never worries, eats three square meals a day, and at night could go to sleep on a nail keg." He had the reputation of staying up all night at his desk, leaving behind a pile of work for clerks at six in the morning. He would return to work at ten, looking as fresh as ever. It wasn't just his iron constitution—he had an iron will.

But as his workload increased, his health began to suffer and he was subject to several breakdowns. The strain was increased by his own chronic deafness. He used an ear trumpet, but that didn't help. That inability to hear properly gave him the reputation of being cold, aloof, even ruthless. It was not easy to be close with him. Certainly he didn't suffer fools. He was ambitious and self-assured. He made enemies but he never complained, never explained.

A strong Methodist, he never drank, though that didn't prevent him from passing out gallons of whisky to his supporters at election time. He was suspicious of Roman Catholics and French Canadians and didn't employ any Quebeckers in his department. Nor did he mingle with his French-Canadian colleagues. That sprang from the traditional Methodism of southern Ontario where the Siftons grew up.

As a politician he had few equals. He was a gold medallist when he graduated from a Methodist college in Cobourg in 1880. He started out adult life as a lawyer, but soon became a politician. By 1890 he was Attorney General of Manitoba. He was a skilled organizer and a tough campaigner. He loved politics with a joy of the battle. They called him the Young Napoleon of the West, after the famous French emperor.

He ran his campaigns like an army general. He had his own intelligence agents. His spies in the opposing camp revealed his opponents' tactics. If he found that they were doing anything illegal or improper, he took them to court.

He ran his campaigns like an army general. He had his own intelligence agents. His spies in the opposing camp revealed his opponents' tactics. If he found that they were doing anything illegal or improper, he took them to court.

He was a good speaker—he'd been a Methodist lay preacher in his youth—"the greatest combination of cold-blooded businessman, machine politician and statesman our country has produced," in the words of a man who knew him well.

He was more than a cabinet minister. He was in charge of the Liberal political machine in the West, totally in control of party propaganda, party patronage, and election tactics.

"The men in sheepskin coats," as Sifton dubbed them, later became his loyal supporters. He made every effort to convince them that it was the Liberal government that had brought them to the promised land. He virtually dictated the texts of political pamphlets that were designed to convince the newcomers to vote for his party.

Even the smallest ethnic groups received his attention. There were about forty Icelandic voters in Manitoba in 1900, but Sifton went after all of them, bringing in speakers of Icelandic descent to spread the Liberal gospel. He even put one Icelandic youth in the local post office after he learned that the clerk, who couldn't tell one Icelander from another, had been blindly handing out Liberal campaign literature to the Conservatives. And of course he found jobs for good Liberals but not for good Tories, the nickname for the Conservatives.

He was not only the most powerful political figure in the Canadian West, but when he bought the *Manitoba Free Press* (later the *Winnipeg Free Press*) in the winter of 1898–99, he became the most powerful journalist. It had its advantages and disadvantages for the country. But it had a great advantage for the poor and dispossessed people of Eastern Europe who arrived in the new country bewildered and unsure of themselves. A great many newspapers were hostile to the newcomers. Sifton's paper tried to tell the other side of the story and thus gave a measure of hope to the men and women in sheepskin coats.

CHAPTER THREE

The Ordeal of the Galicians

IN THE MOUNTAIN TRENCHES OF GALICIA, THE LAND WAS TOO PRECIOUS TO BE WASTED. THE FURROWS OF THE STRIP FARMS RAN TO THE VERY EDGES OF THE HOUSES. COWS AND SHEEP DOTTED THE PASTURE LAND ON THE LOWER SIDES OF THE MOUNTAINS. OATS, RYE, AND POTATOES SPROUTED UP FROM THE VALLEY FLOOR. ABOVE THE HUDDLE OF THATCHED ROOFS THE GREAT MOUNTAIN PEAKS ROSE, COVERED IN OAK, BEECH, AND FIR, EACH RIDGE EFFECTIVELY SEALING ONE VILLAGE FROM THE NEXT, PRESERVING A PEASANT WAY OF LIFE THAT WAS FROZEN IN TIME.

Since there were no fences—only corner stakes to mark personal holdings—each fertile Carpathian valley resembled one gigantic farm under a single management. But appearances were deceptive. Each peasant needed fourteen acres (5.6 hectares) to provide for himself and his family, and yet 70 percent of the farms were no more than half that size. In fact, some families' wages were as low as five cents a day, while the price of land, for those who could afford it, was high. Land, in fact, fetched as much as $400 an acre. Taxes were also among the highest in Europe.

Under these depressing conditions, theft was common and alcoholism universal. The wealthy lords owned not only the forests, meadows, and villages, but also the taverns—there were more than twenty-three thousand of these in Galicia. It was in the interests of the ruling class to keep the peasants drunk and underpaid. The consumption of liquor was almost unbelievable—twenty-six litres a year for every man, woman, and child.

Let us look into the Galician village of Ghermakivka on a spring morning in 1897, a year after the Sifton immigration policy went into high gear. The Humeniuk family is packing to leave for Canada on money borrowed from relatives and friends. Everything the Humeniuks owns takes up no more than twenty cubic feet (0.6 m³). It is carefully stored away in a green wooden trunk built by Nykola Humeniuk himself.

His wife, Anastasia, puts the winter clothes, blankets, and bedsheets at the bottom. Then come the holy pictures, packed between pillows. On top of that are the family's dress clothes for Sunday church. For the emigrants are certain there will be a little church with an onion-shaped spire in whatever community they may reach.

On top of that there is another covering, and then twenty-five little cloth bundles of garden seeds—onions, garlic, horseradish, dried ears of corn. Above that, some religious articles—candles, chalk, a bottle of holy water. Four precious books will also be taken: a prayer book, a history of the Ukraine, a school primer, and a collection of Bible stories. And, finally, Nykola's carpentry and farm tools: hammers and planes, axe and drawknife, saws, bits, chisels, sickles, scythes, hoes, a rake, and a flail.

At last the task is done. Anastasia ties up some food for the trip in a cloth bundle. The neighbours and relatives pour into the house to say goodbye. Everybody is talking at once. There are smiles at first, then suddenly some of the women begin to cry. They hug and kiss Anastasia, apologizing for things left undone and past offences, real and imagined. The children start to cry too. Then some of the men are seen to wipe tears from their eyes.

Somebody shouts for silence. Then, as all bow their heads, he begins to recite a prayer, asking God to bless the family and their two small children, Pettryk and baby Theodore, and to give them a safe voyage, prosperity, and good health in the strange land across the ocean. Write soon, everybody cries, write as soon as you arrive!

The wagon and team are waiting for the journey to the station. Four men hoist the big trunk onto the back as the family climbs aboard. But Anastasia Humeniuk stops and turns back, her baby in her arms. She walks to the doorway, makes the sign of the cross, kisses the frame, and then, in one last gesture, picks up a small lump of Galician earth, wraps it in a rag, and puts it in her hand valise, a memory of a land she will never see again.

Professor Oleskow's plan had been to bring to Canada only the best farmers—the most productive and educated elements—people who owned enough land to finance the long journey and the first years on the Canadian homestead. But that plan was never acted on. The steamship agents, to whom each peasant paid a fee, wanted to sign up as many as possible. And so it was the ignorant and the innocent, like the Humeniuks, who came to Canada and were exploited shamelessly by those who stood to make a profit from them.

There are many examples of this. Let's look at the little Galician town of Oswiecim, now a part of Poland. There, two immigration agents, Jacob Klausner and Simon Herz, were masters at the art of bribery and corruption. They paid off all the local officials, including both the police and the railway conductors, in order to get as many people under their control as possible.

They overcharged shamelessly for ocean passage. They cheated on the exchange rate. They sold worthless advertising cards instead of tickets. If a man was the right age for compulsory military service and thus unable to emigrate legally, they charged double to smuggle him out of the country. And whenever anybody was foolish enough to object, he was locked into a barn and beaten.

There were other swindles. One Polish agent invented a fake telephone on which he received fake "information." It was only an alarm clock. However, when it rang, he claimed it was inquiring about passage. And when the clock rang again, he charged the peasant a special fee for its use. Sometimes he'd use the clock to ask "the American emperor" whether he'd allow the hopeful emigrant to enter Canada. That, of course, meant another fee.

One swindler dressed up as a doctor and pretended to fail emigrants. Then he would accept a bribe and pass them on. Another had a store full of clothing that he sold at high prices, claiming the peasants wouldn't be allowed to wear their native dress in Canada. At the ocean ports, especially in Germany, scores were told they would have to wait for a boat. They would be deliberately held in boarding houses, hotels, and taverns, where they were cheated for lodgings and food.

One group from Bukovina arrived at Winnipeg's immigration hall in May 1897 protesting that everything had been misrepresented to them. They'd been told that the "Crown Princess of Austria" was in Montreal and would see they were given free land with houses, cattle, and farm equipment. All they had to do was telegraph her if these promises went unfulfilled. As a result, many refused all offers of jobs in Winnipeg and sat in the crowded immigration hall. With five hundred more newcomers arriving, the police attempted to move them out. A small riot ensued. Many were flung to the floor and were then dragged or carried off, the women yelling and shrieking.

The former mayor of Winnipeg, William McCreary, was now the immigration commissioner in Winnipeg. He had been working from six in the morning till nine at night, getting a special low rate on the railway to Yorkton for the immigrants. He'd also arranged for fifty days' work for those who were destitute. But that didn't suit the new arrivals. They had been fooled by the steamship agents' promises and so refused to board the train. Some upset the baggage carts. Some, with their goods on their backs, started marching north. Others squatted on the street or seized vacant houses near the track. In the end, of course, they gave in.

McCreary got them some flour and a few bushels of potatoes and finally settled them on homesteads in the vicinity of Saltcoats, Assiniboia, near Yorkton, where eventually they forgot about the non-existent Austrian princess. It was exactly this kind of fraud and exploitation that Professor Oleskow had wished to avoid.

It is understandable that so many immigrants were saddened and rebellious when they reached this country. Apart from the false promises, there was a long journey across Europe from their home villages, and then the stormy ocean voyage in the holds of the immigrant ships. Once they left home, the first stop, usually after a twenty-four-hour train journey, came at a control station between Galicia and Germany. There, everybody had to submit to a medical examination before going further. These stations had been set up after a cholera epidemic in 1892 and were run by the steamship companies. Now everybody coming into Germany from Austria-Hungary or from Russia en route to North America had to take a medical exam.

So let's look at one of these control stations at Myslowitz at the junction of the German, Austrian, and Russian borders. A uniformed official leads the people from the Krakow train through a long hall to a desk behind which stand three more officials: a steamship agent and, in uniform, a Russian policeman and a German officer. The emigrants give up their rail and steamship tickets to the agent, and then, clutching their baggage, are led into two large halls, where the Galicians are separated from the Russians.

This hall has a tiled floor, painted walls, a high ceiling, and windows of coloured glass. It is ringed by wooden benches, under which they stuff their baggage. As many as can find space sleep on the benches; the rest stretch out on baggage or on the floor, men, women, and children all crammed together. The walls are alive with lice.

No one is allowed to leave until the next train arrives. The only available food is sold at a canteen, but the canteen keeper is drunk, and, in spite of a long price list on the wall, the stock consists mainly of beer, wine, and liquor, but no tea or coffee.

More officers arrive with more emigrants. The first emigrants ask for breakfast but are told only the canteen can supply it. At nine, the wife of the canteen keeper turns up and makes some coffee. At noon, for twenty-five cents, they get a dinner of soup, boiled beef, potato salad, and bread. Many can't afford it.

At two in the afternoon a doctor arrives. The emigrants have been waiting almost twenty-four hours to be inspected; others wait much longer. They are driven into another room, pass in single file before the doctor, and wait for their clothing and baggage to be disinfected.

Their tickets are returned and they are packed aboard the train, faced with a twenty-four-hour journey across Germany. The third-class coach is so crowded that many have to stand for all that time. And at Hamburg there is another medical inspection.

At this point, those who have paid steerage fees—for the cheapest accommodations—are told there is no more room on the ship. They will have to wait another ten days, or pay an additional thirty marks for a third-class ticket. Some can't afford the extra fare or the cost of waiting. Cheated by agents, who lied to them that their rail fare had been paid in advance, they have already spent their meagre funds. They can't even afford to send a telegram home.

Now a flurry of counting, consulting, borrowing, and lending takes place as the immigrants pool their money, decide to pay the extra fare, and set off across the angry ocean, gambling that they won't be rejected on the other side for lack of funds.

For most, the ocean voyage was a nightmare. Jammed into tiered bunks in stifling holds of ancient vessels, vomiting from seasickness, half-starved, and terror-stricken by hurricane-force gales, men, women, and children were flung together under conditions that made a mockery of privacy.

But that was not the real horror. It was the storms that raged on the Atlantic that drove them to a state of terror. One of these emigrants, Theodore Nemerski, has left a graphic account of his own experiences on the *Christiana* in the spring of 1896. He was one of the first Galicians to be influenced by Professor Oleskow's pamphlet. Now, here he was, with eight other members of his family. Four days out of port, the storm broke.

"Good Lord! What fear grips one here. You look, and here from the side there appears a great opening. The water has drawn back and the whole ship simply flies into that void, turning almost completely over on its side. And here all of a sudden a huge mountain with a great roar and clatter of the waves tears into the ship, spilling over the top onto the other side. This is no place to be! … escape inside.

"Inside you find complete panic … all are silent … whispering prayers … awaiting the end …

"Some tied their eyes so as not to see this terror, while they hung onto the bed so they would not fall out. Suddenly water is coming in to the inside from the top, splashing from wall to wall. The people are in lament. Some cry, some complain: Did we need this? It was good for us to live in the old country. This is all on account of you … I listened to you and now we shall all perish …"

On the *Arcadia*, another ancient ship carrying emigrants, the crew herded the passengers below and locked the hatches when the storm struck. Fifteen hundred Galicians clung to the four tiers of iron beds, praying and vomiting, the stench so ghastly that those stewards who ventured in were themselves taken sick.

An old man and a child died before the storm was over. But that was not the end. The ship struck an iceberg. When the hole in the side was repaired, the captain discovered that he was locked in the grip of the frozen ocean and couldn't move. All the passengers were herded back on deck and required to race from side to side—back and forth, back and forth—on signals from the ship's whistle, until the *Arcadia* was finally shaken free from her icy embrace. By this time most of the baggage was soaked and ruined. One month after they left their home villages, the hapless passengers finally landed at Quebec City on the St. Lawrence River.

For those who were able to eat, the food was generally terrible: filthy water, rotten herring, dirty potatoes, rancid lard, smelly meat—all eaten from unwashed dishes and cutlery. The staple meat was pork—not the best remedy for a sick stomach. Thirty years later after his ordeal, one immigrant wrote: "To this moment I cannot face the warm smell of pork without sweat starting on my forehead."

Another, who travelled steerage on the *Bavaria* in 1904, claimed that he was served pig's feet three times a day and "had visions of millions of pigs being sacrificed so that their feet could be given to the many emigrants leaving Europe."

The more fortunate travelled third class, which was a bit better than steerage, although it did no more than provide decently for the simplest human needs. As one woman put it, "to travel in anything worse than what is offered in the third class is to arrive at the journey's end with a mind unfit for healthy, wholesome impressions and with a body weakened and unfit for the hardships that are involved in the beginning of life in a new land."

Yet tens of thousands of sturdy men, women, and children, who quit their tiny Carpathian farms to make a new life in a world of strangers, endured it all and somehow managed to survive and prosper.

CHAPTER FOUR

"Ignorant Foreign Scum"

AS ONE MIGHT EXPECT, THE GALICIANS WHO ARRIVED IN HALIFAX IN NOVA SCOTIA OR QUEBEC CITY AFTER A MONTH OF HARD TRAVEL PRESENTED A SORRY AND BEDRAGGLED APPEARANCE. FEW HAD ANY IDEA OF DISTANCE. THEY'D NEVER, UNTIL THIS MOMENT, GONE MORE THAN TWENTY-FIVE OR THIRTY MILES (40 TO 48 KM) FROM THEIR HOMES. THEY DIDN'T REALIZE THE NEED FOR CHANGES OF CLOTHING. EVERYTHING WAS PACKED AWAY IN TRUNKS, BOXES, AND VALISES, TO BE OPENED ONLY WHEN THEY REACHED THEIR PRAIRIE HOMES.

It's important to realize that these were a people obsessed with cleanliness, used to scrubbing themselves regularly. Now, suffering from a lack of washing facilities on train and steamship, they looked and felt unclean.

Maria Olinyk, a nine-year-old girl from the western Ukraine, later remembered how the crowd on the dock at Halifax stared at her and her shipmates, some out of curiosity, some out of contempt. Here were women in peasant costumes and men in coats of strong-smelling sheepskin, wearing fur hats, linen blouses, and trousers tucked into enormous boots, their long hair greased with lard. The Canadians, Maria noticed, stopped their noses. These first impressions of the newcomers helped to encourage the wave of anti-Galician feeling that was fed by the anti-Sifton newspapers.

Thus Sir Mackenzie Bowell, a former Conservative prime minister and leader of his party in the Senate, was able to write in his newspaper, the Belleville *Intelligencer*, that "the Galicians, they of the sheepskin coats, the filth and the vermin do not make splendid material for the building of a great nation. One look at the disgusting creatures after they pass through over the CPR on their way West has caused many to marvel that beings bearing the human form could have sunk to such a bestial level ..."

To many newcomers, the new land, at first glimpse, seemed equally appalling. Dmytro Romanchych, who came out from the mountains of Bukovina as a result of reading Professor Oleskow's pamphlet, never forgot his first sight of Quebec City—streaks of dirty grey snow lying in the ravines. The sad, uninviting landscape made him feel that Canada was sparsely settled and inhospitable. Dmytro felt depressed, for he had left a land whose meadows and glens, three weeks before, had been green with the promise of early spring. Ottawa with its granite Parliament buildings was more impressive, but across the river the land seemed wild, with the bare rock banks and sickly trees making an unpleasant impression.

But these vistas were cheerful compared to the despair that seized the newcomers when the colonist trains rattled and swayed across the Precambrian desert of the Canadian Shield in northern Ontario. Theodore Nemerski, barely recovered from the storm that tore at the *Christiana*, was shaken by the possibility that this broken expanse of granite ridges and stunted pines might in fact be the actual promised land that Oleskow had described. His companions "turned grey with fear." What if there were no better soil than this in Canada? they asked. "Here the heart froze in not a few men ... the hair on the head stands on end ... because not a few think, what if they get into something like this?"

This was not an unusual attitude. When the Humeniuk family came out the following year, 1897, the women in their car began to sob and cry out that "it would have been better to suffer in the old country than to come to this Siberia." Two years later Maria Olinyk felt the same shock of apprehension. "The heart of many a man sank to his heels," she remembered, "and the women and the children raised such lamentations as defies description."

There were other problems. In Montreal, the Galicians were met by hordes of small-time hustlers trying to separate them from their funds, charging high prices for food, hawking useless goods, and urging them not to venture farther west. The situation became so serious in the spring of 1897 that immigration authorities were forced to call in the police and confine the new arrivals to sheds, until they could be put into railway cars with their final destination clearly marked and the tickets in their hands.

The exploitation resumed in Winnipeg, the jumping-off spot for the prairies. Here, a group of Winnipeg real estate agents collared six Galicians, discovered they had twelve thousand dollars among them, and talked them out of leaving Winnipeg. They claimed it was too cold in Alberta and that the very horns on the cattle froze in the winter. The real estate men were a little too persuasive. Four of their victims immediately bought tickets and returned to Europe.

There were other disappointments. Maria Olinyk and her family were among those who took one of the special trains to the Yorkton area, where hundreds of their fellow countrymen were homesteading. A friend who had come out the year before had written to them, boasting of his prosperity, describing his home as a mansion, telling of his immense cultivated fields and how his wife now dressed like a lady. He depicted Canada "as a country of incredible abundance whose borders were braided with sausage like some fantastic land in a fairy tale."

The family hired a rig and, after a thirty-mile (48-km) journey north through clouds of mosquitoes, finally reached their destination. What they found was a small log cabin, partially plastered and roofed with sod, a tiny garden plot dug with a spade, a woman dressed in ancient torn overalls, "suntanned like a gypsy," and her husband, his face smeared with dirt from ear to ear, "weird, like some unearthly creature," grubbing up stumps. Maria's mother broke into tears at the sight, but, like so many others, the Olinyk family hung on and, after years of pain and hardship, eventually prospered. Maria became Dr. Maria Adamowska, a noted Ukrainian-Canadian poet who, when she died in 1961 at Melville, Saskatchewan, left behind a literary legacy that included her vivid memories of those lean, far-off years.

The Galicians did not care to settle on the bald southern prairie. They preferred the wooded valleys of the Saskatchewan River. This baffled the immigration authorities. "These Galicians are a peculiar people," McCreary wrote to Sifton's deputy minister, James Smart, in the spring of 1897. "They will not accept as a gift 160 acres of what we consider the best land in Manitoba, that is first class wheat growing prairie land; what they particularly want is wood; and they care but little whether the land is heavy soil or light gravel; but each man must have some wood on his place …"

There was a reason for this. Wood was precious in the Carpathians—so scarce that it was bought by the pound. In some areas the harvesting of wood was a monopoly; it was a crime to cut down a tree. Thus in Canada the Galicians were allowed, perhaps even encouraged, to settle on marginal lands while other immigrants, notably the Americans, seized the more fertile prairie to the south.

Let us, once again, follow the fortunes of the Humeniuk family whom we saw leaving Galicia some weeks before. They arrived in Winnipeg in June of 1897. In the colonist car they sat quietly on their seats as they had been told, peering curiously out of the windows at the equally curious crowd on the platform peering in. Suddenly they spotted a familiar figure—a Galician searching about for acquaintances. His name was Michaniuk and he soon spotted his old friends.

"Neighbours!" Mr. Michaniuk shouted, "where are you going?"

There was a commotion in the car. Where *were* they going? Nobody seemed to know. "Don't go any farther!" cried Mr. Michaniuk to his former townspeople. "It is good here!"

One of the men in the coach rose to his feet and addressed the assembly.

"This is our neighbour, Mr. Michaniuk. He came to Canada last year. He says it is good here. Let us get off the train."

A stampede took place. Men seized the doors, but found them to be locked. They tried the windows, but those were fastened too. Several, in a frenzy, picked up their handbags, smashed the glass, and began to crawl through the openings, throwing their goods ahead of them. The Humeniuk family was carried forward by the press of people onto the platform.

A conductor ran up with an interpreter.

"What are you going to do now?" the interpreter cried. "We have good land for you near Yorkton. There are no free good homesteads for farming left in Manitoba."

But the newcomers could not be convinced. A spokesman replied: "We are not going any farther. Our old country friend has been here one year. He says it's good where he settled."

Nobody could persuade them to go on to Yorkton. They were moved to the immigration hall, where the women began to cook food, to launder the clothes, and to tend to the children. The men followed Mr. Michaniuk to the Dominion Land Office to file for homesteads near Stuartburn on the Roseau River, near the American border, where thirty-seven Galician families were already located.

It turned out that some land was still available and it was there that they settled. Most of them were still there a half a century later, when Nykola and Anastasia Humeniuk, surrounded by grandchildren, celebrated their golden wedding anniversary on the farm they filed for back in 1897.

The sheepskin people had to make do with essentials. Their homes were built of timber and whitewashed clay, the roofs thatched with straw. Whole families slept on top of the vast stove-furnaces six feet (1.8 m) square. Gardens were dug with spades because they couldn't afford better equipment. Benches and tables were handmade. Plates were hammered out of tin cans found in garbage dumps. Drinking glasses were created by cutting a beer bottle in half.

Browbeaten for centuries, the Galicians didn't find it easy to throw off old habits. W. A. Griesbach, the young mayor of Edmonton, found them timid and frightened and noticed that when a uniformed policeman approached, they drove right off the road, removed their caps, and waited for him to go by. If a well-dressed Canadian gave them an order, they would immediately obey. This made them ripe targets for exploitation.

The sheepskin people had to make do with essentials. Their homes were built of timber and white-washed clay, the roofs thatched with straw. Whole families slept on top of the vast stove-furnaces six feet (1.8 m) square.

One man who worked with them on the railway described them as "naïve, trustful, bearded giants [who] worked like elephants, laughed like children and asked no questions," but were subject to "ruthless, brazen robbery." The food was meagre and barely edible; better fare was available in the company's store, but "for prices that New York night clubs would be ashamed to ask … Those who didn't like it could get out (at their own expense) for there was a never ending stream shanghaied by the mass-procurement agencies of the East … The Ukrainians were held in check by the small Anglo-Saxon element present in every camp, who, being decently treated, were always ready to put down with fists, clubs, and even guns, any outbreak of the 'Bohunks.'"

All the same, the newcomers were changing the look of the prairies. Carpathian villages with neat, whitewashed houses and thatched roofs sprang up. Onion-shaped spires began to dominate the landscape. Mingled with the silhouettes of the grain elevators, and the familiar style of the prairie railway stations, they helped create a profile that was distinctively Western.

To those public figures who had no axe to grind, they were an attractive addition to the prairie mix. William Van Horne, president of the CPR, found them "a very desirable people." Charles Constantine, a veteran mounted policeman at Fort Saskatchewan, used the same adjective. The immigration agent in Edmonton said, "They are settlers, and I should like to see more of them."

Van Horne, in 1899, was astonished to discover that those who had been given railway transportation on credit actually paid the money back. As he said, "We had little hope of ever getting what they owed us, but they paid up every cent." And several who had first opposed their arrival changed their minds.

One doctor described his visit to a Galician colony as "a revelation." He described the colonists as "worthy, industrious, sober, and ambitious to make homes for themselves."

Another who also changed his mind was W. M. Fisher of the Canada Permanent Mortgage Company, who reported that "the Galicians against whom I was prejudiced before my visit … I found to be a most desirable class of settler, being hard working, frugal people and in their financial dealings honest to a degree."

The attitude of the newspapers was predictable. The government papers thought they were wonderful; the opposition papers thought the opposite. The first wave had scarcely stepped ashore when the Conservative papers mounted a vicious attack. To the Belleville *Intelligencer* they were "disgusting creatures," to the Brandon *Independent* "human vermin." The Ottawa *Citizen* objected to Canada "being turned into a social sewage farm to purify the rinsings and leavings of rotten European states." In Edmonton, the *Bulletin* pulled out all the stops. It said the Galicians were "a servile, shiftless people … the scum of other lands … not a people who are wanted in this country at any price."

The attacks were entirely political. In the pro-Sifton newspapers, the Galicians could do no wrong. But the public outcry by the Conservatives in

Parliament finally forced Sifton to put a damper on Galician immigration. The general belief was that the influx of Slavs would dilute and muddy the purity of Canada's Anglo-Saxon heritage.

Hugh John Macdonald, the son of Canada's first prime minister, actually referred to the Galicians as "a mongrel race." Premier Roblin of Manitoba went further. He called them "foreign trash" and proceeded to deny them the vote in order to "defend the 'old flag' against an invading foe."

The Conservatives harped on the belief that these Galicians were subhumans with violent criminal tendencies, subject to greed and uncontrollable passions. Mackenzie Bowell wrote of "tales of murder, arson and brutality, more horrible than anything ever dreamed of by the wildest disciple of the school of realistic fiction." These were not the words of a street-corner bigot— they came from the pen of a former prime minister.

As for real Galician crime, it hardly existed. That same year, the chief of police in Winnipeg released annual figures showing the ethnic origins of convicted prisoners. Of 1,205 criminals, 1,037 were Canadians, and 168 were foreign born, and of these latter, only nine were Galicians.

We have heard the same comments in our own time, especially in those areas where emigrants from the Far East have also been attacked, without evidence, as criminals, thieves, and wife-beaters.

The tales of the Galicians were simple fiction. One newspaper, the Shoal Lake *Star*, wrote of murder, robbery, wife-beating, and other crimes being committed among the Galicians in that area. But when Wesley Speers, of the Immigration Department, went to Shoal Lake and tracked down every story, he found them all to be untrue. He forced an apology from the newspaper, and a correction.

Yet the concept of the Galicians as potentially dangerous criminals stayed in the public mind. That was because every Galician who got into trouble was identified in bold headlines. "GALICIAN HORROR" is the way the Winnipeg *Daily Tribune* headlined a local murder in June of 1899, convicting the man out of hand long before he went to trial.

Another Galician charged with murder was castigated before his trial as "an inhuman wretch." Trial by newspapers was far more common at the turn of the century than it is today. The following month the pro-Conservative Winnipeg *Telegram* reported the murder of Mrs. Robert Lane of Brandon in July of 1895, identifying her assailant as Galician. It titled its story as "ANOTHER SIFTONIAN TRAGEDY." It said that "In order that Mr. Sifton may keep his Liberal party in power by the votes of ignorant and vicious foreign scum he is dumping on our prairies, we are to submit to have our nearest and dearest butchered on our door-steps."

The entire story was a lie. The murderer wasn't a Galician, but an English woman who confessed to the crime and was hanged for it. But the impression of Galician madmen murdering defenceless Canadian women was hard to erase.

As for real Galician crime, it hardly existed. That same year, the chief of police in Winnipeg released annual figures showing the ethnic origins of convicted prisoners. Of 1,205 criminals, 1,037 were Canadians, and 168 were foreign born, and of these latter, only *nine* were Galicians.

CHAPTER FIVE

Fears of "Mongrelisation"

BY 1904, THE ATTITUDE TOWARDS THE SHEEPSKIN PEOPLE HAD BEGUN TO CHANGE, AND FOR A VERY PRACTICAL REASON. THE NEWSPAPERS AND POLITICIANS WHO HAD ATTACKED "SIFTON'S DIRTY SLAVS" REVERSED THEMSELVES. THE VIOLENTLY TORY WINNIPEG *TELEGRAM*, FOR INSTANCE, WHICH HAD ATTACKED THE IMMIGRANTS AS "IGNORANT, SUPERSTITIOUS AND FILTHY," NOW DISCOVERED THAT THEY WERE "INDUSTRIOUS," "THRIFTY," "PROGRESSIVE," AND "PROSPEROUS."

The reason was that there was an election, and everybody was scrambling for Galician votes. Even the Tory premier of Manitoba was having second thoughts. He had once called the newcomers "dirty ignorant Slavs" who lived on rats and mice, but now he rose in the legislature to praise "their diligence, their intelligence, their sobriety, their generally estimable character."

They'd been denied the provincial vote in Manitoba back in 1899. Now the premier gave it to them. He had to do something to defeat the federal Liberal campaign, which was making such great headway among all the immigrants in the West. Immigrants voted for the Liberals because the Liberal party had opened the doors to immigrants and given them free land.

It's doubtful whether many really understood the Canadian electoral system. In Europe they had voted for "electors"—one for every five hundred voters—who, in turn, went to the political centre of their district and voted for the actual candidate, usually a big land owner. That system made the newcomers suspicious of all politicians. And that was reinforced when they discovered that in Canada a vote could be sold for a dollar. Some sold their votes twice—once to each opposing candidate, and then voted as they pleased.

Nor could they understand a word the politicians uttered when they toured the villages. Both parties had to use interpreters. There was a story of one interpreter warming up a crowd of potential Liberal voters by telling them, "I'm going to call upon the local candidate to speak, and I want you to listen carefully. When I start clapping I want all of you to do the same. And when he finishes I want all of you to give him a great ovation. You won't regret it and neither will I." And of course he was paid off by the Liberals for that.

Frank Oliver, a Conservative candidate, once spoke to a group of Galicians in a small general store in his riding near Edmonton. Nobody had any idea of what the man was saying, except for the local party interpreter. If they had known, they would have had little interest in the subject because he was ranting on about free trade.

"What's he say?" one listener finally asked the interpreter.

"He's glad we're here. Canada was lucky to get us …"

"What about the stupid fire regulations?"

"He'll fix them."

"What's he say about the railroad?"

"I forgot to tell you that—he's got it started for sure."

"What about the mudholes around Whitford Lake?"

"He'll fix them—he'll do all he can for our area …"

Frank Oliver was not above dressing up some of his supporters as surveyors pretending to drive highways through Galician farmyards in preparation for an apparent new railway. When the despairing immigrant begged for a changed route, the fake surveyors told him to get in touch with the local Liberal agent who might be able to help them. In every case, of course, the Liberals agreed, and the farmer gave Oliver his vote.

The newcomers were also vague about voting dates. Because they didn't read any English, an effort was needed to get out the vote, or in some cases to keep the vote away. Oliver had his organizers swarm over the Galician communities asking each man whom he intended to vote for. Those who were voting Liberal were told the proper date of the election was Monday. But the Conservative voters were told it was Wednesday.

It was Oliver who replaced Clifford Sifton the following year as Minister of the Interior. Not surprisingly, the concept of unrestricted immigration was tossed aside when the government changed.

There was no talk about multiculturalism then. The big word was "assimilation." The people who ran the country wanted conformity—in dress, in language, in customs, in attitudes, and in religion. Every immigrant who arrived in the West was expected to accept as quickly as possible the Anglo-Celtic, Protestant values of his Canadian neighbours.

In those days everybody agreed that certain races couldn't be assimilated and had no place in Canadian society. Orientals, East Indians, and Blacks were not wanted. Anti-Semitism was universal. The press was racist. They called the Blacks niggers, Orientals were Chinamen, and the Jews were sheenies.

Could the Galicians be assimilated, or would their presence "mongrelise" the nation when they mixed with other races and groups? That was the basis of the argument from the moment they arrived. It was generally agreed they were an inferior race, but that wasn't the problem. The question was whether or not they could be turned into "white" Canadians.

The anti-Sifton newspapers didn't believe it possible. As the Edmonton *Bulletin*, owned by Frank Oliver, said, "They have withstood assimilation in the country from whence they come for many generations. What reason have we to expect their ready assimilation here?" Others were grudgingly optimistic. As the Hamilton *Times* put it, "They may never develop into such perfect Canadians as the Scotch or the Irish, but the chances are they will turn out all right."

As we know now, they did turn out all right. The son of one of those immigrant families, Ray Hnatyshyn, would one day become Governor General of Canada.

The general sentiment was one of optimism. A new century was dawning—"Canada's century," Prime Minister Wilfrid Laurier called it. It was a country capable of working miracles. The men in sheepskin coats would be quickly transformed into well-cropped, bowler-hatted Canadians—or so it was believed. As the *Manitoba Free Press* put it, "the land is here and the Anglo-Saxon race has great assimilating qualities." To William McCreary, the Galicians were "already dressing in a more civilized garb" and "accepting Canadian customs and ways."

One of several reasons that some leading Canadians wanted the Galicians to assimilate was because they wanted them to be sturdy

Protestants, and not Orthodox Catholics. J. W. Sparling, the principal of Winnipeg's Methodist Wesley College, wrote, "there is danger and it is national! Either we must educate and elevate the incoming multitudes or they will drag us and our children down to a lower level. We must see to it that the civilization and ideals of Southeastern Europe are not transplanted to and perpetuated on our virgin soil." In Sparling's view, these ideals, of course, were those of the Catholic religions.

The Methodist publication *Missionary Outlook* summed up the Methodist point of view in 1908, when it wrote: "If from this North American continent is to come a superior race, a race to be specially used of God in the carrying on of His work, what is our duty to those who are now our fellow-citizens? Many of them come to us as nominal Christians, that is, they owe allegiance to the Greek or Roman Catholic churches but their moral standards and ideals are far below those of the Christian citizens of the Dominion … It is our duty to meet them with an open Bible, and to install into their minds the principles and ideals of Anglo-Saxon civilization."

But nobody asked the Galicians whether or not they wished to be ground up in the great Anglo-Saxon mill. They clung fiercely to their religion. And indeed, the presence of Roman Catholic and Greek Orthodox churches in the rural prairies helped them keep their language and culture. Certainly, many wanted to learn English and wanted their children to learn it. In this desire they were often held back by the lack of good teachers. But they also wanted to keep their original language, and this they did to a remarkable degree, producing an impressive body of prose and poetry in their own tongue.

The fears of "mongrelisation" were groundless. The newcomers and their children managed to become Canadians while retaining a pride in their heritage, as the Scots did, as the Icelanders and others did. By the First

World War, when immigration ceased, the talk of assimilation began to subside. By the 1920s, the term "Galician" had died out.

By then, most Canadians were beginning to understand the difference between Poles and Ukrainians, for by then Polish and Ukrainian social and political clubs were scattered across the West. The time was coming when Canadians of every background would be referring to the Canadian "mosaic" and later to "multiculturalism" and, indeed, boasting about it as if it had been purposely invented as an instrument of national policy to preserve the Dominion from the American Melting Pot.

CHAPTER SIX

The Spirit Wrestlers

AT 4 P.M. ON JANUARY 20, 1899—A PERFECT WINTER'S DAY—THE S.S. *LAKE HURON* STEAMED INTO HALIFAX HARBOUR WITH TWENTY-ONE HUNDRED DOUKHOBORS ON BOARD. THIS WAS THE LARGEST SINGLE BODY OF EMIGRANTS EVER TO HAVE CROSSED THE ATLANTIC IN ONE SHIP. SHE HAD TRAVELLED FOR TWENTY-NINE DAYS FROM THE BLACK SEA PORT OF BATUM, IN THE RUSSIAN DISTRICT OF GEORGIA, MANNED BY A SKELETON CREW (TO SAVE MONEY).

Ten persons had died during the voyage; five couples had been married in the simple Doukhobor ceremony. The new arrivals had also survived a dreadful tempest that blew unceasingly for eight days, causing all to give up hope of ever reaching Canadian shores. In spite of this, the ship was spanking clean, scrubbed spotless by the women. The chief health officer said he'd never known so clean a vessel to enter Halifax harbour.

These too were people in sheepskin coats, though not known as Galicians. They came from the valleys of the Caucasus Mountains between the Caspian and Black Seas—a religious group who lived communally, rejected military service, and refused to take an oath of allegiance to the Czar. They called themselves the Christian Community of Universal Brotherhood, but their tormenters jeered at them "Doukhoborski," or spirit wrestlers.

The name stuck and in the end was accepted with pride in the same way the Society of Friends accepted the word "Quaker." They came to Canada as a result of money raised by a group of high-minded Canadians and Russian noblemen—including Count Leo Tolstoy, the world-famous author of the novel *War and Peace*—who could not stomach the persecution they were receiving in Russia. They did not come at the invitation of the Canadian government, but there was little the government could do about them. They were coming anyway—twenty-one hundred of them.

Nothing like this had ever taken place before. Somehow all of these people—men, women, and children, scarcely any of whom understood a word of English—had to be taken halfway across Canada as soon as they got off the boat.

How to find shelter in Winnipeg for these new arrivals? Who was going to house twenty-one hundred people? The immigration shed could handle no more than six hundred. The shed at Brandon held no more than four hundred, and that was ice cold, the wind blowing snow and ice through the cracks in the walls.

Nor was the department equipped to feed such an army. William McCreary, the immigration agent, was planning to throw up a frame shed at Yorkton. There was another at Dauphin, Manitoba, which would hold three hundred, mainly women and children. An additional hundred could perhaps be squeezed into the shed at Brandon, another hundred at Birtle, and upward of fifty at Qu'Appelle. That would still leave another hundred who would have to be crowded into the overtaxed hall in Winnipeg.

McCreary was on the verge of a breakdown from overwork. He felt powerless to cope with the Doukhobor influx. He had no authority to buy anything. No committee had been organized to handle the money raised from the Doukhobors themselves and from well-wishers. He had to find wood, water, harnesses, oxen, sleighs, flour, vegetables. He couldn't locate sixty-gallon (227-L) cooking pots in the West—they would have to be shipped by freight, and that would take ten days or longer if there was a blizzard.

Five trainloads of Doukhobors began arriving in Winnipeg at noon on the afternoon of January 27, 1899. This was the coldest winter in the memory of the city's oldest inhabitants! When the third train pulled in, it was one o'clock in the morning, and so cold on the platform that McCreary froze his nose and fingers.

Train No. 4 was an hour behind, en route to Brandon. The fifth train arrived at 5:30 and collided with a yard engine just as it pulled out for Dauphin. Two cars were damaged and had to be replaced.

But the Doukhobors were in a state of near ecstasy. To them, McCreary's makeshift arrangements felt like heaven on earth. Hot dinners awaited them the moment they stepped off the train. The women of Winnipeg had spent hours peeling potatoes and chopping cabbage and making soup. Thousands turned out the following day to greet them.

An address of welcome was offered by a local church minister, heading a committee especially organized for the purpose. There were tears in the eyes of the onlookers when he spoke.

As far as the Spirit Wrestlers were concerned, their problems were over. But McCreary's were just beginning. He'd managed to house two thousand-odd Doukhobors in temporary quarters, but now he was faced with four new concerns. With winter coming on, he had to clothe these people, move food out to them, provide real housing, and do this before another two thousand arrived. For they were already aboard the Beaver Line's *Lake Superior*, due in Halifax in a fortnight's time.

The Doukhobors were ill-prepared for the 45 below (−43°C) weather. They wore hard leather boots and pieces of blanket around their feet in place of socks. The women wore only a half-slipper with a leather sole. Nobody had mitts. Several froze their toes. McCreary bought two hundred pairs of moccasins, four hundred pairs of socks, and a mountain of warm clothing for the men he was dispatching to prepare the new colonies for the others.

The staple food was simplified. Cheese, molasses, and fish, which some had been fed at Brandon and Portage la Prairie, were cut off because the Doukhobors themselves insisted they all get the same provisions. The regular diet would be potatoes, onions, cabbage, tea, and sugar.

Meanwhile, McCreary had managed to outfit and supply gangs of ten men from each of the three colonies planning to settle in the West. These were out cutting timber for houses. By February 9, one gang had erected three buildings in the settlement, each large enough to hold fifty or sixty people.

So, with their own resources, the Doukhobors rose to the challenge. The young men took any job they could get, from shovelling snow to chopping wood. The older men set up cottage industries, making wooden spoons and painted bowls for sale. The women responded to local demand for fine embroidery and woven woollens. The younger girls took jobs as domestic servants.

Rather than purchase shovels and harnesses, the Doukhobor farmers bought iron bars and leather, built forges to produce implements, and fashioned Russian-style gear that was superior to the mass-produced Canadian harness.

The Dominion Experimental Farm gave advice on crops. The Massey-Harris Company sold equipment on credit. And so, with the help of a number of dedicated and generous friends, these extraordinary people were on the way to self-sufficiency.

In spite of all the problems, Canada, in just over a year, managed to settle seventy-five hundred persecuted and poverty-stricken Russians on the black soil of Saskatchewan in three separate colonies. One, known as the Rosthern Colony, lay just west of that town on the South Saskatchewan River. The so-called North and South colonies lay to the southeast, the first on the Manitoba border, the other just north of Yorkton.

Within a year, their villages were built and their future seemed secure. But trouble was brewing in the North and South colonies. To a small and fanatical group, the true promised land wasn't in Saskatchewan at all, but in the dreams and visions of their leaders.

The Doukhobors believed that Christ lived in every man and so priests were unnecessary and the Bible obsolete. They rejected churches, litany, icons, and festivals. They insisted their only allegiance was to Christ—they would take no oaths to a government. They were fanatically loyal to their leader, Peter Verigin. He was still in exile in Siberia, but from Siberia he could send messages to the Canadian colonies.

The Doukhobors did not believe in the concept of private property, and because of this they were bound to come into open conflict with the Canadian government. The Doukhobors held their property in common, pooling their resources and farming big tracts of land. But the rigid Canadian system didn't allow that. Each quarter section was owned by an individual who had title to it. Each Canadian family lived on that quarter section—often miles from their nearest neighbours. The Doukhobors, however, lived close together in villages.

In that first summer there was scarcely an able-bodied man left in any of the fifty-seven villages. While they worked on the railway, the women broke the sod, often hitching themselves to ploughs—twenty-four to each team.

By the end of 1900, the men were back at work in the fields. Life was hard, but there was also an idyllic quality to it. A choir chanted in the streets each morning to wake the workers. The men divided into gangs and sang as they marched towards the fields. The town meeting made for a rough democracy. Antelope and deer foraged unmolested among the cattle, for these people were vegetarians.

They were incredibly polite: they never passed each other on the street without removing their caps and bowing. It was explained that they were not really bowing to each other but to the spirit of Jesus within them.

The general attitude towards the Doukhobors in Canada was one of curiosity and good nature. After all, they were a persecuted people fleeing from a tyrannical government.

And then, in the fall of 1902, a stunning series of events occurred that would put the Spirit Wrestlers back on the front pages and from then on make the name Doukhobor a synonym for terror, fanaticism, and lunacy.

In all his years on the prairies, Wes Speers, the colonization agent, had never seen anything like it, and he knew he would never see anything like it again. It was October 27, 1902. He was standing on the open prairies, some thirteen miles (21 km) north of Yorkton—a tall, rangy figure, Sifton's appointee as colonization agent for the West—waiting for the Doukhobors.

They came upon him slowly like a black cloud low on the prairie, densely packed, thirty to forty abreast—some two thousand men, women, and children. The procession was headed by an old man with a flowing white beard, chanting and waving his hands. Behind him, two stalwart Russians led a blind man, followed by men bearing stretchers of poplar branches and blankets carrying the sick, and behind them a choir, three hundred strong. The chanting never stopped, the multitude repeating the verses of the Twenty-second Psalm over and over again: "*My God, my God, why hast thou forsaken me?*"

For the next two weeks, Speers would come head to head with the most stubborn group of fanatics in Western Canada—the splinter group of Doukhobors who called themselves the Sons of God. These people seemed intent on killing themselves in the name of the Saviour, not by any sudden action but simply from hunger and exposure on the frostbitten prairie.

The government faced a dilemma: it could not allow them to die, but neither could it interfere with a devout religious sect. There must be no violence: after all, they didn't intend to harm anybody but themselves.

Slowly, the army of men, women, and children advanced on the colonization agent. He knew it was useless to reason with them. They required nothing of him, they said.

"We are going to seek Christ," they told him vaguely. Christ, apparently, was somewhere in the southeast, somewhere in the land of the sun, far from the windswept prairie, in a country where the fruit hung thickly on the trees and vegetables were cropped the year round, where it was not necessary to use a single animal for labour, food, or clothing. A lovely prospect for people facing another bitter winter—but a false one.

The pale prairie afternoon would soon turn to dusk. Speers knew that he must find immediate shelter for these people who believed that God would look after them. Back he rode to Yorkton to arrange for space in the immigration hall, the Orange Hall, an implement warehouse, a pool hall, a grain elevator. Some of the children were crying with hunger. The people were living on dried rosehips, herbs, leaves, and grasses. The women of Yorkton were prepared to feed them—that is, if they agreed to be fed.

Speers had picked up the first rumours of trouble that summer when he heard that some of the Doukhobors in the Yorkton area were acting strangely. They were freeing all their animals, burning their sheepskin vests and leather boots, making sandals from plaited binder twine, refusing to eat eggs, butter, or milk, abandoning their horses and hitching themselves as teams, and making no provision for the coming winter by putting up hay for their stock. Some had come to believe that it was a sin to exploit animals in any way.

The problem had its roots in the complex mind of Peter Verigin, resting comfortably in Siberian exile and daydreaming of a paradise on earth in which the sun would always shine, where men would live on fruit and never exploit their animal brethren, where money would not be needed, and metal, the symbol of an industrial society, would be outlawed.

Verigin's vague ideas took hold. For more than fifteen years, members of the sect had been without anyone to guide them. They were hungry for leadership, especially by 1902, when the Canadian government began to press upon them demands they could not accept. Canada didn't want them to hold land in common. In addition, it wanted every Doukhobor to take an oath of allegiance to the state. Now, out of the blue, came a message from the one man who could stand up for them against the same kind of authority that had forced them to leave Russia.

There was more, surely. There must also have been a longing for the kind of sunny paradise that Verigin dreamed of, where frost never fell, winds did not blow, and prairie whiteouts were unknown. The exiled leader had talked of warmth and energy from the sun: "Man employing food raised by an abundance of solar heat, such as, for instance, raspberries, strawberries ... tender fruits, his organism will be formed, as it were, of energy itself ..."

Slowly, a sect within a sect was forming—the Sons of God. Self-appointed apostles began moving through the villages, spreading the new gospel. And so there they were on the night of October 27—men, women, and children huddled together in a poplar bluff without a fire to warm them.

Their leaders insisted that they would continue to go on to find Christ, but Speers had no intention of allowing that. With the help of the Mounted Police, he herded the resisting women into shelter, guarded by three mounted policemen and fifteen constables. The men, he said, were free to continue if they wanted to. The following day, after standing up praying and chanting all night, they set off again.

They threw away the clothes they'd bought in Yorkton, leaving behind a trail of boots, cloaks, and hats. They slept in ditches, lived on grasses and raw potatoes until their faces grew gaunt and their eyes feverish. And yet they still managed to walk twenty miles (32 km) a day, their feet torn and bleeding from the frost-covered stubble. Speers trailed them, trying to make them listen to reason, but the answer was always the same: "Jesus will look after us."

On November 7, 450 hard-core believers reached Minnedosa, in Manitoba. They intended to carry on, but Speers had no intention of letting them.

All night long the Sons of God, herded into the local skating rink, prayed and sang. The Doukhobors tried to rush the doors but were prevented. A special train was on its way with twenty-three police. It arrived at 4:30 that afternoon. Speers led the men out of the rink. The Doukhobors turned from him and started to head east. The townspeople stopped them.

Several were picked up bodily and flung into the train because the Sons of God refused to strike a blow against their captors. It took forty minutes to pack them into the waiting cars and send them home.

That broke the back of the pilgrimage. The women and children had already been taken back to the railhead near their villages. They refused to ride the rest of the way and insisted on walking the full twenty-seven miles (43 km). Within two hours of their return, they had their furnaces going, vegetable soup on the stove, and were hard at work scrubbing and cleaning their houses.

For the Doukhobors the pilgrimage left a bitter legacy. It turned public opinion against them. The opposition press began to rail against all Doukhobors—whether or not they belonged to the minority sect. The urge to turn them into carbon copies of Canadians was just as strong as it was in the case of the Galicians.

Meanwhile the villages were at peace. Exhausted by their long travail, the Sons of God rested quietly, waiting for the imminent arrival of their leader, Peter Verigin, released at last from his Siberian confinement.

CHAPTER SEVEN

Peter the Lordly

VERIGIN ARRIVED IN WINNIPEG ON A PERFECT WINTER AFTERNOON JUST THREE DAYS BEFORE CHRISTMAS, 1902. HE STARTED DOWN THE PLATFORM TO A CROWD OF GREETERS — A BIG MAN, HALF A HEAD TALLER THAN HIS FELLOW PASSENGERS, WITH A LUXURIANT BLACK BEARD AND DARK, THOUGHTFUL EYES. HE WAS NOT DRESSED LIKE THE OTHERS. UNDER HIS SHORT GABARDINE COAT, ONE COULD SEE LEGGINGS, CLOSE-FITTING, DARK GREY, PIPED WITH BLACK. HE WORE A BLACK FEDORA, AND AROUND HIS NECK ON A LONG CORD DANGLED A SILVER WATCH AND A GOLD PENCIL.

His supporters rushed towards him. He dropped his black nickel-studded valise, removed his hat, and stretched out his arms to embrace the woman who led the greeters. "Anna!" he cried. She was his sister; they had not seen each other for fifteen years.

Both the Doukhobors and the Immigration Department saw Verigin as a saviour. The sect was convinced he would stand up for their rights. The government was hopeful he would calm the fanatics.

For the next three days, from early morning until late in the evening, Peter Vasilivich Verigin received representatives from each of the fifty-seven villages. They called him Peter the Lordly, and the title fitted. Off he went on a tour of all the villages, seated in a six-horse sleigh, with a choir of maidens chanting psalms. The authorities were delighted. They were convinced that Verigin would bring peace.

He was a good bargainer for his people—he got the railway contractors to raise the Doukhobors' wages. One contractor tried to tell him that if he went too high the company couldn't make a profit.

"No company will profit by our work," Verigin told him. "Take it or leave it." The contractor took it because workmen were hard to find.

Verigin swiftly changed from his Russian costume to a tailored suit with a white shirt and turned-down collar. He had his long hair close-cropped and his face clean-shaven except for a bristling moustache. He said he would give his children Canadian names.

The community was still split into three factions. The well-to-do farmers of the Rosthern Colony, southwest of Prince Albert, were opting more and more for independence and free enterprise. The radical Left, especially in the South Colony near Yorkton, were activists who believed in demonstrations to reach their goals. In the centre was the great mass of Doukhobors who wanted to retain the communal system of central villages where personal possessions were all but unknown. That too was Verigin's desire, but he became more and more unsure of achieving it in Saskatchewan.

He travelled about like an Oriental leader, in a six-horse sleigh in winter and in a carriage in summer, wearing a silk hat. The inevitable choir of chanting maidens accompanied him. One, a plump, blue-eyed brunette of eighteen, Anastasia Golubova, he called his wife.

But his power was dwindling. The first of a series of small protest marches engineered by the same fanatics who had led the pilgrimage of 1902 took place the following March. Fifty of them refused to register their lands with the government. They began to travel from village to village, urging their fellows to resist temptation, to turn animals loose, and to seek the sun.

Meanwhile, a new group, the Freedomites, known as the "Sons of Freedom," added two new rituals—first nudity, later arson. The results for Verigin were catastrophic.

The press was intrigued by men, women, and children who burned their clothes and marched naked on the chill prairie. The authorities stopped all efforts to photograph them. Speers tried to find out why they would insist on taking off their clothes, and was told it was part of their religion—that they wanted to go to a warm country and live like Adam and Eve.

That did not endear them to the Canadian public. Some went to jail where, being vegetarians, they lived on raw potatoes and oatmeal. Others followed on charges of arson, and two were judged insane. One died of malnutrition, and the headlines kept on.

The Doukhobors had no political power. Because they refused to swear allegiance to Canada, they couldn't become citizens and vote. Squatters moved onto their unregistered lands, and these had clout in Ottawa. With tens of thousands of settlers moving into the West, the Doukhobors' holdings looked good to them. Pressure began to mount, and then Sifton resigned and Frank Oliver replaced him as Minister of the Interior.

Oliver's intentions were to treat the Doukhobors like any other landowners. They must conform to Canadian customs. There would be no exceptions to the rigid regulations of the Homestead Act. Each must obey its regulations to build his house on his free quarter section and farm it individually.

Communal farming was out. There could be no villages as a result, no common tilling of the soils. The houses would be scattered about, four to a section, in the Canadian fashion. If any Doukhobor continued to live in the villages, his ownership would be cancelled. Only a few people protested this violent attempt at assimilation. Few Canadians seemed to care.

Verigin had seen it coming. He had no intention of submerging his people's religion and lifestyle in an ocean of Canadian conformity. The short haircut and the clean-shaven face had lulled the authorities into believing the Doukhobor leader was like everybody else. He was far more complicated, determined, and far-sighted than outward appearances suggested.

He'd built up a massive war chest by sending the men of his flock to earn money on the railways. With these funds he decided to buy other lands privately in another province—in the Kootenay district of British Columbia—and start all over again. For the first and only time, a substantial body of immigrants rejected the Canadian dream and turned its back on the promised land.

This was an incredible sacrifice. Everything the Doukhobors had slaved for since 1899 was to be abandoned—the neatly ploughed fields, the well-kept villages, the stacks of hay, the lofts bursting with grain. Not everybody followed Verigin. Two thousand independent Doukhobors at Rosthern took the oath and settled on their individual homesteads. Another thousand in two colonies north of Yorkton decided also to remain. But five thousand followed their leaders to the new province.

Suddenly, in June 1907, a quarter of a million acres (100,000 hectares) of prime farmland, abandoned by the Doukhobors, came onto the market—free homesteads for any man who could fight for a place in the long lineups forming at the doors of the land offices.

This wasn't raw land. Some of these homesteads were worth from three thousand to ten thousand dollars. And so the stage was set for the last great land rush in North America.

There were scenes of mob violence in Yorkton and Prince Albert. Over the weekend of June 1 and 2, men waited for forty-five hours in the cold and rain for the Yorkton office to open at nine on Monday morning. The town was crammed with real estate speculators. Hotels were bursting. People paid ten cents a night just to sleep in haystacks.

Far more people queued up each night than there were homesteads available. In Prince Albert, one group of thirty exhausted and shivering men, bone weary from more than twenty-four hours in line, found themselves muscled from their positions by a fresher party. They were crushed so tightly that some were shoved through the glass panes of the land office. Five policemen had to restore order with fists and clubs.

By the first week in June, the police figured that five hundred strangers, representatives of real estate men, were in Yorkton with orders to break into the queue at any cost. During one night a group of these men charged the line and struggled with the Mounted Police. "Mob the police! Mob the police!" they cried, until the sergeant in charge called out the fire department and turned a hose on them. But, dripping wet, they clung stubbornly to their place in the queue.

Thus the reign of Peter the Lordly came to an end on the prairies, with fists and truncheons, cries and catcalls, and the jarring sounds of human beings in collision—a stark contrast to the soft chanting of the choir of maidens, now only an echo in the empty villages scattered along the green valleys of Saskatchewan.

Looking back, the government's new attitude, under Frank Oliver, towards the Doukhobors seems not only racist but foolhardy. Why shouldn't people work communally? Why do they have to be separated by long distances with a house on each quarter section—a lonely life for all immigrants who arrived in Canada? Why couldn't they cluster in villages?

Canada, in those days, was intent on bending all immigrants to its will—not only Galicians and Doukhobors, but also the English, the Americans, and the other nationalities who, a million strong, crowded into Canada in this restless, difficult, and eventually triumphant period.

In the end they managed to cling to their roots and their origins and their culture, while at the same time becoming strong Canadians. Many became important citizens—mayors of cities, leading politicians, lawyers and doctors, journalists and writers, engineers, and some just plain farmers. One, as we've already noted, became Governor General of Canada.

It was this vast horde of strangers filling up an empty land that eventually helped to build a country stretching from ocean to ocean. They helped give their adopted country its greatest natural resource—grain. They remain proud of their origins—and in this sense the government helped them by making Canada the first multicultural country in the world. But they also strengthened the land and were responsible for the great Western boom that helped make the country prosperous in the days before the First World War, when Wilfrid Laurier said the twentieth century belonged to Canada.

INDEX

Barr colonists with wagons and teams at the railway
station in Saskatoon, Saskatchewan, April 1903.
(COURTESY GLENBOW ARCHIVES, NA-118-27)

A PRAIRIE NIGHTMARE

CONTENTS

The Promised Land

THERE WAS A TIME IN THE FIRST DECADE OF THIS CENTURY WHEN CANADA WAS SEEN AS A LAND OF UNLIMITED OPPORTUNITY. THIS WAS ESPECIALLY TRUE OF THE CANADIAN WEST, WHICH HAD JUST BEEN SPANNED BY THE COUNTRY'S FIRST TRANSCONTINENTAL RAILWAY, LINKING BRITISH COLUMBIA WITH THE SETTLED EAST. THERE, SOME OF THE RICHEST SOIL IN THE WORLD LAY BECKONING THE WOULD-BE FARMERS OF EUROPE.

To the Europeans, and indeed to many Canadians, the land seemed empty, waiting to be filled up by settlers. But it wasn't really empty. Long before the white man, it had been the domain of the Cree, the Blackfoot, and the other Indian bands that trapped and hunted in a seemingly endless ocean of waist-high buffalo grass. When the railway was built, the Indian bands still roamed the plains; but in a single decade the wave of white new-comers would fence and till their hunting grounds, leaving only those little islands of native settlement the white people called "reserves."

As far as the Indians were concerned, the white Canadians were all immigrants. They did not welcome strangers to their hunting lands any more than the white Canadians welcomed the new wave of strangers pouring across the Atlantic—especially the Slavs from Eastern Europe.

The average Canadian was in favour of immigration, as long as the immigrants behaved exactly as the original British and French had behaved. It was the British-born who were wanted, not the men in sheepskin coats from the foreign countries of the Ukraine and Poland.

Only after the British arrived did Canadians begin to have second thoughts. Instead of reliable British farmers, they got men and women from the slums of Manchester, or office clerks from London who had never dirtied their hands in "honest" toil. The newcomers were often laughed at as inept—totally unsuited to the raw prairies.

And yet, as people generally do, they muddled through, made the best of the conditions, and in the end prospered.

This is the story of one such group from the British Isles, who, on the face of it, stood no chance of making a new life in the Canadian West. And yet, after incredible hardships, most prospered. We should remember, when we study the strange story of Isaac Barr and his "lambs," that even today Canadians sometimes want to reject new arrivals because they seem unsuitable for life in Canada.

That's how many Canadians looked on the settlers of the Britannia Colony, which became Lloydminster, Saskatchewan. How wrong they were!

CHAPTER ONE

Goodbye, Forever

LIVERPOOL, MARCH 31, 1903. IVAN CROSSLEY, AN EIGHTEEN-YEAR-OLD IRISH YOUTH, STANDS ON THE DOCKSIDE AMONG THE JOSTLING CROWD, LOOKING DOWN AT THE WATERS DAPPLED BY THE SPRING SUN, PREPARING TO WAVE GOODBYE TO THE OLD WORLD.

The day before, he had been part of a similar scene before boarding the channel steamer at Belfast, in what is now Northern Ireland. His mother had prayed and wept. The crowd had sung, "God Be With You Till We Meet Again." But they would never see each other again. Ivan had said goodbye to his mother forever.

Ivan was going to Canada with a party of Irish emigrants, hoping to make a new home on the Canadian prairies. He had already enjoyed a brief adventure in the New World, working on a fruit farm in Florida. Back in Belfast he had been kicking up his heels, wondering what to do with himself, thirsting for excitement, planning maybe to seek his fortune somewhere in the British Empire.

And then his mother received a letter from a relative in England. A pamphlet dropped out of the envelope, describing the wonders of the Canadian West. The writer of the pamphlet was a Christian minister named Isaac Barr.

Crossley wrote Barr at once and got an enthusiastic letter in return. He sent in ten dollars, as required, got back a receipt, and now here he was, preparing to board the old Boer War troopship, *Lake Manitoba*, which was standing out in the harbour, waiting for the tide.

In this spring of 1903, the original trickle of immigrants pouring into western Canada had become a flood. They came from all parts of Northern Europe. Thousands of Swedes, Norwegians, Germans, Poles, and

Ukrainians—as well as thousands more from the British Isles—were heading for the promised land. Some were young men like Ivan Crossley, looking to make a start in life. Others were men down on their luck, hoping to better themselves on the Canadian prairies.

The Canadian government encouraged them to come. The plains had been empty of white settlers, but now the new Canadian Pacific Railway was ready to take newcomers out to till the fertile soil. The government proposed to settle one million immigrants between the Red River of Manitoba and the Rockies of what would become Alberta. It would be one of history's great mass movements, and Ivan Crossley was part of it.

The *Lake Manitoba* had been chartered by the Reverend Mr. Barr, whose enthusiastic pamphlet had appealed so strongly to young Ivan. The ship was built to hold seven hundred passengers, but this strange and often maddening clergyman planned to load it to the gunwales with close to two thousand—"the flower of England," as he called them.

At least five thousand people crowded the dockside that spring morning, all bidding each other goodbye. There were Boer War (1899–1902) veterans here, as well as butchers and bakers and even a few farmers—all turning their backs on Merrie England to start life over in an unknown world.

Great trucks arrived loaded with luggage labelled for Saint John, New Brunswick. Grandmothers cried and prayed—for they knew they would not see their families again. Handkerchiefs fluttered, children sniffled, dogs who were going along on the passage scuffled and whined.

Whole families arrived by carriage, toting baskets of food and shotguns, umbrellas, and birds in cages. A military band struck up a festive air. The crush on the dock became unbearable.

They represented a cross-section of the British Isles—a hundred from Scotland, another hundred from Ireland—men from the coal pits and cotton mills, from the stores and offices. There were fifty clergymen's sons setting off in one group, and five offspring of one Irish peer. They came from points as far away as John o'Groats at the northern tip of Scotland and as close as the River Tweed.

Scores were dressed for the New World—or what they thought was the proper dress for the New World. They turned up in riding breeches, puttees, and broad-brimmed Stetsons, with bowie knives at their hips and pistols at their belts. They were heading for the great Northwest, the domain of the people they knew as Red Indians. There they intended to become gentlemen farmers, living a countrified life.

The Reverend Mr. Barr had told them that their neighbours would be others like themselves—no sweaty Slavs, or German dirt farmers, or grubbing Yankees for him. This was to be an all-British colony and he would allow only proper Britons to join it.

At last the little black and white tug pushed the liner towards the dock. Great heaps of baggage were hoisted aboard. Trunks and boxes were hauled onto the deck by rope, and if some broke open, spilling their contents into the sea, that was too bad. The tide waited for no one.

As the ship moved out into the harbour stern first, the dock became a sea of waving handkerchiefs. There were so many people on one side of the ship that it threatened to tip over. "Get these people topside!" the captain roared up to the mate. And so the long and irritating voyage began.

Standing at the crowded ship's rail not far from Ivan Crossley was another youth, Robert Holtby. As he looked down on the tear-stained faces of the people on the dock, he felt a lump in his throat. Now he too realized that he and his family were saying goodbye forever to their home in Leeds. The chances were he would never see his schoolfriends again.

That thought was too much for him. He could no longer bear the sight of the waving crowd, growing smaller and smaller as the vessel steamed towards the open sea. And so he turned away and went down to his bunk in the hold. When dinner came, the food was so awful that he forgot one misery and replaced it with another. Like many of his fellow passengers, he began to have second thoughts about the Reverend Isaac Barr.

Isaac Barr's Flawed Dream

WE MUST NOW BRIEFLY LEAVE IVAN CROSSLEY AND ROBERT HOLTBY AND TAKE A HARD LOOK AT THE MAN RESPONSIBLE FOR SENDING THEM OFF TO CANADA.

Barr was one of those dedicated enthusiasts driven by a kind of missionary zeal, not to save souls, but to engage in wild projects. At a first meeting he seemed likable, earnest, and thoroughly believable. But he was not quite what he seemed to be.

His plans were impractical, his promises could not be fulfilled, his ability was less than it should have been, his organization was hollow. He was, in short, a charlatan—though perhaps he did not know it. He fooled everybody, but then he also fooled himself.

He had arrived in England from North America in January of 1902 after an up and down career in Canada and the United States. He'd been raised in Hornby, in southern Ontario, and had served as a Church of England priest in a series of posts—none of them for very long. His parishioners obviously didn't care too much for him, for they made no real effort to keep him when he argued about his salary.

In 1875 he became a missionary in Prince Albert, in what is now Saskatchewan, but he left that position too after a few weeks, on the excuse that his wife and son were both sick. He returned to Ontario and lost his job again, and spent the next two decades in the United States, where he held half a dozen posts. He was obviously not a very good clergyman. He had been, by his own account, married and divorced three times—a fact he apparently succeeded in hiding from the church.

When he arrived in London in 1903, Isaac Barr was fifty-three. He had, he said, "a strong desire to take up my abode again under the old flag which I love so well." He applied for a job as a Canadian immigration agent, saying he "had some successful experience in locating people and land, and have for years taken a deep interest in immigration and colonization." That was all pretty vague. When he didn't get the job, he started a scheme of his own. He would set up an all-British colony of immigrants from the old country, somewhere in the North West Territories of Canada—an area that included the present-day provinces of Alberta, Saskatchewan, and much of Manitoba.

By this time he had practically broken with the church, but he did get a licence to preach during the summer at St. Saviour's in London. This allowed him to wear his clerical collar, which gave him an aura of holiness. He himself was short and thickset, with a broad moustache and plump features. He also had the voice of a bull, but he could also be soft-spoken, courteous, and convincing. As one of his future colonists put it, "you could not help but trust him."

Yet there were some flaws in his character. He didn't have any sense of humour; he couldn't stand criticism; he had a quick Irish temper; he tended to be a bit of a dictator. He wasn't able to share his power, and he couldn't accept the truth, when the truth got in the way of his own desires. But he certainly was imaginative, and he certainly had a way with words.

In fact, you could say he was drunk with words. He knew how to use them and he believed in their power. Once the plan took shape on paper, it was, in Barr's curious way of thinking, halfway to completion. All during the spring and summer of 1902 he had been churning out articles for no fewer than thirty-two publications. Thus the grand scheme of an all-British colony in the Canadian West began to expand in his mind.

What a triumph it would be! To place hundreds, even *thousands* of stout British farmers and tradespeople—the finest stock in the world—in a colony all their own. And no foreigners would be allowed to creep in! Barr was British to the core.

In his imagination he had already built a town. It would have shops and schools, churches and a post office, all grouped around a central park, with the farms of the settlers circling it for miles. His enthusiasm about this non-existent city was so infectious that by August he had received two hundred inquiries in writing and a hundred calls. As a result, Barr produced a small pamphlet outlining his scheme. He said it would be cheap to build houses because building materials could be purchased in quantity. Horses, oxen, cows, implements, and seeds would all be arranged for in advance and available for purchase on the spot. And there would be openings for tradesmen and teachers, as well as farmers. He claimed that "agriculture on the prairies is simple," and that "the work is not very hard." Anyone who knew conditions in the Canadian West would not have been impressed by his words.

Barr needed an official okay for his scheme and so sent a draft of his pamphlet to the Canadian immigration office in London. He asked for its help, and also for a year's contract "and a very moderate salary," plus an office and expenses, and free transportation to Canada to choose the site of his proposed community.

He himself was short and thickset, with a broad moustache and plump features. He also had the voice of a bull, but he could also be soft-spoken, courteous, and convincing. As one of his future colonists put it, "you could not help but trust him."

Barr claimed that most of those who had called on him were either practical farmers or the sons of farmers. That just wasn't true. And it was farmers—and only farmers—that Canada wanted. "I know the North well, having laboured as a missionary at Prince Albert in the North Saskatchewan," he wrote. That too was totally misleading. But who could check up on Isaac Barr?

Barr didn't get what he wanted at first because the immigration commissioner was away. That didn't stop him. He produced a second, longer pamphlet in September, which suggested, falsely, that he was a man with wide farming experience in Canada and that he had something resembling an official seal of approval from the Canadian Immigration Department.

Here is an example of the kind of thing he was writing: "Modesty suggests that I should not say anything of myself, but it seems necessary that I should … First, then, before taking action I conferred with the Canadian Emigration Commissioner here in England, and I keep in constant touch with the Emigration Office, although this is a perfectly independent movement." What he suggested, but wasn't able to say, was that he did not have any seal of approval from Canada.

And then he wrote, "I was born on a large farm in Canada, and learned all branches of agriculture. With me, farming has always been an enthusiasm—I might also say a passion, and I have farmed both in Canada and the United States. I have been interested in Colonization for many years, have done some fairly good work as a colonizer, and am now anxious to build up my native Land, and keep it as much as possible in the hands of people of British birth ..."

This was all hokum—but nobody bothered to check. Nobody bothered to find out how much time he had spent in the Northwest. (It was very little.) No one bothered to look into his claims to be a colonizer. Nobody even examined the list of applicants for the colony to see if they were really farmers. No one really *wanted* to know.

Lloyd, like so many of his generation, believed unquestioningly in the rightness of British causes, whatever that cause might be — even if it involved killing Boers, Métis, or Matabele. He believed in those things as strongly as he believed in the evils of alcohol, or the revealed truth of the Gospels.

The British took him at face value because he was a churchman. How could he be dishonest? And Canada was eager to get more British immigrants into the West. The government had been strongly criticized because it was bringing in so many poor Slavs from Eastern Europe instead of well-to-do British farmers.

Unfortunately, the British farmers were well off and perfectly content to stay where they were. It was the industrial and office workers, slum dwellers—city people unfit for the rigours of the Canadian prairie—who hammered on Barr's door.

But here was an apparently imaginative man—a Canadian and, undeniably, a man of the cloth—prepared to bring thousands of Britons, "very generally men of sufficient means," as he put it, into Canada. Clearly they wouldn't be a burden on the country. Nor would they water down Canada's sacred Anglo-Saxon heritage. The press was enthusiastic, and so was the response to Barr's pamphlets.

Now another enthusiast, also a clergyman, joined Barr. This was the Reverend George Exton Lloyd, a tall, gaunt Church of England minister who knew far more about the Canadian Northwest. He had just come back to England after an absence of twenty years. His background was so romantic that it spurred on those who wished to follow him into the promised land.

Born in London, Lloyd had gone out to Canada at the age of twenty. He spent his first five years in the poverty-stricken backwoods of Ontario. Then he fought in the Saskatchewan Rebellion. At the battle of Cut Knife Hill in 1885, with his last cartridge gone and a bullet piercing his side, he was saved by a last-minute rescue from certain death at the hands of the Crees fighting alongside Louis Riel, the Métis leader.

The Queen's Own Rifles made Lloyd their chaplain. Later he became an Anglican minister in Winnipeg, and in 1891 he founded a boys' school near Saint John, New Brunswick. But now, in 1902, at the age of forty-one, he was back in London, as assistant secretary to the Colonial and Continental Church Society.

Lloyd, like so many of his generation, believed unquestioningly in the rightness of British causes, whatever that cause might be—even if it involved killing Boers, Métis, or Matabele. He believed in those things as strongly as he believed in the evils of alcohol, or the revealed truth of the Gospels. That is how most people thought in the early years—even committed Christians.

Lloyd was upright, relatively humourless, but certainly dedicated. And he was also a born leader, a good organizer (though an impractical businessman)—the kind of person that people instinctively liked. But he could also drive people into periods of frustration.

He didn't want "foreigners" watering down the Anglo-Saxon heritage of Canada. He wanted to take a few thousand people "of good British blood" to settle the farmlands of the West. Why didn't they go? he asked. "Are they afraid they'll be going from civilization to barbarism in a wild, unknown land?"

He had certainly struck a nerve. When he offered to answer questions, a deluge of letters swamped him. And no wonder. Britain was overcrowded. The Boer War was over. Thousands of veterans had come home. But jobs were scarce, firms were failing, and vacancies had to be made for sons coming into family businesses. Labour was cheap, wages low.

On the other hand, the Victorian age had reached its peak, and the ambition to bring British ideals to the untamed corners of the globe burned in every Englishman.

Unfortunately, it wasn't farmers who looked across the Atlantic. It was the huddled masses in the cities who yearned for a return to simple rural life. Surely, they figured, their dream could come true in the open spaces of Canada.

One man who answered Barr's call later wrote, "Most of us pictured our homesteads as picturesque parkland, grassy, with gently-rolling slopes, interspersed by clumps of trees, a sparkling stream, or possibly a silvery lake thrown in, the whole estate alive with game of all kinds." But the Canadian Northwest did not resemble the fields and hedgerows of the English countryside.

Still, shortly after Lloyd himself issued a circular letter answering forty-two questions most frequently asked, Barr knocked on his door and the two joined forces. Lloyd would run an office in England and begin to take applications for the Britannia Colony, as it would be called. Barr himself left for Canada.

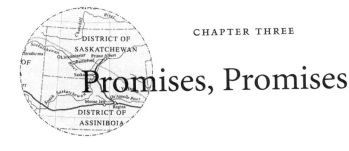

CHAPTER THREE

Promises, Promises

ISAAC BARR WAS A HUSTLER. HE PUBLISHED HIS FIRST PAMPHLET IN MID-AUGUST 1902, RUSHED OUT HIS SECOND IN MID-SEPTEMBER, AND BY EARLY OCTOBER HAD ARRIVED IN OTTAWA FROM ENGLAND. AT THE END OF THAT MONTH HE WAS ONE HUNDRED MILES (160 KM) WEST OF BATTLEFORD, IN WHAT IS NOW SASKATCHEWAN, SELECTING HOMESTEADS FOR HIS NEW COLONY.

He returned to England in time to publish his third and more detailed pamphlet before Christmas.

Barr announced that he would bring out his first shipload of settlers in early March—only a year after his original arrival in Great Britain.

The deputy minister of Immigration, James Smart, was so impressed he agreed to reserve homesteads in eight townships until February or later. All he wanted from Barr was a list of prospective immigrants and fees to register the titles to their land.

"He is most enthusiastic and is also very clever, and I am inclined to think that he probably stands a good chance of making a success of his work," Smart said. Meanwhile, Barr had persuaded the Canadian Pacific Railway to reserve additional homesteads in the same area for sale to the British. Things were moving at a fast clip.

But there were those who were not so enthusiastic. One Tory MP dismissed Barr as a "sharper." Experienced men in the colonization field thought that he was inexperienced. The government itself remained cautious. It refused to hire Barr, give him any expenses, or set him up in an office.

The department became nervous at the speed at which Barr was moving. He was actually talking about bringing his people out in early March! That was the season when the weather was so bad that a previous group of women and children arriving in April had all come down with influenza. March was the month of storms on the prairies—the worst possible time to impress newcomers. The government urged delay. The clergyman, who didn't like anybody getting mixed up in his plans, agreed to postpone the sailing date—but only until the end of March.

The press on both sides of the Atlantic was captured by Barr's eloquence. He had moved so quickly the government couldn't wash its hands of him even if it wanted to. He'd reached Canada at a time when the opposition party in Ottawa was demanding more English immigrants and fewer Slavic paupers. The fanatical Doukhobor sect known as the Sons of Freedom were also on the march, causing the authorities no end of trouble. If Barr were denied a chance to bring out more Englishmen, there would be a public outcry.

The trouble was that Barr had let his imagination run away with him. In his new pamphlet he proposed a series of schemes, such as a "Stores Syndicate" that would operate retail stores in the colony; a "Hospital Syndicate" that would look after the community's health; and a "Transportation Syndicate" to carry the colonists and their goods comfortably from the end of the railway to the site. These weren't much more than pipe dreams.

Was he in it for the money? "I'm not on the make," he declared. And certainly profit was secondary to his grand scheme. On the other hand, he did make money: he got $1.50 per colonist from the steamship company, and commissions from the CPR on the sale of railway lands. He also planned a $5.00 charge on homesteads for those settlers who wouldn't come out with the first group. That was illegal under the Homestead Act.

But in England enthusiasm was building. Barr's newest and longest pamphlet had described his journey to Canada, and outlined the area reserved for the Britannia Colony. "Those who wish to join us must decide at once and deposit passage money," he declared. Ivan Crossley was one of those who put their money down.

Much of what he wrote was sensible and accurate, but some of it was misleading. He managed to give the impression that fruit trees—apple and plum—would grow easily in Northern Saskatchewan. Anyone who knows Northern Saskatchewan would know that that was not true. He suggested that the Canadian Northern Railway would reach the settlement "within a few months." That was not possible. Its construction would take far longer. He said timber was easily available and could be rafted downriver from Edmonton, and that a good road existed between the railway's end and the colony. Those were wild exaggerations.

He also faked the distances. He suggested that a factory for producing sugar from beets was close by. Actually it was three hundred miles (480 km) away. Although he agreed that it was "sometimes very cold," he made a good deal of the "invigorating and enjoyable climate" and "the dry, and highly exhilarating atmosphere." But words like "invigorating" and "exhilarating" were code words for "freezing cold."

He didn't tell his prospective colonists how long the winters would be. He didn't give any details of the kind of sod, log, or frame houses they would have to build. He promised that "at Saskatoon there will be provided horses, wagons, harness and provisions for the journey, also coverings for the wagons, camp stools and other necessary things." He said women and children would go by covered wagon, stage service all the way to Battleford, "where they would be suitably housed and cared for until the men could establish homesteads."

These were paper promises, but they were believed. How could anybody living in England's green and pleasant land imagine a country where a road was nothing more than a rut, a village was a huddle of shacks, and a homestead was a vast expanse of unbroken turf stretching off to the horizon?

The English people knew a good deal about the settled cities in Canada, such as Halifax, Saint John, Montreal, and Toronto. These had streetcars and six-storey brick buildings, banks with marble pillars and theatres—even opera houses. Those who had relatives or friends in Quebec, Ontario, or the Maritime provinces also knew something about the country. They knew about the CPR with its new chateau-style hotels at Banff and Lake Louise, which were advertised throughout England. As for Winnipeg—traveller after traveller wrote of its miraculous growth, its electric railway, its brick buildings, and its block pavement. Winnipeg was the West, wasn't it?

Few Britons, alas, realized that after Winnipeg civilization came to a stop. Canada was really two countries—one half-sophisticated, the other as empty of European settlement as the desert. In a country like England, where you couldn't travel a mile without seeing a cluster of little homes, it was difficult to imagine a realm where your nearest neighbour was a quarter of a mile away, a realm peopled by nomadic natives, Métis, and a few white trappers.

Who in crowded England could conceive of the vast distances west of Winnipeg? No map could convey the emptiness, the loneliness, the desolation. And so, to most of Barr's prospects, the Britannia Colony was just around the corner from the nearest big city.

By the end of January 1903, Barr's scheme had, in his own words, reached "immense proportions." He claimed he could bring out as many as six thousand settlers that March, but since he couldn't handle that number he was closing off the movement. He would settle for about two thousand.

This represented an enormous change—the previous fall he had only figured on a few hundred. The Canadian officials in London had already become disillusioned with Barr. Unfortunately, in Canada the enthusiasm was snowballing. Now the government knew it would have to step in to prevent a disaster.

Barr had sent advance agents from England to the Canadian West with instructions to scout out supplies. Unfortunately, they had neither the money nor the authority to buy anything. Several members of the so-called Stores Syndicate arrived from England with big plans to start business in the new colony—but they also had very little money. In fact the Stores Syndicate did not really exist.

That was March 10, just two weeks before the Barr party was due to leave England. Meanwhile, Barr's advance agent, Charles May, who had been sent to Battleford, apparently to buy supplies, turned up in Winnipeg to reveal that he had no money to buy anything. Barr kept firing his agents. By March 19 he hadn't spent a dollar in Canada.

The Minister of the Interior in charge of immigration was Clifford Sifton, a tough-minded member of Wilfrid Laurier's cabinet. He began firing off telegrams to London urging that Barr be brought to his senses because he was clearly misleading everybody. Without waiting for Barr, Sifton hired two farm instructors to teach the newcomers practical agriculture as well as land guides to help them find their homesteads.

The minister had lost all faith in Barr's arrangements. He sent his colonization agent, Wesley Speers, to Saskatoon to see that big tents, firewood, and fodder for the animals were spaced at regular intervals along the trail that led to Battleford and on to the colony.

Meanwhile in England, his deputy, James Smart, was trying his best to push back the sailing date. He got nowhere with Barr, but the shipping company agreed to pretend that slight repairs were needed to cause a delay until perhaps April 1.

Barr's enthusiasm had not lessened, nor had his self-delusion. As late as March 21 he suggested to *The Times* of London that all of his projects were thriving. But he didn't leave it at that. He went on enthusiastically to talk about "lumber yards, creameries, mills, grain elevators, schools, post offices, and a newspaper," which, he claimed, would be set up without delay.

Barr was a man who, simply by promising that something would be done, made it a fact in his own mind. The truth was bleaker. It turned out the Indians couldn't furnish any lumber for the colony until the middle of May, when it would be too late. The Battleford contractor, who had been hired to provide portable sawmills, refused because Barr's plans were so flimsy. There was no plan for hay or oats for the horses. And Barr's brother, Jack, who had gone to Calgary to buy two carloads of broncos for the so-called transport service, found that half of the horses had suffocated to death.

In Canada Barr's house of cards was collapsing. In spite of this he was on the high seas heading for Saint John, New Brunswick, with two thousand colonists. Somehow, this idealistic, if incompetent clergyman had managed to pull off a coup. He had slithered around the cautious Canadian bureaucrats, bedazzled two thousand generally unromantic Britishers with his wild dream, shocked the Canadian government into sudden action, and bamboozled everybody into taking part in an adventure whose outcome was uncertain and, for some, would be horrific.

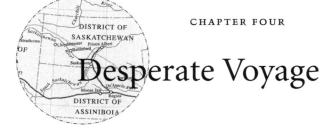

CHAPTER FOUR

Desperate Voyage

WITH CLOSE TO TWO THOUSAND PASSENGERS CRAMMED INTO SPACE INTENDED FOR SEVEN HUNDRED, THE VOYAGE ACROSS THE ATLANTIC WAS CLOSE TO BEING A DISASTER.

The steerage passengers were divided into sections, each with its own cook: single men in one hold, married couples in others. The better off travelled in second-class cabins, but there was no first class.

Thirteen-year-old Paul Hordern, the son of a dry goods merchant from Leicestershire, scrambled about with his father looking for their bunks. They finally found themselves in the forward hold with seven hundred others. At first sight, as they made their way downward, the setting seemed shipshape, the walls painted gleaming white. Only later, when the big waves hit and the whitewash peeled off the walls, revealing a layer of manure, did the Horderns realize that this had been a cavalry ship loaded with horses.

The murky holds, full of smoke, had two or three tiers of bunks. One second-class passenger, Stanley Rackham, visited one of these gloomy caverns to locate his vast array of luggage (he was travelling with 350 pounds [159 kg]). Now he thanked his maker he didn't have to spend much time below. What would it be like, he wondered, when the weather grew rough and people crammed into these bunks grew seasick? He shuddered to think of it and decided never to go below again.

But almost everybody was seasick. Paul Hordern was overcome so suddenly in his upper bunk that he didn't have time to shout a warning. Fortunately, somebody across the way shouted, "Duck!" and the man below jumped aside, reproaching Hordern: "Why the devil didn't you holler?" he asked.

"How can I, with my mouth full?" Hordern replied. There was a six-inch (15-cm) layer of sawdust below his bunk to handle such emergencies.

Young Robert Holtby was so sick he wished somebody would come along and pitch him overboard. After a few days he recovered enough to swallow solid food, but he found he couldn't face the food in the hold, with its smell of soup and potatoes and sour sawdust, and a foot and a half (0.5 m) of bilge water slopping back and forth.

Robert shovelled some food onto a plate and went up on deck, and there he found a hundred people like himself, sniffing the salt air and trying to balance their plates on their knees.

Here, when the weather was fine, they could hear the strains of a portable organ and youthful voices singing familiar hymns. This was Miss Laura Sisley, a banker's daughter from London, and her charges, a dozen underprivileged boys from the church club she ran in downtown London. She had come into a small fortune on her father's death, and she was using that money to bring them all out to the new country, where she hoped to settle them together in their own community near the Barr reserve.

Miss Sisley's organ was welcome because shipboard life had taken on a sombre tone. Barr was not a diplomat. By the time the ship reached Saint John, he managed to anger a good percentage of the passengers, especially those below in steerage. One of these, Harry Pick, wrote that "it speaks well for British love of law and order to record that only eleven fights, seven incipient mutinies, three riots, and twenty-two violent interviews with Barr ... occurred during the voyage." He may have been exaggerating, but this was certainly a stormy voyage.

A lot of that was Barr's fault. He'd painted the rosiest possible picture. Now, with the reality facing them, his flock turned against him. Barr wouldn't mix with the passengers as Lloyd did, but kept to himself in his cabin. Lloyd gave regular lectures on Canada, complete with question and answer sessions. In dealing with scores of complaints, he was tactful, clear, and forthright. More and more, as the voyage progressed, the passengers looked to him as their natural leader. Barr seemed to have a dislike for contact with any of them.

What an odd pair they were. The squat, heavy-set Barr was quite a different character from the reed-thin Lloyd, with his gaunt features and his long side-whiskers. Lloyd was leaving England forever. With his wife and five children he would make his home in the new colony that would one day bear his name and be known as Lloydminster. When Barr did meet with the colonists, he often lost his temper. Once, in a fury, he threatened to turn a fire hose on them.

No sea voyage in those days was pleasant, but this vessel was so badly overcrowded that whole groups of families were squeezed together below decks with little privacy. There weren't enough lifeboats for all the passengers. And there wasn't nearly enough fresh water. The colonists had to get along on partially distilled salt water, so brackish it ruined the tea.

The food was terrible—the potatoes rotten, the meat tough, the knives and forks dirty. There was no butter and no bread, only ship's biscuit. "We didn't die, but we damn near starved to death," Ivan Crossley wrote later. He and his comrades from Ireland sat at a long table in steerage. When the waiters arrived with a basket of hard-boiled eggs, they'd roll them down the table, the diners grabbing at them as they whirled by.

Many of the dining room and kitchen staff had signed on for the voyage, but they quit before the ship sailed when they heard there were so many immigrants aboard. Barr had to hire replacements for them from among the passengers, but not before some ugly scenes occurred. Lloyd was called to one dining room to settle a fight involving a group of Boer War veterans. One of the ex-soldiers had thrown a pot of jam at a waiter.

"Sure, I threw the jam tin at him," the veteran barked.

"What, a little fellow like that?" said Lloyd mildly. "You might at least help him to scrape the jam off."

With that the soldier complied and the two shook hands. Barr, on the other hand, was the kind of man who always ran from trouble. Driven half-crazy by complaints, he shut himself up in his cabin and refused to see anybody.

At one point Ivan Crossley and his friends went to Barr's cabin to demand he come down to the dining room to see how bad the food was. Barr agreed, and that night in the hold he stood up on a wooden box and tried to explain that he was doing his best to improve both meals and conditions. At that point, somebody threw a ship's biscuit at him. It was three inches thick and the size of a saucer, and it hit him squarely in the nose, knocking him off the box and touching off a big fight. The crew finally rescued the clergyman, who retired to his cabin for the rest of the voyage, crying out that his people were nothing but a bunch of savages.

On April 5, Lloyd conducted the Sunday service with the ship twelve hundred miles (1,930 km) out of England. The setting provided a contrast to the hurly-burly of the dining rooms. One twenty-seven-year-old colonist, William Hutchison from Southey Green, thought it the most interesting and impressive service he'd ever attended.

It was held in one of the holds, with the men sitting on their cots or leaning on the rails of their bunks, smoking their pipes and listening as three violinists accompanied the hymns.

Looking about, Hutchison couldn't help noticing the strangeness of the surroundings—the gun cases, coats and hats, kit bags hung on nails, boxes, trunks, bundles of rugs, and bedding strewn about. It wasn't what he was accustomed to at the Evensong services in the Anglican church back home in Southey Green.

In spite of what Barr had told the Canadian government, few of these men were farmers. The problem was that Barr was inclined to tell people just whatever they wanted to hear. This was the flaw in his pamphlets and in the rosy interviews he continued to give to the press.

The few colonists who had had some farming experience were surrounded by a group of men eager to learn what they could from them. As one remembered: "Very few had the remotest conception of what conditions actually were, or what difficulties would have to be overcome, but trusted blindly toward our leader and all his promises ..."

Barr had a large map on which he invited people to pick out their homesteads. They did it sight unseen. But he said it would save time and confusion, and then he told them that the ground was so uniform that it didn't matter where they settled, because every quarter section was like every other one. That was a bald lie.

One stonemason asked for a homestead that had enough rocks on it to build a house, and Barr cheerfully agreed that this was easy to get. "I've got just the thing for you," he said and marked out a quarter-section on the map. And yet he had already told Lloyd that "not a stone will be found in the new colony that was bigger than a walnut."

The ship reached Saint John harbour on April 10, 1903, but it couldn't dock because this was Good Friday. One group got together and raised three hundred dollars to buy Lloyd a buggy and two ponies. It's hardly surprising that there was nothing given to Barr. In fact, the passengers grew angry when they learned that Barr had ordered eight thousand loaves of bread, which he intended to sell them at double the going price.

"The old rogue is trying to make some money out of us," Robert Holtby wrote in his diary.

The next day, Saturday, the immigrants found they faced days of waiting while customs officers tried to inspect the mountain of luggage. And what luggage! Few had any idea of a country where vans and lorries did not shuttle back and forth between villages.

Barr had promised a transport service and they took him at his word and brought all their worldly goods to the new country. One man had brought a ton (907 kg) of baggage. Others brought pianos, heaps of furniture, and cases of books. There were bathtubs, jewellery, banjos, bicycles, gramophones, sewing machines. None of this would be of any use in the desolate land for which they were headed. But they had vast wardrobes of clothes, including formal wear, and they had parrots and canaries in cages, and, being English, they had well over a hundred dogs, tied up on the afterdeck, all howling to be exercised.

And then at this point, when everybody was out of sorts, Barr, unable to take responsibility, vanished. And so Lloyd did the job, going directly to the CPR, which was eager to get the trains moving. He managed to have the customs inspection cancelled, and so the ship was able to dock at five in the morning on Easter Sunday. At nine that evening, the first of four trains left for the West.

They couldn't sort out the luggage. Piles of boxes and trunks jammed the freight shed so solidly that owners couldn't squeeze between them to identify their own. Everything was piled onto the baggage cars to be sorted out later at Saskatoon—and that even included the blankets the passengers had brought with them. There was, however, a pile of blankets, which the Stores Syndicate had bought for sale, and these were piled on the dock. Lloyd doled them out to the shivering immigrants, keeping a careful record of those distributed.

And then, just before the last train left at midnight, Barr turned up, apparently drunk, and got into a screaming fight with his partner, charging that Lloyd was stealing the blankets. He even tried to sell some at four dollars apiece, but in his befuddled state, had difficulty counting the money.

Ivan Crossley watched in amusement as Barr tried vainly to make change. When Barr gave him back two dollars too much, Crossley returned it. "You're the first honest man I've seen in the community," Barr told him. Typically, he didn't travel with his charges but left for Saskatoon on the regular train.

The two Horderns, father and son, refused to buy Barr's bread. Instead they stocked up at a local grocery, having learned that food would be hard to get on the train trip. They bought cheese, beans, and canned goods, which they ate cold because there was only one small stove on each of these crowded colonist cars, and that was used by women brewing tea.

The trains swayed so badly one night that young Paul in the top bunk was thrown directly across the passageway, tumbling onto two sleeping people. "Where'd you come from?" one of them asked, surprised.

"Leicester," said Paul Hordern, sleepily.

But the Barr colonists were welcomed by the newspapers. The *Globe* found them "a splendid class," the Winnipeg *Tribune* "a fine-looking lot, above the average." To the *Manitoba Free Press* they were "strong, manly, clean, well-dressed, intelligent."

The Toronto *News* went wild over them. It described the women as "rosy-cheeked English farmers' help, sinewy and graceful, and with a glitter of gaiety and intelligence about their eyes." The paper added that "the hands that rocked the West's cradle will be strong enough to rule the world of Canada in a few years." These papers spoke for the British-born population, who felt that the only pure immigrants from Europe would be Anglo-Saxons.

The government people guided the colonists to Winnipeg. There the newcomers were astonished to discover that the immigration offices had been kept open all night to greet them. At this point two hundred bachelors left the train to seek work.

After Winnipeg, the journey offered several diversions: a herd of five thousand antelope crossed the tracks and barred the way; sportsmen produced their rifles and potted gophers, prairie chickens, and rabbits, shooting from the train windows. In spite of this, the group was uneasy.

Stanley Rackham noted a general feeling of unrest among the group. What lay ahead of them after Winnipeg? They couldn't know, but rumours were beginning to circulate. At Brandon, during a twenty-minute stop, Rackham cheered up a little after talking to an old settler. The settler described the hard times he'd had, but explained that he had come through all right and told the colonists they'd do the same if they just stuck to it.

After Brandon, the real West began to unfold. Now the colonists gazed out at the empty prairie, the cold brown grass covering the tough sod—flat, treeless, hedgeless as far as the eye could see stretching off to the horizon.

For many this was their first inkling of the future. At last they began to understand what they faced in the land of promise. Here, in this grey realm, the villages—mere clusters of log shacks or hovels of corrugated iron—were dumped down as if by chance. They weren't perched on a hillside or nestled in a valley as in English villages—but stood stark on the level plain.

This was not what they'd expected. But then what *had* they expected? Barr had never told them that the Canadian West was anything like the English countryside. Like the Canadian government's own pamphlets, his had ignored that kind of descriptive detail and talked instead about the promise of the future. He had let the colonists dream their own dreams and conjure up their own visions. Like all good con men, Barr had allowed them to con themselves.

CHAPTER FIVE

Not What They Expected

THE BULK OF THE BARR COLONISTS ARRIVED IN SASKATOON ON THE MORNING OF APRIL 17, 1903, A STEAMING HOT DAY WITH A TEMPERATURE AT 85°F (29°C). BARR'S AGENT, THE REVEREND DR. ROBBINS, WAS THERE TO GREET THEM ON THE PLATFORM AND TO INTRODUCE THEM TO A BIG, BROAD-SHOULDERED MAN WITH A WEATHER-BEATEN FACE AND BRISK MOUSTACHE. THIS WAS WESLEY SPEERS, THE COLONIZATION AGENT.

Speers chose the occasion to make a speech, which Stanley Rackham thought was more than a little flowery.

"I have a vision of teeming millions in the great valley to the West where you are going, and you are the forerunners," he cried in his deep voice. "You will not be disappointed. The valley contains the richest land in the Dominion and the Government has provided you with shelter here and will see you safely settled. March westward ho! There are your tents, march!"

The government had been smart enough not to wait for Barr to supply shelter. Instead, Speers had arranged for additional bell tents and marquees. This was a wise move because most of Barr's own tents were on the baggage cars running more than a day behind the main trains.

To the newcomers, used to cozy English villages with ivy-covered cottages, Saskatoon looked bleak. Young Paul Hordern was bitterly disappointed. He'd heard a lot about Saskatoon from Canadians at the various stops. "Oh, that's some town," they told him. "That's a big town!" But a big town in Canada wasn't like a big town in the old country. There wasn't even a cobblestone on the wet and muddy main street down which Hordern splashed his way.

Saskatoon was scarcely a year old. It was just another huddle of shacks, with two small hotels, and a few stores—"large boxes rushed up without regard to architecture or comfort," as one newcomer commented. A single stone building, the Windsor Hotel, stood out.

A year before, fewer than one hundred people had lived in the town. Now there were six hundred permanent residents and close to two thousand more passing through. This was the West, raw and new—a few houses clustered around a grain elevator and a railway station, the core of a community no different from scores of others springing up along the rail line.

But Saskatoon, like so many western villages, was on the verge of a boom that would see entire streets built in less than three weeks. Tents began to blossom everywhere. Cowboys, Mounted Police, Indians and Englishmen in broad sombreros crowded its single wooden sidewalk. The atmosphere was that of a lively carnival.

The newcomers had other matters on their minds. Those who had paid four dollars for a tent found now they must pay an extra dollar for shipping costs from Saint John. They began to hold indignation meetings; but Barr hadn't yet arrived in camp so the first meeting came to nothing. They paid their money reluctantly and scheduled a second meeting for Sunday.

By this time they were in another frenzy about their luggage. It finally arrived, jammed into eighteen cars with nobody to sort it out. Some remained on the train. Some lay in heaps dumped alongside the tracks. Barr now turned up and pleaded for patience. But he made the mistake of warning the crowd the Mounted Police would fire on any who tried to rush the baggage cars. From that point on the wretched clergyman could do nothing right. A brief, wild rush for the baggage cars destroyed the Sunday quiet, blows were struck right and left, and goods captured and retaken.

That Sunday the immigrants jammed into the restaurant marquee and listened to the drone of an Anglican service. Saskatoon had never seen anything like this. A sea of dainty hats met the eyes of the old-timers as the neatly gloved women in their tailored suits bowed their heads. Beside them, the men mumbled their responses, sober in broadcloth and tweed, with clean shirts, white ties, and neatly polished boots.

The text of the lesson seemed appropriate. It dealt with the rebellion of the children of Israel against Moses. At the same time, here on the Canadian prairies, Barr's children were rebelling against him. The curate read the lesson and described how the rebels were blasted by fire and swallowed by the earth. It was not a passage likely to soothe the rebellious colonists.

Now the minister, Archdeacon Mackay, a veteran of twenty years in the Northwest, gave as the text for his sermon: "The wilderness and the solitary places shall be glad for them; and the desert shall rejoice and bloom." He welcomed his temporary flock, warned against faint-heartedness, and talked of the pluck and grit needed to make a fortune from Saskatchewan's soil.

Out into the muddy street the congregation poured, with the men in sombreros and fedoras and bowlers, and one even in a silk hat. What a strange spectacle that was! Who but an Englishman would bring a silk hat into the West? It was as if he was walking out into the green and manicured English countryside rather than the yellow prairie.

But of course this was not England. On the west side of the tracks, one hundred acres of white canvas fluttered in the breeze—close to five hundred bell tents and marquees. The tents were pitched every which way in the elbow of the South Saskatchewan, a river red with mud and impossible to reach because of the gigantic blocks of blue ice thrown up on its banks. Scores of men and women were chipping away at these blocks, which were the only source of fresh water in the overcrowded community.

Others were struggling to put up more tents, although many had never seen one before. Many more didn't know how to use an axe. A group of Boer War veterans helped these people. And so the Lord's day rolled on, the air alive with the sounds of axe and hammer, wagons creaking and oxen lowing, children crying, men cursing, dogs yapping.

As dusk fell, an ominous glow lit up the sky—not a sunset, but a prairie fire roaring towards the camp. The colonists gaped and wondered. They had never imagined anything like this. Would they be destroyed like the rebellious children of Israel? But the village road acted as a firebreak, and for the moment at least the newcomers were spared the ravages of nature in the great Northwest.

They were all impatient to get moving towards their new home, but Barr wasn't ready yet. Indignation meetings continued all week. The colonists were furious over the prices charged for food and equipment. But Barr had no control over the Saskatoon merchants who had raised the prices to make an extra dollar.

He tried to escape from one mass meeting, but Wes Speers hauled him back. And there he faced a barrage of questions. Why was he trying to charge his people a guinea each ($50 in today's money) for the privilege of joining the party? Why was he trying to take money from late arrivals for holding their homesteads for them? Why was he charging young girls $10 each for future homesteads? Why was he taking a commission from the leading Saskatoon merchants?

Instead of trying to explain and turn aside these questions, Barr turned ugly. He shouted that it was nobody's business, flung out of the tent, and then cried that he wasn't making a cent of profit. He called one man a liar. Pandemonium resulted. Some of the newcomers wanted to toss Barr into the river. Others wanted to kick him out of the camp.

But it must be remembered that many of these complainers were tenderfeet, not used to rough conditions. They tended to magnify the smallest troubles. And they were looking for a scapegoat. Barr provided an easy target. He probably didn't make much out of his project, although he certainly tried. He did receive a 10 percent commission on gold sold to the colonists. He bought oats in town for 40 cents a bushel and sold them for a dollar, when the going rate was only 23½ cents. On his livestock, which he also sold, he got a profit of between 20 and 100 percent.

Nor did he attempt to calm his critics. A group of colonists asked the member of the North West Territories legislative assembly, James Clinkskill, to discuss the situation in a meeting in the restaurant tent. Barr wouldn't have any of that. He shook his fist in Clinkskill's face and called him an "infamous scoundrel." The meeting broke up as the colonists sang their new song:

Barr, Barr, wily old Barr
He'll do as much as he can.
You bet he will collar
Your very last dollar
In the valley of the Sask-atchewan.

Now, Wesley Speers, faced with what he called this "constant turmoil and excitement," realized two things. First, most of the colonists had no farming experience at all. Second, many of them didn't have enough money to run a homestead. Something would have to be done, or the Liberal government would have a political black eye.

Speers took matters into his own hands. He called another meeting to find out who was broke, who needed more money, and who needed to work to earn more. About fourteen hundred people turned out. Speers learned that two hundred had less than ten pounds left apiece. And so he went to work setting up an employment bureau which got jobs for 135 in Moose Jaw and 50 more in Prince Albert. He got jobs for the rest with local surveying parties, and for the others he arranged practical talks on farming from government inspectors.

By this time the major Canadian newspapers had sent reporters to Saskatoon. The newspapermen were astonished by the naiveté of some of the colonists. The Toronto *News* reported:

"Women who spend their time in dressing and kissing ugly little pug dogs talk of going out to earn money the first year by working in the cornfields, quite blind to the fact that there can be no cornfields there, until they sow the first crop in 1904. A pork packing factory is projected while, as a Westerner points out, there isn't a hog nearer the colony than Battleford."

One western farmer placed in charge of the government horses, J. J. Dodds, was scathing in his criticism. He discovered that not one man in twenty even knew how to hitch up a team. Canadian schoolboys could learn the work faster.

Paul Hordern was convinced that the number of real farmers could be counted on the fingers of one hand. The Horderns decided to leave Barr. A few days after arriving in Saskatoon, they simply packed their goods and located on a homestead near Dundurn, south of Saskatoon.

Mrs. Hordern, who was handling the dry goods store back home in Leicestershire, sold the business and brought the rest of the family out to join her son and husband in 1904. Half a century later, when Saskatchewan celebrated its fiftieth jubilee, Paul Sylvester Hordern was still in Dundurn to join the festivities. He died in Saskatoon in 1983 in his ninety-fifth year.

Not all were as practical as the Horderns. The government and, in fact, the country were beginning to realize that Barr's rosy promises about stout English yeomen were so much eyewash.

The long-suffering government agent, Wes Speers, had his problems.

One day in April, while he was working in his tent and planning his employment agency, a thirty-five-year-old Englishman came in, obviously in distress. Behind the Englishman was his wife, slender and dark-eyed, cuddling a tiny fox terrier in her arms. Speers recognized her at once, for she had been the talk of the camp, skipping about, patting her dog, crooning to it as if it were a child. She was clearly a romantic who saw herself as a brave pioneer's wife—a heroine helping her husband to future fortune.

However, her husband was not so optimistic. He had sunk all his money into Barr's failing Stores Syndicate. If he bought a yoke of oxen and a wagon and a breaking plough, he wouldn't have more than seven pounds to his name. "I cannot live on seven pounds for a year and a half," he told Speers. "What am I going to do for food, for a house, for barns and horses?"

"Why, hire yourself out to Mr. Barr to break sod," Speers told him. "Mr. Barr says he'll give you three dollars an acre for the work."

"But I cannot break sod, donchaknow, I never did it before."

"You can learn."

"But where will I live?"

"Build a sod house."

"What's that?"

"A house of sod, built on a ravine side."

"I don't think I could possibly do it."

"Yes, you could. Go ahead and buy your oxen and take your stuff out there. Make some money carrying another man's goods along with you."

"Whom shall I get to drive these oxen?"

"Drive them yourself!"

The Englishman looked dumbfounded.

"Come on down tomorrow and we'll pick out your cattle for you," Speers told him.

She would be kind to the oxen, the wife said. They would be like household pets. She would feed them bread and butter. *Did she say bread and butter?* Yes, she did! A reporter for the Toronto *Star* who had been viewing the scene scribbled those words in his notebook. Speers suppressed a smile. His mind went back to the day when he chased a yoke of oxen up a furrow with a cordwood stick.

"You'll have enough to do to feed yourself bread and butter," he snorted.

"And we shall have some delightful little piggies," she burbled. "I shall go out and bustle in the harvest field with my dear husband." That was too much for Wesley Speers.

"Go and buy those oxen and your plough," he said shortly. "And go ahead if you haven't got a loaf of bread left. The government of this country isn't going to let anybody starve."

There were other bizarre incidents in the tent city as each family bought its equipment and animals and prepared for the long trek to Battleford and then on to the colony. A dozen women cooked for their husbands—all wearing gloves! One six-foot (1.8-m) Englishman washed his fox terrier in a dishpan. One wretched woman, half-drunk, was rescued from the open prairie by the Mounted Police after she had been rushing through the camp shrieking that the Indians had been trying to kidnap her.

And there was more: a crush of three hundred people crammed into the tent post office waiting for the mail; but when it arrived there were only 43 letters. An Englishman was spotted invading the male preserve of the local bar and calling in vain for "an harf'n harf," a British brew no Canadian had ever heard of. And there was another struggling with an ox, striking it with a sudden fury, then begging the animal's pardon, saying he didn't mean it.

By Friday, April 24, the first colonists were ready to move. But the news wasn't good. Barr's Transportation Syndicate had collapsed. There would be no wagons for the women and children. Charles May, Barr's former agent in Battleford, had quit and was taking up a homestead of his own. And the pioneer party that Barr had sent out to prepare the new site returned in disarray. Its members had lost their way on the prairie, lost their cattle in the muskegs, and starved for three days before reaching civilization.

CHAPTER SIX

A Trail of Flood and Fire

ISAAC BARR'S ORIGINAL PLAN HAD BEEN TO ESTABLISH CONVOYS OF TWENTY OR THIRTY WAGONS TO COVER THE TWO-HUNDRED-MILE (320-KM) DISTANCE BETWEEN SASKATOON AND THE NEW COLONY. THE WOMEN AND CHILDREN WOULD TRAVEL SEPARATELY. HOWEVER, THE COLONISTS WERE NOW STRIKING OUT ON THEIR OWN WITHOUT GUIDES.

Each had to find his own way through slough or muskeg and care for his family at nightfall. Many of these were driving horses and oxen for the first time. Some had pocket charts showing that part of the animal's body where the harness could be attached. Others actually used marking chalk to sketch diagrams directly on the horses' sides.

Most spent the best part of a week searching out and bargaining for animals, for wagons, for harnesses, farm equipment and supplies. On April 23 the first party got away. The last stragglers didn't set out until May 5. And so, for the best part of a month, the trail that led to Battleford and then westward to the colony was dotted with wagons.

Stanley Rackham had planned to leave on the 23rd, but he found that the wagon he had chosen had been sold to somebody else. He had to wait until the CPR freight arrived with more. He finally got away at 10 o'clock the following morning, a blistering hot day.

His oxen were soft after an idle winter. He took a long rest at noon, as much for the animals as for himself. By four o'clock he was stuck fast in a bog. A Russian immigrant turned up and helped haul him out. Rackham's experience was repeated again and again that Friday. Even before they found themselves out of sight of Saskatoon, a dozen wagons were stuck in the mud. Matthew Snow, one of the experienced farm instructors hired by the government, helped pull them out.

That was only the beginning. Barr's "road" was nothing more than a deeply rutted trail through the scrub timber made by the Red River carts of the Métis packers bringing in furs from Battleford. The entire country that spring was a heaving bog, dotted by sloughs, little streams, and ponds left by the rapidly melting snow.

William Hutchison of Sheffield, whom we last met attending Rev. Lloyd's church service on the *Lake Manitoba*, took the advice of old-timers and delayed his departure until prices came down and the ground was firmer. He was told that a day's delay in Saskatoon would save him two days on the trip, and as a result he and his brother, Ted, reached Battleford without mishap in a fast five days.

Just five miles (8 km) out of Saskatoon, Hutchison came upon four teams of oxen, all stuck fast in the mud. Exhausted from trying to pull themselves out, they had given up the struggle and were looking around for something to eat. A local farmer took time off from his spring seeding to help haul them free. But Hutchison's own ordeal was yet to come.

The colonists had been warned not to carry more than a thousand pounds (454 kg) per wagon. A team of oxen could manage no more. But most of the carts were overloaded with a ton (907 kg) or a ton and a half (1,360 kg)—even, on occasion, two tons (1,814 kg). Some looked like gigantic Christmas trees, hung with lamps, kitchen chairs, oil cans, baby buggies, plough handles, bags, parcels, tools, women's hats, dogs, and even pianos.

Jolted over the uneven ground, flour sacks burst open and coal oil spilled into the food. The loads were so heavy the women and children had to walk. A bitter wind sprang up. Half an inch (1.3 cm) of ice formed on the ponds. This was the worst spring weather in the memory of the oldest packers. And so the women were forced to trudge numbly onward with the children crying with the cold.

Wagon after wagon sank to its axles in the white alkali mud of the bogs and sloughs. Every time that happened the entire load had to be taken off while the drivers waded through gumbo to find a dry spot. Then the team would be hitched to the rear axle and the wagon hauled out with a logging chain.

These frustrating delays took the best part of a day. There were other problems. The horses, up to their knees in mud, would often lie down and die in the swamps. Many more died from lack of feed or overwork at the hands of men who had never handled a team. One packer counted eighteen dead horses on the trail to Battleford.

A young student missionary, J. A. Donaghy, remembered that "some never seemed to realize how much a horse must eat to live, and the whole country was full of the finest pasture along the trail. It was painful to see horses staggering under the weight of the harness until they dropped." Many horses ran away. Some settlers, afraid of losing their teams, tied them to trees, but with such a short rope they couldn't graze properly and so starved slowly to death.

Barr had planned to have marquees with freshly baked bread and newly butchered meat all along the route. That plan collapsed. The government's plan to set up large tents at regular intervals saved a good deal of misery. The first comers crowded in and wolfed tea and porridge, the main food on the trail. The latecomers had to unload and pitch their own tents.

In England it was spring. But here in the Canadian West, blue patches of old snow could still be seen in the bluffs of naked poplars. The settlers grew homesick. Robert Holtby, trudging along mile after mile in the drenching rain—twenty-five miles (40 km) a day behind the family's wagon—thought longingly of the cricket field at home, green as emerald.

Stanley Rackham stared at the brown grass, bleached by the frost, and the gaunt, lifeless trees, and realized that it was May Day back home. And that brought to his mind a familiar vision of primroses, violets, and cowslips surrounding the cottages in his native Mayfield.

But spring was on its way. Water gurgled down the slopes and coulees and into the swelling sloughs, barring the route. For the latecomers there were purple anemones poking out of the grasses. In June the sweet perfume of briar rose filled the night air. Frogs chorused after dark, and wild fowl burst from the willow groves. The crack shots feasted on rabbit, duck, and prairie chicken.

And then suddenly, in the heart of this wilderness, a wilderness of rolling brown hills, white alkali, scrub willow—an astonishing spectacle greeted the trekkers. William Hutchison could scarcely believe his eyes. Here, surrounded by furrowed fields, was a Russian village. Here were houses of trim logs, carefully plastered and neatly arranged along a wide street, their verandahs all gaily painted. This was a Doukhobor settlement, and here the weary travellers rested. The hospitable Slavs took the women and children into their own homes and fed them on fresh eggs and butter.

Hutchison came upon a party of children walking two-by-two to Sunday school. In their brightly coloured dresses they looked like a living rainbow. He was reminded of a children's ballet at a Christmas pantomime. He and his brother were impressed by the Doukhobors' progress. Here were solid buildings and barns, and droves of fat cattle, and piles of equipment. If these people could make it, so could they! Before they left they took careful note of what they'd seen, storing it in their minds for the day when they might benefit from that lesson.

Not far ahead lay the dreaded Eagle Creek ravine. This was a vast chasm, five miles (8 km) across, with a raging river at the bottom, and sides as steep as the walls of a house. Robert Holtby, gazing at it in awe, thought it must have been torn up by a gigantic earthquake.

Down this dizzy slope ran a bit of a track at an angle so steep it seemed impossible to get down it. Few of the wagons had any brakes. Some of the tenderfeet actually hobbled their oxen before attempting the descent. As a result, the careering wagons rammed into the rumps of the terrified beasts, overturning the whole load, and scattering the contents on the slope. The more experienced drivers locked their rear wheels with chains and stood by with long poles to brake the front wheels should the wagon get away.

The climb upward was equally dismaying. Some wagons required four horses or three teams of oxen to haul the heavy loads up to the rim of the valley. Here, the Holtby family came upon a pitiable sight—a horse had struggled to the top, only to drop dead of fatigue. The ants and hawks were already turning the corpse into a skeleton. By the time the Holtbys reached the government tent at ten that night, young Robert was so tired he could scarcely finish his tea. But the endless squalling of young children kept him awake.

At last they reached Battleford, the midway point on the trail. Here in this historic community, the newcomers got a glimpse of the old West—of fur traders and Indians—now vanishing before the new invasion. Here were the Mounted Police barracks, white and trim, the Hudson's Bay post with its pink roof, and the Native school across the river.

The little community, untouched until now by the successive waves of immigrants, sat on the flat tableland between the North Saskatchewan and

Battle Rivers. A government marquee was already in place. The overflow was put up in the nearby agricultural hall. Some of the colonists didn't bother to go any farther. They looked for their homesteads in the neighbourhood. Others caught their breath, reorganized their loads, and pressed on to the colony, a hundred miles (160 km) away.

Now they entered wilder country—the empty haunt of Indians and wild animals. Apart from a single farm, there was no white settlement for three hundred miles (480 km)—only rolling hills, little lakes, scrub willow, prairie grass, and pea vine.

Barr had reached Battleford on May 2. That day a large contingent took off for Britannia. Barr spent four days in Battleford, constantly attacked by indignant colonists, many of whom flew into a rage at the mere mention of his name.

The unfortunate clergyman was now seen as a dictator who wanted the absolute right to assign each man a homestead and force him to accept it. Few now believed his shipboard promise that all the land was equal. That was fantasy. Some farms were flat, some were rolling. Some were wooded, some bald. Some were fertile, some stony.

Barr had insisted that all the settlers wait until he personally reached Britannia to dole out homesteads. The Dominion Lands Agent, R. F. Chisholm, told them to ignore that. They could move out of the settlement and find their own land. That angered Barr. "If there's bloodshed and destruction of the colony as a result, I throw the whole blame on you," he shouted at the government man.

He left for Britannia with Lloyd and, travelling light, reached it on May 9. Lloyd was dismayed by the number of Barr's immigrants who were going back to Battleford in disgust. He began working his way back along the trail to try to talk them out of leaving the colony and going home to England.

These people were bitterly disappointed. They'd reached Britannia ahead of Barr and found nothing there except three large marquees, two of them government tents, the other occupied by Barr's Stores Syndicate. There were no buildings and not a stick of lumber to be had. Despite his promises, Barr had made no arrangement to supply doors and sashes and float them down the Saskatchewan. There wasn't even a post office. The mail had been dumped on the floor of the stores tent.

The prices the advance party was charging were so high that many packed up and left on the spot—they had bought oats near Battleford at a quarter of the Barr prices.

The only farm in the area, forty miles (64 km) out of Battleford, belonged to Peter Paynter, a ex-Mounted Policeman. For hundreds of outfits strung out along the dreadful trail, this farm was an oasis. Here were herds of horses and cattle, flocks of turkeys, and grunts of pigs. The Holtby family stayed here for two days to give their exhausted horse time to rest. Mrs. Paynter, whose kitchen was full of women and children warming themselves, let Mrs. Holtby use her oven to bake bread while the men put up the tents.

Ahead lay devastation. Fires had charred the land, leaving a wilderness of ruin. No sliver of green could be seen through the black, ashen world that greeted those travellers who'd had the good fortune to escape the flames. Some lost everything—tents, wagons, horses, supplies—everything but their lives.

In this gloomy part of the country, the sloughs and the bogs were the worst the colonists had yet encountered. The Hutchison brothers, who had managed to avoid every swamp on the trail, were stuck fast on three occasions. With their wagon mired to the axles and tilted on its side on the muddy bank of a small torrent, they were struck by a blizzard that blocked their passage for four days.

In all that time they were never dry. Their clothing, greatcoats, and blankets were drenched and encrusted with mud. From Saturday night to the following Thursday they lived on starvation rations: a plate of boiled rice and one pancake made from flour, water, and snow, per meal. When they were able at last to push forward, very little else was moving. They passed scores of tents pitched in the snow beside the trail, their occupants depressed and sick—many of them trying to sell their ploughs and equipment to earn enough to pay for their ticket home.

Meanwhile, at the settlement, Barr became the focus for every complaint. Ivan Crossley watched while one group demanded to know what had happened to all the fresh meat he had promised. At that, Barr seized an axe and knocked down one of his own oxen. "There's fresh meat for you, now!" he cried. "Help yourselves." And they did.

Barr left the colony May 13, taking with him three nurses brought out for the Hospital Syndicate. On May 15 he was back in Battleford, and there he encountered more angry demonstrations. Two Boer War veterans lit into him over their purchase from him of CPR land in the colony. The railway had no record of the transaction. The homesteads had already been sold. Barr blustered, but when threatened with violence he gave them their money back.

It was obvious to all that he *had* been on the make. He'd not only tried to sell supplies at huge prices and collect money for CPR land without approval from the company, but he'd also charged absentee Englishmen $5 apiece to reserve their homesteads. He'd got $10 from single girls in England, promising to settle them later. He'd tried to collect a premium of $5 or more from every settler. He'd taken another $5 from each member of the Hospital Syndicate that he knew was collapsing.

That was the end for Isaac Barr. On May 16, in Battleford, a mass meeting took away any control he had left. Lloyd was appointed in his place as head of a twelve-man committee, quickly dubbed the Twelve Apostles.

In one final moment of bluster Barr shouted that they were all ruffians, and brandished a revolver. But then he meekly gave in, surrendered his records, resigned all claims to a homestead for himself, and turned over everything of value to the community, which all agreed would be named Lloydminster. Barr went back to the settlement where he spent most of his time giving back money to those who felt they'd been cheated. He left forever in mid-June. When he reached Regina, he narrowly escaped being pelted by eggs. In Ottawa he tried to get the bonus the government paid to all colonizers, but he was turned down. He was told that he not only caused the government more expense than the total payments would allow, but he'd also tried to squeeze money illegally from British settlers.

That was the end in Canada of Isaac Barr. He married his secretary (his fourth wife, thirty-five years his junior), became an American citizen, and for the rest of his life dreamed unfulfilled dreams of settling people in the far corners of the Empire. He died in Australia in his ninetieth year, still scribbling away in the end papers of a book he was reading, building more imaginary communities in non-existent promised lands.

CHAPTER SEVEN

Survival

ALL THE QUALITIES OF THE BRITISH IN GENERAL AND THE ENGLISHMAN IN PAR-
TICULAR—THEIR AMATEURISM, THEIR CLANNISHNESS, THEIR ENDURANCE—
CAN BE SEEN IN LLOYDMINSTER'S EARLY YEARS. FOR LLOYDMINSTER WAS
UNIQUE. IT WAS THE ONLY COLONY IN THE WEST THAT WAS 100 PERCENT
BRITISH. ITS LEADERSHIP WAS ENTIRELY ENGLISH, ITS OUTLOOK IMPERIAL.

Lloydminster colony started out with everything against it. The leadership was incompetent. The people weren't practical farmers. They refused
to learn from other immigrants. And yet in the end it succeeded. There were
many reasons for this—the richness of the Saskatchewan River valley, the
coming of the Canadian Northern Railway, and the growing prosperity of
the Canadian West. But not the least of these reasons was the peculiar
English habit of being able to hang on and muddle through.

In exchanging the leadership of Isaac Barr for that of the Reverend Mr.
George Exton Lloyd and his twelve-man committee, the colonists weren't
out of the woods. Lloyd was likable but hopelessly incompetent. George
Langley, the land agent, called the Twelve Apostles "one of the most inca-
pable bodies of men that ever got together." J. A. Donaghy described Lloyd
as "the blind leading the blind."

Speers reported an absence of all business methods among Lloyd and
his council. The hospital plan collapsed. The Stores Syndicate went out of
business. Free enterprise replaced the cooperative effort. Power went to
Lloyd's head and he became a dictator.

One problem was Lloyd's super patriotism. He and his committee
insisted that nobody except Englishmen would be allowed to settle in the
colony. That was Barr's original plan. He had written, "We hope to keep the
colony free from any foreign admixture, even of American people ... I think

it not wise to mix that people with this colony. I hope to keep it British in actuality as well as in settlement."

As a result, the English tenderfeet had no practical farmers from Iowa and Nebraska as neighbours to help them by example and advice. The colony's doctor, who stayed behind when the Hospital Syndicate folded, found his work was constant but pretty monotonous. His biggest daily chore was stitching up axe wounds. Scores of colonists had never before had an axe or hatchet in their hands.

This lack of experience and of knowledgeable neighbours held up the colony's development for at least a year and caused untold hardships. Some of the buildings being erected on the homesteads were among the poorest in the Northwest. Some were almost useless. Many were so badly built the roofs were in danger of collapsing.

To understand the problem facing these green arrivals, let us go out into the empty prairie with Ivan Crossley and see what he and his Irish friends were up against.

The land agent brought them here, located the survey posts and left them standing behind their wagon on their new homestead—640 acres (260 hectares) of unbroken prairie, some twelve miles (19 km) southeast of the colony. What a lonely scene this was! There wasn't a sign of human habitation—nothing as far as the eye could see except for the prairie blackened by fire, and a few skeletal clumps of charred cottonwood.

The scene was not unique. It had already been repeated thousands of times in the open country that lay between the Red River and Rockies. It would be repeated thousands of times more before the plains were broken and fenced, and would remain engraved on Ivan Crossley's memory for all of his life, as well as on the memories of thousands of others—British, American, German, Scandinavian, Slav, and Dutch. None would ever forget those first despairing moments on the limitless ocean of the prairie.

This was home. This was where they must live. This hard turf on which they stood—as tough as human gristle—would be their building material. Before they could prosper, before they could plant a single grain, they would have to attack it, break it, turn it over, rip it apart, and finally nurture the black soil beneath. That became the folk memory of the West.

Crossley knew that some of their compatriots faced with a challenge had already packed up and fled. He and his partners were almost broke. But they didn't have wives or children, they had enthusiasm and energy, and they were young. And so they pitched their tent, unloaded their walking plough, and went to work.

They had a sketchy idea of how to build a sod house. So they set to work ploughing long strips of various lengths, dragging them to the site on a stone boat of fire-killed trees. They learned by trial and error. The house would be sixteen by twelve feet (4.8 by 3.6 m). They simply marked out a space, laid a row of sods along it, and kept on building until the walls were eight feet (2.4 m) high.

There would be no windows—they couldn't get any glass. But they made a door out of split poles, and they covered it with blankets. They made a kind of roof out of small poplar poles, laid close together and shaped to shed the rain. They piled more sods on top of the poles and chinked them with earth. That would have to do—even though it wasn't watertight. But then, no sod house was. There was a saying in the West that if it rained three days outside, it rained for two weeks inside. They would have to get used to that.

They installed their stove, built bunks out of more poles, and made mattresses of branches. As Crossley said, it would take a lot of imagination to call this hovel a house. But it would be their only shelter in the winter to come, and before many weeks crept by they would start to think of it as home.

It was one thing, of course, to throw up a house of sorts, but quite another to begin practical farming. Crossley and his friends tried to plant a garden in a bare spot where the sods had been stripped away, only to discover too late that they had removed the best soil. The vegetables withered and died and the men were forced to go to work for wages.

Scores left the colony to seek jobs. Scores more would have gone had Lloyd and his committee not persuaded them to stay, promising jobs in the town itself, jobs that never appeared. Others sat in their homesteads trying to break up the land with little success.

Matthew Snow, the government farm inspector, had great trouble getting the colonists to move quickly to break the land and get it ready for the following year's crops. The breaking season was quickly passing and yet

70 percent had no chance of getting a crop in the following year, let alone in that summer of 1903. Teams stood idle, some animals straying away because their owners were so lazy. They didn't seem to realize the prairie could be broken only in the summer. Many thought, in their ignorance, that they could work late in the fall, after their houses were finished.

In fact, these middle-class Englishmen from Leeds and Birmingham, London and Manchester, had no comprehension of the harshness of the prairie climate. They'd never known a western winter. They'd never faced a blizzard or a whiteout. They'd never felt their eyelids freeze together, or their skin peel off when they pressed it against icy metal. The Slavs and Scandinavians, the Nebraskans and Iowans were used to this. The Englishmen weren't. By fall it was clear that the average amount of farmland broken by the plough, let alone planted, was less than two acres (0.8 hectares) a homestead.

That winter, in the course of a snowshoe patrol, Sergeant D. J. McCarthy of the Mounted Police came upon a queer scene some miles to the southeast of Lloydminster. Here he found one of the colonists, crouched in his shack with the door partly open, sitting close to his stove, wearing all his outer clothing, including his cap and mitts, and calmly reading Shakespeare.

The door wouldn't close because he'd pushed a long tree from the outside into the door of the stove. When the fire died down, he just pushed the tree farther in. He seemed quite cheerful, and invited the policeman in for a spot of tea, and explained that he was the son of a former British ambassador to Turkey.

In sharp contrast was the example of those who *had* farming experience. They did well. By July 22, William Rendell, whose family had farmed in England for two centuries, managed to break and plant three acres (1.2 hectares) of oats, an acre and a half (0.6 hectares) of barley, another acre and a half of potatoes, and a quarter acre (0.1 hectares) of vegetables. His family bungalow, the largest of the settlement, was within two weeks of completion, even though Rendell had to haul the lumber thirty miles (48 km).

But Rendell was one of the few who knew his business. He'd refused the homestead Barr had offered, had chosen another one, and started to plough the day after he got there. That winter his wife, Alice, wrote her friends in England an enthusiastic letter, in which she said, "I would never advise anyone to come out here who is afraid of work. They are better off at home. There is room to breathe in this country and if the work is hard the freedom, which is the indispensable attribute of the life here, makes one far less susceptible to physical fatigue … Here one feels that each week's work is a step forward whilst in the old country oftentimes a year's hard work brought nothing but disappointment …"

The Rendells were in a minority. Less than 10 percent of the people had farming experience. Wesley Speers called a meeting to see who needed government aid, but was hampered by the pride of the English. As one woman told him: "I will not become the object of charity."

He was appalled at the conditions among the destitute. The worst example was that of J. G. Bulmer, whose ailing wife was the mother of eighteen children, one no more than three weeks old. While Speers was visiting the family, she fainted dead away. Bulmer had a fine piece of land, but he hadn't broken a foot of ground, so Speers packed the entire family off to Battleford.

An equally pathetic case was that of Alexander Carlyle-Bell, who had somehow dropped his wallet, stuffed with $200 in cash, on the prairie and then lost a bank draft for $500. The wretched man could do nothing right. He'd managed to break seven acres (2.8 hectares) on a quarter section of land, only to discover it was the *wrong* section. The last straw came when his wife fell off the wagon and broke her arm. That was the last the colony saw of the Carlyle-Bells.

The wretched man could do nothing right. He'd managed to break seven acres (2.8 hectares) on a quarter section of land, only to discover it was the wrong section. The last straw came when his wife fell off the wagon and broke her arm. That was the last the colony saw of the Carlyle-Bells.

And yet the settlers muddled through—and somehow they made it through the winter. Some men took jobs during the cold weather, not always successfully. Speers was frustrated at the settlers' ineptitude. By the following spring very little land was broken. Three-quarters of the horses were dead of exposure, and the rest were ailing.

Speers was fed up with Lloyd and his committee, who thought in city terms rather than country terms. Speers was convinced Lloyd and his council were wasting the colonists' time at the planting season with endless meetings, organizations and sub-committees. They were all planning in a most optimistic fashion for a glorious future—discussing taxes and lot sizes and all the details of municipal organization, "troubling about small things that should give them no concern ... trying to build up a commerce without cultivating their good lands ..."

Speers himself was a rugged and practical farmer, but his patience was sorely tried. Like all Canadians, he'd welcomed the British. But now, in their own way, they were proving a maddening group. What were they doing, organizing musical societies, tennis clubs, theatrical performances, and literary circles in the town, when they ought to be in the fields, building up their quarter sections? In Speers's view, they couldn't afford such indulgence. What these people lacked, he thought, was not culture, but common sense.

Yet they were beginning to prosper. The impossible cases had been weeded out. Those left behind were learning slowly by trial and error. In 1905 they broke more land than they had during the previous two years combined.

By November Lloyd was out of the way—promoted to Archdeacon of Prince Albert. Now there arrived in the area a group of Americans and Canadians with farming experience. And that fall of 1905 the Canadian Northern Railway arrived at last.

By February of 1907, the local immigration agent was able to report that Lloydminster had surpassed all expectations. In 1908, the Lloydminster board of trade felt justified in putting out a pamphlet boosting the town as "the Banner District of the West."

By that time all the heartache and controversy that had marked the settlement's early days were forgotten. As one old-timer put it many years later, "Strangely enough, as the years rolled by, it was apparent that several among the most successful settlers were men with no previous farming experience."

That was certainly true of William Hutchison, who, by 1905, was able to write an article on "How to Become a Farmer" for his hometown paper in England. Stanley Rackham was another who did well. In fact he could have afforded to make regular trips home to the old country. But he never left the site of the Barr Colony, and he was still in Lloydminster in 1937 when he died at the age of sixty.

Like many others, Ivan Crossley alternately farmed his homestead and added to his income by taking temporary jobs. When he needed money, he'd go to work ploughing another man's field, or taking a winter mail contract from Battleford or Saskatoon. In between he'd go back to his homestead, break ground, work on his shack, put up a barn, until he owned the land outright.

In 1906 Crossley ran into his former shipmate, Robert Holtby, bringing a load of hay into town for sale. Robert Holtby's pretty sister was sitting astride the load. Crossley took her to lunch and soon became a regular visitor at the thriving Holtby homestead, seven miles (11 km) out of town. The pair were engaged that fall, and married in Lloyd's log church the following spring. They enjoyed forty-eight years of married life—the memories of those early struggles on the long trail from Saskatoon slowly fading as the years wore on and Lloydminster prospered and the grandchildren of that pioneer union began to arrive.

INDEX

A Canadian Pacific Railway passenger train with
Engine 147 in Calgary, 1884.
(Courtesy Glenbow Archives, NA-967-12)

STEEL ACROSS THE PLAINS

CONTENTS

The Shape of the Nation

CANADA IS DECEPTIVELY VAST. THE MAP SHOWS IT AS THE LARGEST COUNTRY IN THE WORLD AND PROBABLY THE GREATEST IN DEPTH FROM NORTH TO SOUTH. IT IS ALMOST TWICE AS DEEP AS THE UNITED STATES AND MUCH DEEPER THAN EITHER CHINA OR RUSSIA.

But that is an illusion. For practical purposes Canada is almost as slender as Chile. Half its people live within a hundred miles (160 km) of the U.S. border, 90 percent of them within two hundred miles (320 km). It is a country shaped like a river or a railway, and for the best of reasons. In the eastern half of the nation this horizontal bunching of the population is due to the presence of the St. Lawrence River, in the western half to the Canadian Pacific Railway.

More than most countries, Canada owes its existence to its transcontinental railways. It was the promise of a railway to the Pacific that brought British Columbia into Confederation. It was the presence of that railway—the Canadian Pacific—that brought one million immigrants to the Canadian prairies at the turn of the century.

The American symbol of western expansion is the covered wagon. The Canadian symbol is the CPR colonist car. Every country has in its background a great national moment—a revolution, a military victory, a civil war. Ours is the building of a railway. The Trans-Canada Highway, which follows the railway route, is a continuation of that effort to tie the country together.

The CPR was the natural extension of the route used by explorers and fur traders in their passage to the Northwest. If that natural extension had been continued as was originally planned, Canada might today have a different shape. But in the spring of 1881 a handful of men gathered around a cluttered circular table in an office in St. Paul, Minnesota, and altered the shape and condition of the new country west of Winnipeg.

That decision affected the lives of tens of thousands of Canadians. It created a new network of cities close to the border that might not have existed for another generation, if ever—Broadview, Regina, Moose Jaw, Swift Current, Medicine Hat, Calgary, Banff, and Revelstoke.

It doomed others—Carlton, Battleford, Eagle Hill, Bethlehem, Grenoble, Baldwin, Humboldt, Nazareth, Nut Hill.

It affected aspects of Canadian life as varied as the tourist trade and the wheat trade. And it gave the CPR something very close to absolute control over the future of scores of new communities along the line of the railway.

That was not what the government had originally intended when it began planning the railway in 1871, or even in 1881, when the job was taken over by a private company. The original route led northwest, away from the U.S. border, along the old Carlton Trail in the wooded valleys of the North Saskatchewan River. The three directors of the Canadian Pacific—George Stephen, the president, Richard Angus, and James Jerome Hill—decided to run the line south as close to the border as possible.

They had their reasons. They wanted to go through land that had not been settled so that they could control the real estate around their own railway stations. In this way they could prevent real estate speculators from making all the profits on the land. These people bought land cheaply in the belief that the railway would cross it. Then they could sell it to the CPR for much more than they had paid.

More than most countries, Canada owes its existence to its transcontinental railways. It was the promise of a railway to the Pacific that brought British Columbia into Confederation. It was the presence of that railway — the Canadian Pacific — that brought one million immigrants to the Canadian prairies at the turn of the century.

The CPR abandoned the careful route that government surveyors had explored and laid out in the previous decade at great cost in life, hardship, and expense (see *The Railway Pathfinders*). It would be another thirty years before that original route would be used by another railway—the Canadian Northern—now a part of the Canadian National Railway system.

The CPR's directors were encouraged by a bright-eyed amateur botanist named John Macoun. He had visited the so-called Palliser Triangle in the southern prairies in a particularly wet season. He told the three directors, quite wrongly, that there would be no problems for future farmers.

The Palliser Triangle is a continuation of the Great American Desert. It has its wet years, and as every farmer now knows it has its dry years when almost nothing will grow without irrigation. But Macoun didn't know about the dry years. The railway builders took him at his word, and so the route of the CPR was changed, and the whole structure of the Canadian West was changed with it.

CHAPTER ONE

The Birth of Brandon

JOHN McVICAR WAS CERTAIN HE WAS GOING TO BE RICH. HIS FARM AT GRAND VALLEY, MANITOBA, LAY DIRECTLY IN THE PATH OF THE NEW CANADIAN PACIFIC RAILWAY, WHICH HAD BEEN FORMED IN 1880. NOW, IN THE SPRING OF 1881, McVICAR WAS EXPECTING AN OFFER FOR HIS FARM IN GRAND VALLEY. HE WAS ABOUT TO BE BITTERLY DISAPPOINTED.

Railway lines, like the CPR, are cut up into divisions, just as provinces are cut up into townships or counties. The little settlement of Grand Valley lay clustered on the banks of the Assiniboine River about 130 miles (208 km) west of Winnipeg. McVicar realized that the first divisional point on the prairie line after Winnipeg would have to be established right on his farm. It would become a headquarters for trainmen, conductors, and railway workers. Marshalling yards would spring up, and freight and passenger cars would be shunted about to make up new trains. Supplies would pour in and so would settlers. Grand Valley would become a big community.

McVicar increased the size of his house, doubled the capacity of his warehouse, and waited for an offer. It came quickly that April from the Canadian Pacific Railway's chief surveyor, General Thomas Lafayette Rosser, a tall Virginian who had fought on the Southern side in the American Civil War (1861–65). Rosser offered him $50,000.

John McVicar was about to take the money when his friends urged him to hold out for more. He asked Rosser for $60,000—a big mistake. Rosser turned on his heel. "I'll be damned if a town of any kind is built here," he said.

He ordered his horse saddled, crossed the Assiniboine River and made straight for the shack of D. H. Adamson. He bought Adamson's property for a fraction of the price he'd offered McVicar. That was the end of Grand Valley, and the beginning of the new town of Brandon.

The railway wouldn't bargain with anybody. It simply moved its Grand Valley station two miles (3.2 km) farther west into the Brandon Hills. That would be the CPR's method for all future dealings when private citizens tried to hold it up.

The new town was born on May 9, 1881. That was the day on which a Winnipeg surveyor arrived to subdivide it into avenues, streets, blocks, and lots. The main street was named after General Rosser, who insisted the lots be small so more money could be made. The survey took until mid-August, but the lots went on sale long before it was finished. Once the location of the new town was known, people began to appear and tents blossomed all along the high bank of the Assiniboine.

When it became clear that Grand Valley was dying, its leading grocery store moved to Brandon. It was floated in sections by barge to the new townsite. By June two more stores and a billiard hall had also moved to Brandon. The CPR's clear intention was to destroy Grand Valley as a community.

Lots on both townsites went on sale at the end of May. A brief advertisement proclaimed that "McVicar's Landing" was a CPR crossing. But the name of the new town of Brandon first appeared May 30. Brandon lots sold at prices that ranged from $63 to $355. Grand Valley lots went badly and sold for an average of $33. The original community was clearly doomed.

The first newcomers had difficulty finding the new Brandon. James Canning trudged across the prairie looking for work. He arrived at the corner of 10th and Rosser and asked a man where the town was.

"Right here," came the reply.

Canning looked about him. There was only one other building in sight. "I don't see any town," Canning said.

"Well, it's only a paper town yet," his acquaintance replied.

The paper town blossomed swiftly into a tent community. The first post office was nothing more than a soapbox with a slit for mail placed outside a tent. The first restaurant was a plank laid across two barrels on the trail that was to become Pacific Avenue. The first church services were held out of doors in a driving rainstorm that June. The local harness maker held an umbrella over the minister's head while the congregation, composed entirely of young men, sang lustily in spite of the downpour.

In that golden summer of 1881, the pattern of the new Canada began to take hesitant shape along the line of the railway. Brandon was the beginning—the first of the scores of raw communities that would erupt from the naked prairie. Its birth pangs would be repeated again and again as the rails moved west. There was a kind of an electric feeling in the atmosphere—a sense of being in on the start of a great adventure—that the newcomers who arrived that summer would never forget.

In future years, when other memories became blurred, those early pioneers would always keep the bright memory of those first months when the sharp, spring air was ripe with the scent of fresh lumber and ringing with the noise of construction; when lasting friendships began among the soiled tents on the riverbank; when every man was young and strong and in love with life; and when the distant prairie, unmarked by shovel or plough, was still a mysterious realm waiting to be claimed.

For those who planned to stay, the opportunities were almost unlimited. Of the first seven lawyers who arrived, four became cabinet ministers and a fifth Leader of the Opposition in the Manitoba legislature. The first organist in the church became the mayor of the city four times running. From grading the bumps on Sixth Street, Douglas Cameron rose to be Lieutenant-Governor of Manitoba. A jovial young Irish ploughman from Ontario named Pat Burns went on to become the meat packing king of the Canadian West.

He arrived at the corner of 10th and Rosser and asked a man where the town was.

"Right here," came the reply.

Canning looked about him. There was only one other building in sight. "I don't see any town," Canning said.

"Well, it's only a paper town yet," his acquaintance replied.

By August the town had acquired a dozen frame buildings, including two hotels. On October 11 the first passenger train pulled into the station and a boom of epic proportions was in full swing. The coming of the railway was transforming the West and the changes were spectacular enough to set the continent buzzing. But Grand Valley lapsed into decay. John McVicar and his brother, Dugald, tried to sell their townsite and failed. In the end they took $1,500 for it.

One man passing through early in '82 described Grand Valley as "a living corpse. The few buildings were forlorn. The business that was still being done … made a noise like a death rattle. The CPR had refused to stop trains there."

Some years later a surveyor named Charles Shaw came upon John McVicar ploughing in the vicinity with a team of mules. The farmer ran out onto the road. "Oh Mr. Shaw, I was a damn fool. If I'd only taken your advice, I would have been well off now!" For future speculators the fate of the little community on the Assiniboine was an object lesson in how not to deal with the railway.

CHAPTER TWO

The Railway General

WILLIAM CORNELIUS VAN HORNE WAS MADE THE CPR'S GENERAL MANAGER IN JANUARY OF 1882. WHEN HE ANNOUNCED THAT HE WOULD BUILD FIVE HUNDRED MILES (800 KM) OF TRACK ACROSS THE EMPTY PLAINS IN A SINGLE SEASON, VERY FEW PEOPLE BELIEVED HIM. THE WHOLE PRAIRIE COUNTRY FROM BRANDON TO THE ROCKIES WAS VIRTUALLY EMPTY OF PEOPLE, EXCEPT FOR BANDS OF ROVING INDIANS AND A FEW TRAPPERS AND FUR TRADERS.

There were no roads, no bridges, and no trees. To build five hundred miles of steel in a single summer, the new-formed Canadian Pacific Railway company would have to bring every scrap of timber for bridges, railway ties, and buildings from hundreds of miles away. They would also have to bring in steel rails, bridging material, food for the employees, work tools and giant scrapers—all on rails as the line of steel was constructed. Only a man of Van Horne's determination could even consider such a thing.

The Canadian Pacific Railway company was a brand new organization only a year old. The job of this private firm was to construct a line of steel all the way from North Bay on Lake Nipissing, in Ontario, to the Eagle Pass in the Gold Range of British Columbia. The government contractor would finish the line to the west coast. The government had also tried to build a railway across the Canadian Shield in Northern Ontario, without much luck. The new CPR company was hired to finish that job. But its first task was to open up the prairies.

The CPR directors wanted that done as quickly as possible. They had been given ten years to finish the railway, but they were planning to complete it in a much shorter time. It was absolutely necessary to get the whole line into operation as quickly as possible because they knew that for many years there would be very little local traffic.

It was the transcontinental trade that counted. A cargo such as silk demanded speedy transport, for silk is perishable. The CPR would have an advantage over its United States rivals because its route was much shorter. The coast of British Columbia was closer to the Orient than that of California. But the railway couldn't turn a dollar of profit until the last spike was driven.

Among railwaymen south of the border, Van Horne had a reputation for doctoring sick railroads until they were made to pay. He was also known as a fighter who had battled grasshoppers, labour unions, and other railways. Up to this point he had always won.

He told the CPR directors in Montreal that he could lay five hundred miles (800 km) of prairie line in one year—an announcement that was greeted with skepticism. As one man said, "It was a feat unparalleled in railway history." A previous manager hadn't been able to lay more than 130 miles (209 km) of track in a single year, and here was Van Horne offering to quadruple that.

Still, this new man seemed to know a terrifying amount about railroading. He knew all about yards and repair shops. He understood the mysteries of accounting. He could work out a complicated system of scheduling in his head, while others sweated with pins and charts. He could understand the chatter of a telegraph key. He could operate any locomotive built. He even redesigned railway stations to his own taste. He was a product of his times—there is no one quite like him in today's business community.

He was probably one of the most engaging and versatile immigrants that this country has ever attracted across its borders—cheerful, capable, ingenious, temperamental, blunt, forceful, boyish, self-reliant, imaginative, hard-working, mischievous, and courageous. All those adjectives apply, but the one that sums him up best is the word "positive." As J. H. E. Secretan, his chief surveyor, said, "The word 'cannot' did not exist in his dictionary."

If he knew failure, he never showed it. Nor did he ever show any emotion behind the grave mask of his face or his penetrating blue eyes. He believed in coming to the point swiftly with the fewest possible words. It was the same with railway lines. The best run lines he knew were the ones that reached their destination with the shortest number of miles. And so one of his first jobs was to make sure the CPR would reach the Pacific Ocean by the shortest possible route.

His first decision—on January 13, 1882—was to change the point at which the road entered the Rockies. Several of the passes in the mountains had already been surveyed. One, the Yellowhead, had been chosen by the chief engineer of Canada, Sir Sandford Fleming. But Van Horne felt it was too far north.

The CPR chose the Kicking Horse Pass, well to the south, not far from the present site of Calgary. This pass had not been surveyed but Van Horne was sure it would work. So here he was, proposing to drive steel directly across the plains at the mountain barrier without knowing exactly how to get through.

He had been hired as general manager of the CPR; someday he would be president. A man of great ambition, his love of power had its roots in his childhood and youth. He had started out as a telegraph operator. When he was eighteen, he was struck by the sight of the general superintendent of the Michigan Central Railway coming forward to meet his assistants. The man radiated power and dignity. Young Van Horne gazed at him with awe. He wondered if he might himself someday reach the same rank and travel about in a private car of his own.

"The glories of it, the pride of it, the salary … all that moved me deeply and I made up my mind then and there that I would reach it," he said. And he did. Just ten years later, at the age of twenty-eight, he became the youngest railway superintendent in the world. Nobody in Canada had Van Horne's experience or expertise. After all, Canada had never built a railway as ambitious as the CPR.

His boss in the CPR was George Stephen, who was a financier, not a rail-roadman. A Scot, born in poverty, trained as a haberdasher, of all things, he had risen to be the president of the Bank of Montreal. Stephen was a Highlander. Van Horne was a mixture of Dutch, French, and German. He had a quality of enthusiasm that Stephen must have admired, for Stephen had it too. When Stephen threw himself into a project, he went all the way. So did Van Horne. And what they were planning to do between them was to build the first transcontinental railway in Canadian history.

Stephen only had one passion—finance—unless you counted salmon fishing. But Van Horne had half a dozen hobbies. He was a brilliant gardener and horticulturist; he even bred new varieties of plant life. He was an amateur geologist who had actually discovered and named new species of fossils; in fact, he carried a rock collection about with him. He was a clever cartoonist, a sketch artist, and an amateur magician.

Born in an Illinois log cabin, he had been left fatherless at eleven and at fourteen had to quit school to support his family. He was a hard worker but he played hard too. In his youth as a train dispatcher, his workday was twelve hours, but when it was over he didn't go home. Instead he hung around the yards and shops and offices, soaking up the railway business. He believed that any persistent person could always do what he set out to do.

One of Van Horne's first jobs was to fire General Thomas Rosser, who he felt was incompetent. As a result, the two almost got in a gunfight on the steps of the Manitoba Club in Winnipeg one hot July evening. Van Horne was no man to back away from a fight. As a child he had taken on every boy in school. The two men drew pistols, but others stepped in to prevent a shootout.

With Rosser out of the way in mid-February, 1882, Van Horne told Secretan, his replacement, that he wanted the "shortest commercial line" between Winnipeg and the Pacific coast. He said he would not only lay five hundred miles (800 km) of track that summer, but would also have trains running over it by fall.

Secretan, a great, bulky Englishman with a waxed moustache, thought that was doubtful. Van Horne told him that nothing was impossible. If Secretan couldn't lay out the railroad, he said, then he would have his scalp. Van Horne didn't much like surveyors, but Secretan admired him as "the most versatile man I have encountered."

He noticed that as Van Horne talked he had a habit of making sketches on blotting pads, so well drawn that they were worth framing. Throughout his life, Van Horne had been a frustrated artist. As a small boy unable to afford paper, he had covered the whitewashed walls of his house with drawings. As a child he had fallen in love with a book called *Elementary Geology*—he liked it so much he decided to copy it. Night after night by candlelight the determined boy copied the book in ink onto sheets of foolscap—every page, every note, and every picture, right down to the index.

As he later admitted: "It taught me how much could be accomplished by application; it improved my handwriting; it taught me the construction of English sentences; and helped my drawing materially. And I never had to refer to the book again."

In later life he became a skilled amateur painter, attacking great canvasses as he attacked the building of the railway—with huge brushes at top speed. He believed that work was best done when it was done as rapidly as possible.

His drawings were so realistic that they were sometimes mistaken for actual engravings by other artists. He once got a copy of *Harper's Weekly Magazine* before it reached his mother and with great care transformed a series of portraits of American authors into bandits. He did it so well the pictures didn't appear to have been altered. His mother actually complained to the editor about his apparent policy of insulting the images of great Americans. The issue became a collector's item.

He had the high spirits of a small boy. He left one school because he drew caricatures of the principal. He was a bit of a joker and it cost him his first job when he set up an electric plate that gave a mild shock to any man who stepped on it. His boss stepped on it and fired him. As one of his colleagues said after he died, "He possessed a splendid simplicity of grownup boyhood to the end."

Van Horne loved to eat. When he was travelling around on the railway, he used to wire ahead for roast chicken dinners to be set up for two, and when he arrived he'd eat both of them himself. He believed the men who worked for him should eat well too. Secretan had prepared a list of the food he needed in the field when he was surveying the line, but the company's new chief purchasing officer cut their order in half. Secretan made sure Van Horne heard about that. The general manager was indignant. After all, he knew what it was like to be hungry. So now he called the chief purchasing officer into his office and tore into him.

"Are you the God-forsaken idiot who buys the provisions? If so, I'll just give you till six o'clock tonight to ship a car-load of the very best stuff you can find up to Secretan, the engineer at the front; and see here, you can come back at six o'clock and tell me you have shipped it, you understand, but if you have not, you need not come back at all, but just go back to wherever you came from."

All that summer small luxuries continued to arrive at Secretan's camp.

But Van Horne faced greater problems than food. Some of his staff were against him because he hired more Americans than Canadians. But the Americans had railway building experience. Indeed, this most nationalistic of all Canadian enterprises was to a very large extent managed and built by Americans. No major railroad line had been built in Canada since the days of the Grand Trunk almost thirty years before.

Van Horne hired people he knew he could depend upon. Many of the Americans who came to Canada to build the CPR stayed on and became dedicated Canadians. As someone had remarked, the building of the CPR would make a Canadian out of the German Kaiser. It certainly made Canadians out of Van Horne and many of his colleagues. As Van Horne once told a newspaperman, "I'd keep the American idea out of this country."

That spring, serious floods had thrown out his careful schedule. Construction was held back for nearly a month. But Van Horne was making his presence felt. An iron man who never knew a moment's sickness, he didn't seem to need any sleep. Years later he summed up the secret of his stamina: "I eat all I can; I drink all I can; I smoke all I can and I don't give a damn for anything."

"Why do you want to go to bed?" he once asked Secretan. "It's a waste of time; and besides, you don't know what's going on." He could sit up all night in a poker game and then at seven o'clock rub his eyes, head for the office, and do a full day's work.

He was a great poker player. Indeed, he loved all card games. That may have been his secret—the ability to turn from one form of activity to another, to switch on and off, and not to get too anxious about any of his enterprises.

When Van Horne had finished his work he was free to play games, to eat a good supper, to smoke one of his gigantic cigars, to work with his rock specimens, or to beat a colleague at billiards or chess.

He loved to play and he loved to win. He didn't like to leave a poker table when he was losing. His memory for obscure detail was remarkable. He liked to dare his friends to duplicate the feats of memory with which he astonished everybody.

He was the terror of the railway, a kind of superman with an uncanny habit of always turning up just when things went wrong. Here's how one newspaper columnist in Winnipeg described the arrival of Van Horne at the unsuspecting settlement of Flat Creek west of Brandon.

> The trains run in a kind of go-as-you-please style that is anything but refreshing to the general manager. But when Manager Van Horne strikes the town there is a shaking up of old bones. He cometh in like a blizzard and he goeth out like a lantern. He is the terror of Flat Krick. He shakes them up like an earthquake and they are as frightened of him as he were the old Nick himself. Yet Van Horne is calm and harmless looking. So is a she mule, and so is a buzz saw. You don't know their true inwardness till you go up and feel of them. To see Van Horne get out of the car and go softly up the platform, you would think he was an evangelist on his way west to preach temperance to the Mounted Police. But you are soon undeceived. If you are within hearing distance you will have more fun than you ever had in your life before. He cuffs the first official he comes to just to get his hand in and leads the next one out by the ear, and pointing eastward informs him the walking is good as far as St. Paul. To see the rest hunt their holes and commence scribbling for dear life is a terror. Van Horne wants to know. He is that kind of man. He wants to know why this was not done and why this was done. If the answers are not satisfactory there is a dark and bloody tragedy enacted right there. During each act all the characters are killed off and in the last scene the heavy villain is filled with dynamite, struck with a hammer, and by the time he has knocked a hole plumb through the sky, and the smoke has cleared away, Van Horne has discharged all the officials and hired them over again at lower figures.

As another railway president once remarked, "Van Horne was one of the most considerate and even-tempered of men, but when an explosion came it was magnificent."

Yet he rather enjoyed people who stood up to him. One was Michael J.

Haney, a flamboyant Irish construction boss who was as tough as nails. Haney was in the Winnipeg freight yards one day when his secretary came hustling down the track to warn him that Van Horne was on the warpath.

"He's hot enough to melt rails," Haney was told. "If you've got any friends or relatives at home who are fond of you I'd advise you to hunt a cyclone cellar."

But Haney was feeling pretty hot himself. It was a day on which everything had seemed to go wrong. And he was in a mood to look for somebody with trouble. So instead of getting out of Van Horne's way he stalked right down the yards to meet him.

Van Horne began an exhaustive lecture on the system's defects. His profanity turned the air blue. Haney waited until the general manager stopped for a breath, then lit into him.

"Mr. Van Horne," he said finally, "everything you say is true and if you claimed it was twice as bad as you have, it would still be true. I'm ready to agree with you there but I'd like to say this: Of all the spavined, one-horse, rottenly equipped, badly managed, badly run, headless and heedless thing for people to call a railroad, this is the worst. You can't get anyone who knows anything about anything. You can't get materials and if you could it wouldn't do you any good because you couldn't get them where you wanted them."

Haney followed up this outburst with a list of counter-complaints far longer than Van Horne's, since he was in closer touch with the work. His tirade made Van Horne's explosion "sound like a drawing room conversation." The general manager waited patiently as Haney unleashed his torrent of complaints; by the time Haney had finished he was grinning.

"That's all right, Haney. I guess we understand one another," he said. "Let's get to work."

CHAPTER THREE

Five Hundred Miles of Steel

THE CONTRACT TO BUILD THE PRAIRIE SECTION OF THE CANADIAN PACIFIC RAILWAY WAS PROBABLY THE LARGEST OF ITS KIND EVER UNDERTAKEN. AT THE END OF JANUARY 1882, AN AMERICAN FIRM GOT THE PRIZE. THERE WERE TWO PARTNERS — GENERAL R. B. LANGDON, A ONE-TIME STONEMASON OF SCOTTISH HERITAGE, AND D. C. SHEPARD, A FORMER RAILROAD ENGINEER WHO HAD HELPED BUILD THE CHICAGO, MILWAUKEE AND ST. PAUL RAILROAD.

The two men agreed to build 675 miles (1,090 km) of railroad across the plains from the end of track at Flat Creek in Manitoba to Fort Calgary on the Bow River in what is now Alberta. That was a formidable task. This section of the railway would only be fifteen miles (24 km) shorter than the entire length of the Central Pacific Railway in the U.S., which ran from California to Utah.

The day after the contract was signed, Langdon and Shepard advertised for three thousand men and four thousand horses. The work would have to be parcelled out to no fewer than three hundred subcontractors hired to do specific jobs on specific sections of the line.

Between Flat Creek and Fort Calgary they would have to move ten million cubic yards (7.6 million m³) of earth. They'd have to haul every stick of timber, every rail, fishplate, and spike, all the pilings used for bridge work, and all the food and provisions for 7,600 men and 1,700 teams of horses across the naked prairie for hundreds of miles.

To feed the horses alone they would have to distribute four thousand bushels (145,500 L) of oats every day along 150 miles (240 km) of track. No wonder his colleagues and rivals had laughed at Van Horne when he said he could build five hundred miles (800 km) of that section in the one summer!

By the spring of 1882 Winnipeg was a gigantic supply depot. Stone began to pour in from every available quarry. Railroad ties came from Lake of the Woods country to the east, lumber from Minnesota, and rails from England and from the Krupp works in Germany.

Since the St. Lawrence would still be frozen well into the construction season, Van Horne had the steel shipped to New York and New Orleans, and transported to Manitoba by way of St. Paul along the St. Paul and Pacific Railway, which ran between the American cities and Winnipeg.

Trainloads of material heading for the Canadian West were constantly passing through American cities. There, hundreds of checkers reported on them daily so that the exact moment of their arrival could be plotted.

As fast as the supplies arrived they were hauled to the "End of Track." Long trains loaded with rails, ties, fishplates, and provisions rattled westward to Flat Creek, dumped their loads, and returned empty. No newly completed line of steel had ever known such activity in the first year of its construction.

Spring floods put a halt to all this activity, causing logjams of supplies in Winnipeg and St. Paul. The Red River valley was overflowing. The country between Winnipeg and Portage la Prairie looked like the ocean.

The Assiniboine near Brandon spilled over its banks and covered the valley. If the CPR bridge hadn't been held down by flatcars loaded with steel rails it would have been swept away. Settlers moving west had to move on foot and swim their cattle and horses across swollen rivers. Even oxen were sunk in the mud.

On the cart trail leading towards Qu'Appelle, a carpenter named William Oliver came across a strange spectacle of three wagons and six oxen, all lying half-buried in an ocean of gumbo. Their owners, six mud-caked Englishmen, sat helplessly by, downing a breakfast of bread and ale. Oliver hauled them out with the help of 200 feet (60 m) of rope.

The work came to a standstill. Flat Creek, which seemed to have more railway material piled up in its yards than any other place in the world, was a quagmire. Tents of every size and shape, some brand new and some filthy and tattered, stretched out in all directions on a gloomy expanse of swamp.

It was an entirely male population—freighters, farm labourers, bull-whackers, railroad navvies, muleteers, railway officials, and, of course, whisky peddlers. There was no place to sleep. The food was terrible and sometimes non-existent. But Flat Creek's life was very brief. When the railroad blockade ended and the tracks began to creep west once more towards the newer community of Broadview, the town disappeared. Even the name was changed to the pleasanter one of Oak Lake.

By the time the floods ended, scores of would-be homesteaders were ready to quit the Northwest. Building was at a standstill in Brandon because the CPR was rushing all available construction materials to the front. Even before the floods began hundreds of men were idle.

The railway yards themselves looked like a great country fair. Trunks were piled up along the tracks like cordwood as high as men could throw them, but many of the owners were already trying to sell their outfits and leave.

In May a blizzard struck, destroying scores of tents and causing great suffering. Fuel was so scarce that men resorted to stealing lumber, stick by stick. One man, Charles Alfred Peyton, who lived in a small tent on the riverbank at Brandon, would remember all his life trying to crawl on his stomach towards a pile of dry poles his neighbour had collected. Just as he seized a stick, a bullet whizzed through the wood not more than a foot away.

That was not uncommon. People began to tell each other it would be better to leave the land to the Indians. "Why should we take such a country away from them?" was heard on all sides. The first passenger train out of Brandon for the East after the flood contained three coaches loaded to the doors with men and women quitting the Northwest, never to return.

At last the water subsided, the blizzards ended, and the sun came out and warmed the frigid plains. The prairie evenings grew mellower. The sweet smell of wolf willow drifted in from the ponds and sloughs to mingle with the more familiar odours of salt pork, tamarack ties, wood smoke, and human sweat. The early spring blossoms—wild pansies, strawberries, and purple pasque flower—began to poke their tiny faces between the brittle grasses. Then as a flush of new green spread over the land, the oxcarts of the first settlers started west again until they were strung out by the hundreds ahead of the advancing line of steel.

Now a mountain of supplies descended upon Winnipeg. On a single day, May 15, eighteen thousand dollars' worth of freight poured into the city. The following day eighty freight cars arrived from St. Paul. The next day fifty thousand bushels (1,820,000 L) of oats and eleven carloads of mules were checked into the yards.

With the freight came people. By June three thousand immigrants were under canvas in Winnipeg, all buoyed up by the expectation of an entirely new life on the Canadian prairies. Few people now believed it would be possible for the CPR to achieve its season's goal or anything close to it after the delays.

But Van Horne was immovable. Langdon and Shepard had signed the contract promising to drive five hundred miles of steel that year. Five hundred miles it would have to be. The general manager made it clear he'd cancel the contract if they didn't live up to it.

And so they responded by increasing their army of men and horses. They added an extra shift to track-laying. They lengthened the total work day from eleven hours to fifteen. "The iron now is going down just as fast as it can be pulled from the cars," Shepard announced. "We shall show a record of track-laying which has never been surpassed on this continent."

A whirlwind of construction followed. One magazine called it "absolutely unparalleled in railway annals." The track, winding snakelike across the plains, moved so swiftly that Secretan and his surveyors were barely able to stay ahead. Sometimes, indeed, they were awakened at night by the rumble of giant scrapers being dragged past their tents. "We had never seen the like in Canada before," Secretan wrote in his memoirs.

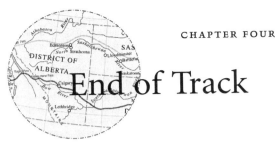

CHAPTER FOUR

End of Track

THE PRAIRIE SECTION OF THE CPR WAS BUILT LIKE A TELESCOPE, EXTENDING FROM A SINGLE BASE. THAT, SAID A LEADING LONDON JOURNAL, WAS IMPOSSIBLE. BUT WITH VAN HORNE NOTHING WAS IMPOSSIBLE. WINNIPEG WAS THE ANCHOR POINT. FROM THERE THE STEEL WOULD STRETCH OUT FOR A THOUSAND MILES (1,600 KM) INTO THE MOUNTAINS. THERE WERE NO SERVICE ROADS, AND NO SUPPLY LINE FOR THE RAILWAY BUILDERS OTHER THAN THE RAILS THEMSELVES.

The previous year's operations had seen small knots of men working in twos and threes with loaded handcars pushing the track forward at about three-quarters of a mile (1.2 km) a day. Van Horne aimed to move at five times that speed. That would require the kind of timing that army generals insist on in the field. Van Horne's army worked that summer with a military precision that astonished all who witnessed it. "Clockwork" was the term used over and over again.

The heart of the operation was at "End of Track"—a unique, mobile community that never stayed in one place for more than a few hours at a time. Here was a hive of industry in which teamsters, track-layers, blacksmiths, carpenters, executive officers, and other trades and professions all had a part. At the end of each day's work, this town on wheels moved another three or four miles (4.8 or 6.4 km) west.

The nerve centre of End of Track was the line of boarding cars—eight or nine of these, each three storeys high—that housed the track-laying crews. The ground floors served as offices, dining rooms, kitchens, and berths for contractors and company officials. The two storeys above were dormitories. Sometimes there were even tents pitched on the roofs.

These huge cars formed part of a long train that contained smaller office cars for executives, cooking cars, freight cars loaded with track materials, shops on wheels, and, on occasion, the private car of the general manager himself.

Van Horne was continually seen at End of Track, spinning yarns with workmen, sketching buffalo skulls, organizing foot races and target shooting at night, and bumping over the prairie in a buckboard, inspecting the track.

Every day some sixty-five carloads of railroad supplies, each carload weighing eighteen tons (16 tonnes), were dumped at End of Track. Most of these supplies had been carried an average of a thousand miles (1,600 km) before reaching their destination.

To a casual visitor this scene was chaotic: cars constantly being coupled and uncoupled, locomotives shunting back and forth, pushing and pulling loads of various lengths, little handcars rattling up and down the half-completed track at the front, teams of horses and mules dragging loaded wagons forward on each side of the main line—and tents constantly rising like puffballs and vanishing again as the whole apparatus rolled steadily towards the Rocky Mountains.

Actually this confusion was an illusion. The organization was carefully planned, down to the last railway spike. Each morning two construction trains set out from the supply yards far in the rear, heading for End of Track. Each train was loaded with the exact number of rails, ties, spikes, fishplates, and telegraph poles required for half a mile (800 m) of railway. One train was held in reserve on a siding about six miles (9.6 km) to the rear, while the other moved directly to the front, where the track-laying gang of three hundred men and seventy horses waited for it.

The track-layers worked like a drill team. "It was beautiful to watch them gradually coming near," one observer wrote, "each man in his place knowing exactly his work and doing it at the right time and in the right way. Onward they come, pass on, and leave the wondering spectator slowly behind while he is still engrossed with the wonderful sight." The ties were unloaded first on either side of the track. They were to be picked up by the waiting wagons and mule teams—thirty ties to a wagon—and hauled forward and dropped along the embankment for exactly half a mile. Two men with marked rods were standing by. As the ties were thrown out, they laid them across the grade, exactly two feet (0.6 m) apart from centre to centre.

Right behind the teams came a hand truck hauled by two horses, one on each side of the track, each loaded with rails, spikes, and fishplates, which held the ties down. Six men marched on each side of the track, and when they reached the far end of the last pair of newly laid rails, each crew seized a rail among them and threw it into the exact position. Two men gauged these rails to make sure they were correctly aligned. Four men followed with spikes, placing one on each end of the four ends of the rails, four others screwed in the fishplates, and another four followed with crowbars to raise the ties while the spikes were being hammered in.

All these men worked in a kind of rhythm, each man directly opposite his partner on each separate rail. More men followed with hammers and spikes to make the rail secure. By this time the hand truck had already moved forward over the newly laid rails even before the job was finished. All the men had to keep in their places and move on ahead; otherwise, they would be caught up by those behind them.

As each construction train dumped its half-mile of supplies at End of Track, it moved back to the nearest siding to be replaced by the reserve train. No time was lost. As the track unfolded, the boarding cars were nudged ahead constantly by the construction train locomotive so that no energy would be wasted by the navvies in reaching their moving mess halls and dormitories.

The operation was strung out for hundreds of miles across the open prairie. Far in advance were the survey camps. These were followed by the grading gangs, scraping the soil off the prairie. Behind them came the bridge-builders. Far to the rear were other thousands—saddlers and carpenters, cooks and tailors, shoemakers, blacksmiths, doctors, and provisioners.

Vast material yards were set up at hundred-mile (160-km) intervals between Winnipeg and End of Track. Supply trains moved out on schedule heading west, unloading thousands of tons of goods at the yards. There all the material was sorted daily into train lots and sent off—as many as eight trains a day—to the front.

Nothing was left to chance. Just in case the track-laying should move faster than expected, extra supplies were held on the sidings and in the yards themselves. Thus, there were enough rails always available for three hundred miles (480 km) and enough fastenings for five hundred (800 km), all within a hundred miles (160 km) of End of Track.

When the steel moved past the hundred-mile point, the yards moved too. An entire community of office workers, sorters, dispatchers, trainmen, labourers, and often their families as well, could be moved a hundred miles in a single night without the loss of an hour's work. The houses were portable and easily fitted onto the flat cars.

The telegraph teams moved right behind the track-layers. They camped in tents, moving their gear forward every afternoon on handcars. The construction trains that brought half a mile (0.8 km) of track supplies also brought half a mile of poles, wires, and insulators for the front. And so, just one hour after the day's track was laid, End of Track was in telegraphic communication with the outside world.

Miles to the west on the barren plain, the bridging crews, grading units, and survey teams felt themselves driven forward by the knowledge that the track-layers were pressing hard behind. The work was so arranged that no weak link could hold up construction. The head contractor had a special group standing by, prepared to finish any work that seemed unlikely to be ready in time for the track to be laid.

The grading was done by immense scrapers pulled by teams of horses. It was their job to build an embankment for the railway four feet (1.2 m) above the prairie and to ditch it for twenty yards (18.3 m) on each side. At that height the rails would be protected from the blizzards of winter, and costly delays from snow blockage could be avoided.

The bridgers worked in two gangs, one by day, one by night. Every sliver of bridging had to be brought from Rat Portage (now Kenora), 140 miles (225 km) east of Winnipeg, or from Minnesota south of the border. Thus the bridge-builders were seldom more than ten miles (16 km) ahead of the advancing steel. The timbers were unloaded as close to End of Track as possible and mostly at night so as not to interfere with other work.

The nation was amazed at the speed with which the railway was being forced across the plains. One man said it seemed to move as fast as the oxcarts of the settlers who were following along behind.

The Northwest was being transformed by the onslaught of the rails. One young man and his sweetheart were able to elope successfully by commandeering a handcar and speeding towards Winnipeg along the line of steel, thus throwing off their pursuers.

The progress of construction was so swift that antelope and other game migrating north were cut off on their return that fall by the lines of rails and telephone posts. They gathered by the hundreds on the north side, afraid to cross it. This would be the last summer in which herds of buffalo and antelope would freely roam the prairie.

Father Albert Lacombe, the voyageur priest who had spent so many years ministering to the Indians of the Northwest, watched the approach of the rails with both sadness and resignation:

"I would look in silence at that road coming on—like a band of wild geese in the sky—cutting its way through the prairies; opening up the great country we thought would be ours for years. Like a vision I could see it driving my poor Indians before it, and spreading out behind it the farms, the towns and cities … No one who has not lived in the west since the Old-Times can realize what is due to that road—that CPR. It was Magic—like the mirage on the prairies, changing the face of the whole country."

The Indians watched in silence as the steel cut through their hunting grounds. They would arrive suddenly, squat on their haunches in double rows, and take in the scene with only the occasional surprised murmur. If they realized their wild, free existence was at an end, they gave no sign.

Onward the track moved, cutting the prairies in two. It moved through a land of geese, snipe, and wild ducks, whose eggs the navvies searched out and ate. It moved through a country fragrant in the soft evenings with a scent of willow and balsam. It cut across fields of yellow daisies, tiger lilies, purple sage, and briar rose. It bisected pastures of waist-high buffalo grass and skirted green hay meadows which, in the spring, were shallow ponds.

As it travelled westward it pushed through a country of memories and old bones—furrowed trails made decades before by thousands of bison moving in single file towards the water—vast fields of grey and withered brush, dead lakes rimmed with tell-tale crusts of alkali.

Day by day it crept towards the horizon. There, against the gold of the sunset, flocks of fluttering wild fowl, disturbed by the clamour of the invaders, could be seen in silhouette. Sometimes a single Indian, galloping at full speed in the distance, became no more than a speck crawling along the rim of the prairie.

This had been once known as the Great Lone Land, unfenced and unbridged. The line of steel made that phrase out of date, for the land would never again be lonely. All that summer it rang with a clang of sledge and anvil, the snorting of horses and mules, the hoarse puffing of great engines, the bellowing of section bosses, the curses of sweating thousands.

History was being made, but few had time to note that fact. William Oliver, a carpenter and future mayor of Lethbridge moving west in his oxcart, had no time to think of history. Later he wrote: "It never came to my mind in watching the building of the railway … that in the next fifty years it would play so important a part in the commerce of the country and in fact of the world … We were more interested in our own affairs and the prospects of a future home …"

The railroad workmen—known as "navvies"—were a mixed lot. They ranged all the way from a gang of Italians who "looked like guys who would cut your throat for a dime," as one observer put it, to younger sons of wealthy Englishmen and graduates of public schools. Some came for adventure, some because they wanted to become Canadians, some because they were down on their luck, and some because the pay was good.

A Winnipeg newspaperman was introduced to a track-laying gang by a section boss who identified some of them: "Do you see that person yonder, that man can read and write Greek and is one of the most profound scholars on the continent; that man next to him was once one of the foremost surgeons in Montreal, and that man next to him was at one time the beloved pastor of one of the largest congregations in Chicago."

The navvies were paid between $2.00 and $2.50 a day—good wages for those times. Often, after they made a little money they quit. Swedes who had learned how to lay track in the old country were highly prized. One Broadview pioneer claimed that "if they were given enough liquor they could lay two or three miles of track in a day." But liquor was prohibited by law in the Northwest although it existed in private hiding places all along the line. The construction workers were plagued by whisky peddlers who sold a mixture that was described as "a mixture of blue ruin, chain lightning, strychnine, the curse of God and old rye."

As autumn approached, the pace quickened. At the end of August one crew managed to lay four and a half miles (7.2 km) of steel in a single day. Next day they beat their own record and laid five miles (8 km).

It was all horribly expensive. There were those who thought that Van Horne "seemed to spend money like a whole navy of drunken sailors." Actually he counted every dollar. In the interests of both speed and economy he allowed steep grades and tight curves which he planned to eliminate once the line was operating.

The contractors didn't reach their goal of five hundred miles—the spring floods had prevented that. However, by the end of the season they had laid 417 miles (671 km) of completed railroad, built twenty-eight miles (29 km) of sidings, and graded another eighteen miles (24 km) for the start of the next season. In addition, Van Horne had pushed the southwestern branch line of the CPR in Manitoba a hundred miles (160 km) and so he could say that, in one way or another, he had achieved what he sought.

The public thought that he had worked a miracle.

CHAPTER FIVE

The Birth of Regina

WITH THE RAILS SPEEDING WEST AT TOP SPEED AND THE SETTLERS MOVING BEHIND THEM, IT WAS NECESSARY TO ESTABLISH A CAPITAL FOR THE NEW NORTH WEST TERRITORIES. THIS VAST AREA INCLUDED ALL THE LAND BETWEEN THE ROCKY MOUNTAINS AND THE PROVINCE OF MANITOBA FROM THE FORTY-NINTH PARALLEL TO THE ARCTIC.

The former capital had been Battleford on the North Saskatchewan River. But Battleford was no longer on the route of the railway and so it no longer counted. The new capital, wherever it was, would be the most important city between the Red River and the Bow, in the foothills of the Rockies. And, because the capital would have to be at a divisional point on the line, the owners of the railway would have a good deal to say about its selection.

The man picked by the prime minister, Sir John A. Macdonald, to choose the site of the new capital was the Honourable Edgar Dewdney. He was Lieutenant-Governor of the North West Territories and Indian commissioner as well. A handsome giant, with his fringed buckskin jacket and his flaring mutton chop whiskers, he made an imposing figure as he stalked about accompanied by his huge Newfoundland dogs.

The speculators knew that when the site was chosen it would become the most profitable piece of real estate in the country. Throughout the winter of 1881–82 they had been sending bands of men to occupy every prominent location. That is one reason why the CPR changed its survey in Saskatchewan and moved the line about six miles (9.6 km) to the south. The company wanted to frustrate the profit takers.

One likely townsite had been at the crossing of the Wascana or Pile o' Bones Creek. Wascana is a corruption of the Cree word "Oskana," meaning "bones." The bleached skeletons of thousands of buffalo lay in heaps along the banks of the river—hence the name—marking the site of an old buffalo corral into which the Indians had driven the bison to be slaughtered.

Because water was so scarce, the riverbank seemed a probable site, not only to the first surveyors, but also to the squatters who followed and sometimes got ahead of them. Not far from the pile of buffalo bones was a well-wooded area, where the original survey line crossed the creek. But when the railway was moved a half-dozen miles to the south, the land sharks were left out in the cold.

That change in the route took place on May 13, 1882. At the time there were only three settlers on the dry and treeless plain at the point where the new line crossed the creek. One of these was a surveyor himself, Thomas Gore. The new site, Gore said, was "by far the best I've seen in the North West."

Most of the speculators and settlers disagreed. They felt that the only possible site for a capital city of the plains lay a few miles to the northeast in the broad, wooded valley of the Qu'Appelle River, one of the loveliest spots on the prairies.

Everything that was needed for a townsite was there—an established community, plenty of sweet water, sheltering hills, good drainage, and timber for fuel, lumber, and shade.

The railway builders, however, planned to skirt Qu'Appelle. They claimed the banks of the valley were too steep. Probably more important was the company's policy of bypassing settled communities in the interests of greater land profits. There were just too many squatters looking for easy money in the Qu'Appelle area.

Another factor was Lieutenant-Governor Dewdney's own interest in the land surrounding Pile o' Bones crossing. He and several friends had formed two syndicates in great secrecy to purchase big chunks of Hudson's Bay Company land along the future route of the railway. One of these syndicates owned 480 acres (194 hectares) on the very spot that Dewdney now selected as a site of the future capital.

The property, of course, was not bought in Dewdney's name, but in the name of a trustee. All the other members of the syndicate kept their names secret; they stood to profit greatly if their land was chosen for the capital.

Dewdney himself was a surveyor. He had helped to lay out the town of

New Westminster, and also the trails and roads between the communities that led to the Cariboo gold fields in the B.C. Interior. He was also a close supporter of the prime minister and was now prepared to reap the rewards of that support. And so there he was, suffering from rheumatism, hobbling about on a stick that May, as he examined the banks of Pile o' Bones Creek.

A few days later a man named William White arrived—he had learned that the line had been moved and so he and five others made a dash for the new townsite. They brought a complete farming outfit, a yoke of oxen, tents, wagons, bobsleighs, and provisions. They took the train as far as Brandon and in mid-April pushed off into the snows, which were then two feet (0.6 m) deep on the trails.

The ruts on the trail were so deep and the ponds so treacherous the party rarely covered more than a dozen miles (19 km) a day. In fact, on one day it took them seven hours to move two miles (3.2 km). When they reached Pile o' Bones Creek they almost drowned when the ferry sank in midstream from overloading. On May 17 they were caught by a shrieking blizzard that held them for three nights; but on May 20 they reached their goal.

White immediately grabbed a 160-acre (65-hectare) homestead near the banks of the river where the survey line crossed it. This was to be the exact site of the business section of the new capital. To White it looked so desolate he couldn't believe anyone would be foolish enough to locate a capital city on that naked plain. He gave up his homestead and took another two miles (3.2 km) away, thereby losing one of the most valuable parcels of real estate on the prairies.

By this time rumours were flying in the Qu'Appelle valley about the choice of a new capital. More tents were rising. Speculators were keeping a careful watch on Dewdney. In the midst of the Dominion Day festivities Dewdney took advantage of the celebration to slip quietly away. Late in the afternoon of June 30 he posted a notice near Thomas Gore's tent, reserving for the government all the land in the vicinity. His own syndicate property adjoined the government reserve directly to the north.

And so the city of Regina, as yet unnamed, was quietly established. When the news reached Fort Qu'Appelle, there was frustration, disappointment, and frenzy. Most of the settlers hitched up their teams and moved everything to the banks of Pile o' Bones Creek. Squatters, advancing like an army, poured towards the embryo city. A few were bona fide homesteaders. Most were Winnipeg speculators, or people who had been paid by these speculators to squat on the land and hold it.

By mid-August the word was out: the capital would be on Pile o' Bones Creek. It was not announced officially until the following March. The Governor-General, Lord Lorne, was consulted about the name. He left the matter to his wife, Princess Louise, and she chose Regina in honour of her mother, Queen Victoria.

Nobody liked that name. Princess Louise was not very popular. Her boredom with Ottawa was widely known. The Winnipeg *Sun* ran a poll of leading citizens on the subject of the name. "That's a fool of a name," cried Joseph Wolf, a well-known auctioneer who wanted an Indian name. Another citizen, Fred Scoble, referred to the name as "a double-barrelled forty-horse-power fool of a name." A third insisted on calling the city "Re-join-her."

The choice of the site caused even more controversy than the name. When the Canadian Press Association visited the townsite in August, the eastern reporters were dismayed to find nothing more than a cluster of tattered tents huddled together on a bald and arid plain. One paper called it a "huge swindle." Another said it should have been named "Golgotha" because of its barren setting.

As the Toronto *World* declared, "No one has a good word for Regina." To Peter McAra, who later became its mayor, Regina was "just about as unlovely a site as one could well imagine." Even George Stephen, the president of the CPR, was dubious. He would have preferred Moose Jaw.

But Dewdney believed he had chosen the best possible location. He had told Macdonald (quite accurately, as it turned out) that the new capital was in the very heart of the best wheat district in the country. That statement was greeted with jeers because it was well known that he and his partners stood to make a million and a half dollars from their property if they could sell it.

Dewdney's Regina interests inevitably led to a clash with the CPR. The railway was already hard-pressed for funds. Its main asset was the land it owned on the sites of new towns. It didn't intend to share these real estate profits with outsiders.

Its interests were identical with those of the government, which was also in the land business in Regina. Under the terms of the CPR contract, the railway owned odd-numbered sections along the railway right of way, except for those originally granted to the Hudson's Bay Company. In Regina and in several other important prairie towns, the government and the CPR pooled their land interests, placed them under joint management, and shared the profits.

That summer, the railway, in order to raise funds, agreed to sell an immense slice of its land—five million acres (2,023,500 hectares)—to a British-Canadian syndicate, the Canada North-West Land Company. The company would manage land sales in forty-seven major communities, including Moose Jaw, Calgary, Regina, Swift Current, and Medicine Hat. The railway would get half the net profits. And so in Regina a quarter of the land profits went to the railway, a quarter to the land company, and one half to the government.

Now there was a struggle, with Dewdney on one side and the land company and the railway on the other, as to where the public buildings of Regina were to be situated. The railway, of course, wanted the centre of the new capital on its own lands and those owned by the government. Edgar Dewdney wanted them on his property.

The CPR had the advantage. It could locate the railway station anywhere it wanted, and wherever the railway station was, the business section would follow. And so it built its station two miles (3.2 km) east of Dewdney's river property in a small and muddy depression far from any natural source of water.

As a result Regina began at first to grow up on two locations. The magnet of the station was too much for the settlers, whose tents started to rise in clusters on the swampy triangle known as The Gore in front of the makeshift terminal.

Both sides attempted to sell land. Dewdney's syndicate tried to show that its land was the more popular and pointed out that the railway land lacked water. The railway countered by promising a large reservoir that would supply the city.

Of course, the railway won. It sold a half-million dollars' worth of real estate that winter. The Dewdney syndicate sold very little.

There was a second struggle: where to put the government buildings? Dewdney, naturally, wanted them near the river next door to his own land. The railway and the government wanted them near the station. In the end the police barracks and the lieutenant-governor's residence were on the river, but the customs office, the land office, and eventually the post office were placed near the station, two miles away. The offices of the Indian commissioner and North West Council were placed halfway between the station and the river. Later, when the registry office went up, it was on a block of its own.

And so the queer community straggled for two and a half miles (4 km) across the prairies, the various clusters of official buildings standing like islands in the prairie sea. Regina was a city without a centre.

CHAPTER SIX

The Promised Land

BY THE SPRING OF 1883 CANADA WAS A COUNTRY WITH HALF A TRANSCONTI-
NENTAL RAILROAD. TRACK LAY IN PIECES LIKE A CHILD'S TRAIN SET—LONG
STRETCHES OF FINISHED ROAD SEPARATED BY LARGE GAPS. BUT A CONTINUOUS
LINE OF STEEL NOW RAN 937 MILES (1,500 KM) FROM FORT WILLIAM AT THE
HEAD OF LAKE SUPERIOR TO THE TENT COMMUNITY OF SWIFT CURRENT.

As the track began to move west again on the prairie section, thousands
of people were invading the land of the Blackfoot. Little steel shoots were
sprouting south, west, and east of the main trunk line in Manitoba. And
wherever the steel went, the settlers followed with their tents and their tools,
their cattle and their kittens, their furniture and their fences.

They poured in from the famine-ridden bog country of Ireland, the
bleak crofts of the Scottish hills, and the smoky hives of industrial England.
The land moved past them like a series of painted scenes on flash cards—a
confused impression of station platforms and very little more, because the
windows in the wooden cars were too high and too small to give much of a
view of the new world.

They sat crowded together on hard seats that ran lengthwise, and they
cooked their own food at a wood stove placed in the centre of the car. They
were patient people, full of hope, blessed by good cheer. In the spring and
summer of 1883, some 133,000 arrived in Canada. Of that number, two-
thirds sped directly to the Northwest.

No one had expected such an onslaught. The demand for passage across
the Atlantic was unprecedented. The CPR didn't have enough trains to handle the invading army. It was forced to use its dwindling reserve of cash to
buy additional colonist cars second-hand.

In Toronto, in May alone, ten thousand meals were served in the overflowing immigrant sheds—as many as had been prepared in the entire season of 1882. The young Canadian postal service was flooded with twelve thousand letters destined for the Northwest. The number had quadrupled in just two years.

The settlers from the old world—some had come from places as remote as Iceland—had been joined by farmers from the back roads of Ontario. Off to the west the trains puffed, every car crammed with people clinging to the steps and all singing the song that became the pioneer theme, "One More River to Cross." By April the CPR was able to take them as far as the tent community of Moose Jaw, four hundred miles (640 km) west of Winnipeg, and sometimes 150 miles (240 km) further on to Swift Current.

As many as twenty-five hundred settlers left Winnipeg every week. It was impossible to tell blue blood from peasant. The man in the next homestead or the worker serving in the tent restaurant might be of noble birth.

The son of the English poet laureate Alfred, Lord Tennyson, was breaking sod on a homestead that spring. Nicholas Flood Davin, a well-known journalist, on his first day in Regina was impressed by the manner of a waiter in the tent where he took breakfast. The waiter turned out to be the nephew of a duke. He was helping to manage a tent-hotel for the nephew of an earl.

Many settlers arrived without funds. They brought everything to the prairies from pet kittens to canaries. One arrived with a crate full of cats, which were snapped up at three dollars apiece by immigrants lonely for company of any kind. Another early pioneer, Esther Goldsmith, always remembered the wild scene at the Brandon station, where a birdcage was sucked from a woman's hand in the scramble for the train. A typical menagerie was brought to Moosomin in 1883 by the Hislop family. It included two horses, four cows, three sheep, a little white sow, a dog, a cat, eleven hens, and a rooster.

It was gruelling work for settlers to break up the prairie sod. The land was dotted with small rose bushes whose interwoven roots added to the toughness of the turf. A man with a good team of oxen was lucky if he could till three-quarters of an acre (a third of a hectare) in a day. It was a harsher life than most had bargained for.

Most settlers counted themselves lucky that first year if they could build a hovel out of the hard-packed sod. One typical sod house built near Regina in the fall of 1884 consisted of a big cellar dug out of the side of a hill, over which were laid poles in the shape of a gabled roof, the ends resting on the ground. On top of these was placed hay to the depth of a foot and over the hay huge squares of sod chinked with dried earth. At the ends of the gables were small poles plastered together with a mortar of yellow clay and straw. Tiny windows were cut in one end and a door in the other. The floor was a mixture of clay and straw and water, about six inches (15 cm) thick, tamped tightly to the ground. The inside walls and ceiling were plastered with mud and then whitewashed. In such cave-like dwellings entire families existed winter after winter. The central piece of furniture and sole source of heat was the cookstove.

They expected to find a town in the old country sense. Instead they discovered a ragged cluster of tents rising from the muddy prairie. When they were sent to a hotel they found it was a tent too, with nothing between their bedroom and the next but a partition of stretched blankets.

Few settlers saw the inside of a general store more than once or twice a year. For most, a shopping trip meant an exhausting journey of fifty or a hundred miles (80 to 160 km) by oxcart. Pork was a staple meat, when meat was available at all. Molasses did duty for sugar. Coffee was often synthetic, made from roasted barley, rye, or wheat—or even toast crumbs.

Many a settler lived almost entirely on potatoes, bread, treacle, porridge, and rabbit stew. Often families went hungry. John Wilson of Saltcoats always remembered the winter of 1883, when, as a boy of seven, he and other members of his family were reduced to a single slice of bread each three times a day. The snow was so deep they couldn't reach their nearest neighbours six miles (9.6 km) away.

Nine-year-old May Clark arrived in Regina from England with her family on a soaking wet day in May, 1883. They expected to find a town in the old country sense. Instead they discovered a ragged cluster of tents rising from the muddy prairie. When they were sent to a hotel they found it was a tent too, with nothing between their bedroom and the next but a partition of stretched blankets.

Regina that spring was mainly a city of women and children. Most of the men were off on the prairie looking for a homestead. After several days May's father located a suitable quarter section about thirteen miles (21 km) to the northeast. The six members of the family packed everything, including pigs and chickens and bowie knife to ward off "wild Indians," and then took a covered wagon—or prairie schooner, as it was called—across the hummocky plain behind two oxen, with a milk cow bringing up the rear.

They seemed totally unfitted for pioneer life. May's mother was sickly and frail. Her father, thin-faced and pale, had never driven a team before. They were used to the gentle beauty of the English Midlands and were appalled by the sweeping loneliness of the prairie.

When the Clark family first reached their homestead it seemed as remote as a desert island. There was nothing to be seen to the distant horizon. There was a vague smudge off to the north which the children were told was a copse of trees. That was all.

The Clarks spent their first summer tilling a few acres of soil and trying to build a log house. Septimus Clark over strained himself and was confined to his bed. When he recovered he found he did not know how to build the roof, doors, or windows. There was never enough to eat. The children were always hungry. They tried to fill their stomachs with wild leaves and berries. Polly, the cow, refused to give milk. One night both parents became lost on the open prairie, and the children spent a terrifying twelve hours alone wondering if they would ever see them again.

In spite of it all, the family survived and thrived in both health and spirits. Hard work acted as a tonic. Life may have been harsh, but it was clearly invigorating. When May Clark, who became Mrs. Hartford Davis, published her memoirs at the age of eighty-one, four of the five Clark children were still alive to share them.

Government land such as the Clarks' was free up to a limit of a quarter section—160 acres (65 hectares). Anybody who worked it for three years could have it. And you could also take on the next quarter section. If you bought CPR land along the railway, you paid five dollars an acre but got back $3.75 if you were able to crop three-quarters of it within four years.

Meanwhile, as the rails pushed steadily towards the mountains, new communities began to take shape. "These towns along the line west of

Brandon are all the same. See one, see all," the Fort MacLeod *Gazette* reported. They all had the same houses, mostly board frames with a canvas roof.
Moose Jaw, with its "bare, freckled and sunburnt buildings" and Medicine
Hat, another canvas town, were in this category. And yet Moose Jaw already
had three newspapers and six hotels, though most of these were mere tents.

And still the trains roared by to End of Track. By July of 1883 the organization had been perfected to the point where ninety-seven miles (156 km)
of track were laid instead of the monthly average of fifty-eight (93 km).

As Langdon and Shepard approached the end of their contract, the
track-laying guides were seized by a kind of frenzy. On July 28, about two
weeks out of Calgary, they set another record. It's one that has never been
surpassed for manual labour on a railroad: 6.38 miles (10.2 km) of finished
railway—earthworks, grading, track-laying and ballasting—were completed in a single day.

It was, of course, a stunt. Special men were brought in, including the
tireless Ryan brothers, world champion spikers, who could drive a spike
home with two blows, and Big Jack, a Herculean Swede who was said to be
able to hoist a thirty-foot (9-m) rail weighing 560 pounds (254 kg) and
heave it onto a flatcar without assistance.

The city of Calgary was not yet born, but some of its future citizens were
at work along the line of track oblivious to the fact they would help to build
the foothills community. Turner Bone, a railway engineer, recalled in his
memoirs how many of the men he bumped into later became prominent
Calgarians. When Bone arrived in Moose Jaw late one night, the CPR's
watchman guided him with the aid of a sputtering lantern to a large marquee pretentiously named Royal Hotel. This man was Thomas Burns—he
later became a city assessor and city treasurer of Calgary. In a Medicine Hat
office he encountered a messenger boy just twelve years old who answered
to the name of George. He became the mayor of Calgary, George Webster.

In the company boarding house Bone ran into a former supply officer
who had opened a law office in Medicine Hat. This was James Lougheed,
soon to become the most noted lawyer in the West, Conservative leader in
the Senate, cabinet minister in the Canadian government, and the grandfa-
ther of a future premier of Alberta, Peter Lougheed.

As the railway towns began to prosper, jealousies sprang up between nearby communities. A three-cornered battle took place between Winnipeg, Moose Jaw, and Regina. The argument, supposedly over the choice of Regina as the capital, was really over real estate.

The battle was fought out in the newspapers. But Regina had none and so a group of citizens got together, raised $5,000, and talked Nicholas Flood Davin, one of the most distinguished journalists in Canada, into starting the Regina *Leader*.

Davin named it that because he intended to make it the leading newspaper in the Northwest, and in this he was successful. Once established, he struck back at Regina's critics. He referred to Moose Jaw as "Loose Jaw" and engaged in a running battle with that town's newspaper. He attacked the real estate sharks trying to get the capital moved and, when he ran out of prose, he turned to poetry.

Five thousand dollars was a lot of money for Regina to raise in the 1880s—it was enough to keep a man and his family in luxury for four years. But reading Nicholas Flood Davin's sweet invective, the citizens who paid the editor's bonus must have reckoned that they had been given their money's worth.

CHAPTER SEVEN

The Displaced People

THE WHOLE COUNTRY MARVELLED THAT SPRING AND SUMMER OF 1883 OVER
THE FEAT OF BUILDING THE RAILWAY ACROSS THE PRAIRIES — EVERYBODY
EXCEPT THE PEOPLE IT WAS DISPLACING.

To the Indians the railway symbolized the end of a golden age. The
Natives, liberated by the white man's horses and the white man's weapons,
had galloped freely across the open prairie for more than a hundred years.
The game seemed unlimited, and the zest of the hunt gave life a tang and a
purpose. This charmed existence came to an end with the suddenness of a
thunderclap, just as the railway, like a glittering spear, was thrust through
the ancient hunting grounds of the Blackfoot and Cree.

Within six years the image of the Plains Indian underwent a total transformation. From proud and fearless nomads, rich in culture and tradition,
they became pathetic, half-starved creatures, confined to the semi-prisons
of their new reserves, and totally dependent on government relief for their
existence. Actually, the buffalo on which the Indian depended were gone
before the railway came, victims of the white man's overkill. But they
could not have survived on a land bisected by steel and crisscrossed by
barbed wire.

Without the buffalo, which had supplied them with food, shelter, clothing, tools, and ornaments, the Indians were helpless. By 1880, after the three
most terrible years they had ever known, they were forced to eat their dogs
and their horses, to scrabble for gophers and mice, and even to consume the
carcasses of animals they found rotting on the prairie.

On top of this they were faced with a totally foreign culture. And the
railway made that impact immediate. It did not arrive gradually as it had in
eastern Canada. In the Northwest it happened in the space of a few years.

The government's policy was a two-stage one. The starving Indians would be fed at public expense—temporarily. Over a longer period, the Indian Department would try to bring about a change that usually took centuries. It would try to turn a race of hunters into a community of peasants. The Indians, in short, would become farmers—or that was the idea. The Indian reserves would be on land north of the railway, far from the hunting grounds, and so the CPR became the visible symbol of the Indian's tragedy.

The famine had been so great that thousands of Indians reluctantly trekked to the new reserves. Others, led by such Cree chieftains as Big Bear and Piapot, continued to oppose the authorities, hoping to hunt the non-existent buffalo. By the winter of 1882–83, with the railway snaking across the prairies, five thousand disillusioned Indians were starving in the neighbourhood of Fort Walsh southeast of Calgary. In the end everybody moved north to the reserves. To the south lay the railway—a steel fence barring them from their past.

The native peoples, Cree and Blackfoot, had no concept of the white man's idea of "real estate." In their society, land was not something that was *owned*, any more than the air or the waters were owned. The whole principle of private property was foreign to them. The idea of fencing in the prairie, parcelling it out to strangers, buying it and selling it for profit, was difficult to grasp. For white Canadians, the coming of the railway was the climax of a grand plan for a nation extending from sea to sea. For the native peoples it was a cultural disaster, the tragic consequences of which have lasted until our time.

Some of the chiefs accepted the coming of steel fatalistically. Chief Poundmaker, for instance, urged his followers to prepare for it. He had negotiated a treaty with the Canadian government in 1879 and settled on the reserve on the Battle River. But when he realized the buffalo were gone he told his people to work hard, plant grain, and take care of their cattle.

On the other hand, Chief Piapot ran afoul of survey crews in 1882 and pulled up forty miles (64 km) of surveyors' stakes west of Moose Jaw. These were his hunting grounds, and he ordered his people to camp directly upon the right of way. He blamed the railway for all his troubles.

Many of the native peoples greeted the stories of the snorting locomotives with disbelief. They watched the construction in silence. The women pulled their shawls over their heads in terror of the whistle and refused to cross streams on the new trestles, preferring to wade up to their armpits. Some of the younger men, their faces painted brilliant scarlet, would try to race the train on their swift ponies. Few would actually touch the cars.

A slender, intelligent man with a classic Roman nose, he carried himself with great dignity and was renowned for many feats of bravery. He had fought in nineteen battles, been wounded six times, and had once rescued a child from the jaws of a grizzly bear, killing the animal with a spear while the whole camp watched.

Piapot believed the smoke of the locomotives was evil medicine that would ruin his people. His fears were not groundless, but his personal appeal to the Lieutenant-Governor was fruitless.

Not far from Calgary the railway builders encountered the most remarkable Indian leader of all—Crowfoot, chief of the Blackfoot nation. A slender, intelligent man with a classic Roman nose, he carried himself with great dignity and was renowned for many feats of bravery. He had fought in nineteen battles, been wounded six times, and had once rescued a childfrom the jaws of a grizzly bear, killing the animal with a spear while the whole camp watched.

He had many good qualities—eloquence, political skill, charity, and, above all, foresight. Long before his people, he foresaw the end of the buffalo, and so signed a treaty in 1877. When the tents of the construction workers went up on the borders of his reserve, there was anger and bitterness among the tribe. The white man was invading the land of the Blackfoot. The chief sent messengers to warn a foreman that no further construction work would be allowed. Seven hundred armed braves stood ready to attack.

At this point, Father Albert Lacombe, the Oblate missionary to the Blackfoot band, stepped into the picture. He, too, had been concerned about the creeping advance of civilization. When he learned of the trouble on the reserve, he rode immediately to the construction camp—a homely priest in a tattered cassock, bumping over the prairie, his silver curls streaming out from beneath his black hat.

At End of Track Lacombe met with a rude rejection. He was told the Indians could go to the devil. And so he made his appeal to a higher authority. Lacombe knew Van Horne, having met him during his term as chaplain to the railway workers in the Thunder Bay branch. Now he sent him a telegram. Back came the order straight to End of Track—cease all work until the Indians are satisfied. Lacombe was asked to appease the Blackfoot any way he could.

The priest had known Crowfoot for years. Once he had led a party of starving Crees for twenty-two days through a blizzard to apparently miraculous safety. Another time, when an entire Blackfoot camp came down with scarlet fever, he had worked tirelessly for twenty days among the sick before he himself contracted the disease. When he nursed the Indians during a smallpox epidemic in 1870, hundreds were so moved by his selflessness that they became Christians.

Now the priest set out to placate his old friend. He came into the camp bearing gifts: two hundred pounds (91 kg) of sugar and a similar amount of tobacco, tea, and flour. Then Crowfoot called a grand council where the priest, standing before the squatting braves, spoke.

"Now my mouth is open; you people listen to my words. If one of you can say that for the fifteen years I have lived among you, I have given you bad advice, let him rise and speak …"

No one budged. It was a dangerous, electric situation. Lacombe kept on:

"Well, my friends, I have some advice to give you today. Let the white people pass through your lands and let them build their roads. They are not here to rob you of your lands. These white men obey their chiefs, and it is with the chiefs that the matter must be settled. I have already told these chiefs that you were not pleased with the way in which the work is being pushed through your lands. The Governor himself will come to meet you. He will listen to your griefs; he will propose a remedy. And if the compromise does not suit you, that will be the time to order the builders out of your reserve."

Crowfoot agreed. He'd already consulted with Lieutenant-Colonel A. G. Irvine, the Commissioner of the North West Mounted Police, and asked him if he thought he, Crowfoot, could stop the railway. Irvine replied by asking Crowfoot if all the men in the world could stop the Bow River running.

The chief resigned himself to the inevitable. He didn't believe in foolhardy gestures. Not long after, Dewdney arrived and agreed to give the Indians extra land in return for the railway's right of way.

CHAPTER EIGHT

The Birth of Calgary

WILLIAM MURDOCH, A HARNESS-MAKER, PUT UP THE FIRST COMMERCIAL SIGN ON THE SITE OF CALGARY IN MAY 1883. TO HIM, A NEWCOMER FROM THE EAST, THE EMBRYO TOWN SEEMED LIKE A DISTANT PLANET. "I WAS DREAMING ABOUT HOME ALMOST ALL NIGHT," MURDOCH WROTE IN HIS DIARY ON A BITTER, WINDY JUNE DAY. "HOW I LONG TO SEE MY WIFE, MOTHER, AND LITTLE ONES. MY HEART CRAVES FOR THEM ALL TODAY MORE THAN USUAL."

Murdoch would become the first mayor of this new city. But he couldn't get so much as a sliver of dressed lumber because there were no sawmills in the foothills. All that was available were rough planks—whipsawed vertically by hand. Fresh fruit was so scarce that when half a box of apples arrived they were sold at fifty cents each.

The settlement watched the railway approach with a mixture of worry and excitement. Where would the station be located? Under the terms of its contract, the CPR had title to the odd-numbered sections along the right of way. Fort Calgary and surrounding log structures, together with all the squatters' shacks, were situated on an even-numbered section—number 14—on the west bank of the Elbow River near its junction with the Bow.

The neighbouring section, 15, on the opposite bank of the Elbow, had been reserved by Order-In-Council for the police horses to graze. So everyone figured the town would have to be put on the east bank, where the fort was located.

On June 1, the giant scrapers lumbered through, tearing up the prairie soil. An army of graders followed close behind. The tension began to mount. The bridgers finished spanning the Bow on August 10. Two days later the first construction train puffed in. On August 15, a train carrying a temporary station arrived and the community held its breath.

Where would it stop? To everyone's surprise and dismay, it shunted directly through the settlement, crossed the new bridge, and stopped at a siding on Section 15 on the far side of the river.

The people living on the banks of the Elbow had no idea what to do. No survey had been taken. The ownership of Section 15 was in dispute. The town was growing rapidly on the east bank, but because everyone wanted to wait for the decision about the townsite, no one wanted to go to the expense of building anything permanent. And so, for all of 1883, Calgary was a tent city.

On August 20 two men arrived from the East, put up a tent and started to publish a newspaper, the *Herald*. Its first edition, dated August 31, said it would always have the courage of its convictions and wouldn't be afraid to speak its mind freely when wrongs had to be righted.

That same edition announced that, four days before, the leading directors of the CPR had come to Calgary aboard Van Horne's private car. They had made the trip from Winnipeg over the new track travelling at an average rate of more than thirty-five miles (56 km) an hour. At some points the locomotives, fed from recently discovered coal deposits near Medicine Hat, had pulled the cars at a clip of sixty miles (96 km) an hour.

The directors invited Father Lacombe, who had saved them from so much grief, to be their guest at luncheon. Then they voted to make Lacombe president of the CPR for one hour. Taking the chair, the priest immediately voted himself two passes on the railroad for life and, in addition, free transportation of all freight and baggage necessary to the Oblate missions, together with free use for himself for life of the CPR's telegraph system. The railway was only too happy to give him that because of what he had done.

All the promises made that day were honoured by the CPR. Lacombe used to lend out his passes to anyone who asked for them. And this too was tolerated. On one occasion, the two passes, which became familiar along the line, were presented by two nuns who had just arrived in the West. "May I ask," the conductor politely inquired, "which one is Father Lacombe?" But he let the blushing sisters go on their way.

After honouring the priest, the visitors left Calgary without leaving the puzzled settlers any the wiser about their future. All they knew was they had no control. This state of indecision continued throughout the fall with half the community swearing it would not budge an inch to accommodate the railway.

The *Herald* continued to demand in vain that the matter be settled one way or the other. "The people in Calgary have by this time the elements of suspense and patience reduced to a science," it wrote that November.

In December the paper reported that "we have much pleasure in announcing that our friends east of the Elbow have definitely decided upon the permanent location of the city in that quarter. Already the surveyors are hard at work on the subdivision of the Denny Estate, and our next issue will contain the date of the sale of this beautiful spot so well adapted for the future capital of Alberta."

But the CPR itself and nobody else—editor, banker, merchant, or real estate man—would make the decision as to where Calgary was to be. In January, when the Order-In-Council regarding the police pasturage was finally cancelled, the CPR spoke. The city would not be on the east, after all, it would be on the west side of the Elbow right where the station had been placed. To underline the point, the government, which stood to profit equally with the railway, moved the post office across the river to the west.

In vain, the Denny subdivision on the east side advertised that it was "the centre of Calgary city." As soon as the post office crossed the river, James Bannerman followed with his flour and feed store. All the pledges about staying put and refusing to follow the railway were forgotten. A wild scramble ensued as butcher shop, jeweller, churches, billiard parlour, and hotels packed up and moved to the favoured site.

The *Herald* reported that buildings were suddenly springing up "as though some magical influence was being exerted," and that what had been barren prairie just three weeks before "is now rapidly growing into the shape of a respectable town."

Once again the railway, in truth "a magical influence," had set the pattern for the new Northwest. From Brandon to Calgary, the shape of the settled prairies was totally dictated by the CPR.

INDEX

The first Canadian Pacific Railway through train from the
Atlantic to the Pacific, Port Arthur, Ontario, June 30, 1886.
(COURTESY LIBRARY AND ARCHIVES CANADA, C-014464)

STEEL ACROSS THE SHIELD

CONTENTS

One Thousand Miles of Rock and Muskeg

THE STORY OF THE BUILDING OF A RAILWAY FROM ONTARIO TO THE PACIFIC OCEAN IN THE 1870S AND 1880S IS ALSO THE STORY OF THE CREATION OF A NEW CANADA. AT THE TIME OF CONFEDERATION, IN 1867, THERE WAS NO "WEST" AS WE NOW KNOW IT. FROM A POPULATION POINT OF VIEW, THE COUNTRY STOPPED AT OTTAWA AND DID NOT BEGIN AGAIN UNTIL THE WEST COAST OF BRITISH COLUMBIA.

Most people didn't believe that this vast, empty gap between the tiny communities of Victoria and New Westminster and the growing cities of the East could be crossed by a line of steel. There were too many barriers.

First, a thousand-mile (1,600-km) desert of rock and muskeg stood in the way—the roots of the ancient mountains we call the Canadian Shield. Next, a thousand miles of waving buffalo grass had to be crossed—empty country, the domain of only a handful of trappers and nomadic bands of Indians. Finally, three mountain walls, each nearly two miles (3.2 km) high, barred the way. Only after these were conquered could the wrinkled British Columbia coast be reached.

But if British Columbia was to be part of the new Dominion, and if the prairie country was to be filled with farmers, then somebody—government or private contractor—would have to build a railway to the Pacific. It would be a steel band joining up with the other railways in the East to bind the country together.

In the days before the automobile and airplane, the railway was king. But the project to build a Pacific line was fraught with danger. Hundreds of men would die blasting the railway through the mountains, bridging the muskegs and canyons, and hammering their way across the ancient rock of the Shield.

The Shield! It barred the way to the fertile plains—700 miles (1,130 km) of the hardest and most ancient rock in the world, followed by 300 miles (480 km) of swamps so treacherous they could swallow locomotives at a single gulp.

This vast ocean of rocks, older than time, is the anchor that holds North America together. But it also splits Canada in two. No covered wagon could cross it; no immigrant could farm it, which explains why so many would-be Canadians moved into the United States to follow easier routes to the prairies.

The Shield! It barred the way to the fertile plains — 700 miles (1,130 km) of the hardest and most ancient rock in the world, followed by 300 miles (480 km) of swamps so treacherous they could swallow locomotives at a single gulp.

Today when we drive the Trans-Canada Highway out of Toronto and North Bay, we are both awed and surprised by the raw beauty of this rocky desert, which our landscape painters have already made famous. In our comfortable automobiles we travel through a dark and haunting land of stunted pines and spruce, little gunmetal lakes, and Persian carpets of moss and lichen. Here we can sense the problems the early railway builders faced. And we can also see why another eighty years went by before this second link could be forged from sea to sea—today's Trans-Canada Highway.

Back in 1871, Prime Minister John A. Macdonald had promised British Columbia a railway. But Macdonald was driven from office two years later, and a more cautious Liberal prime minister, a solemn stonemason, Alexander Mackenzie, scrapped Macdonald's ambitious scheme. He wanted to do the job on the cheap, using the Great Lakes as a water highway to substitute for the line of steel. Beyond the lakes he planned to hire contractors to build a railway in sections from Lake Superior to the Red River. After that, he felt, a simple wagon road could do the job across the plains.

And so the story of the building of the railway across the Canadian Shield, from the end of steel at North Bay to Selkirk (near the future site of Winnipeg), is a stop-and-go tale. The line was built in bits and pieces, first by the Mackenzie government and later, when Macdonald returned to power, by a private company, the Canadian Pacific Railway (CPR).

This is the story of two separate railways built across the Shield. One led west out of North Bay heading for Lake Superior. The other, to which the first segment would eventually be linked, started at Fort William and moved west in fits and starts towards Selkirk.

Those two lines, blasted from the ancient rock and floated over vast swamps, were designed to link up with each other and with the line being driven across the plains and over the mountains to the Pacific.

This is also the story of Canada's beginnings, from a small, constricted country centred on the St. Lawrence valley to a transcontinental nation stretching between two oceans. Without the railway, Canada, as we know it, would not exist.

CHAPTER ONE

Bogs Without Bottom

According to Harry Armstrong, a resident engineer for the railroad in the mid-1870s, the "construction of Canada's greatest highway [began] at a dead end." He was right. One chunk of the railway began at Red River and ran east towards the muskegs on the Ontario/Manitoba border. Another was built westward from Fort William literally to nowhere. These two pieces were useless because they didn't connect.

A third chunk of railway from Lake Nipissing to Thunder Bay had not even been considered and would not be started until the government got out of the railway business in 1881, turning construction over to a private company, the Canadian Pacific Railway (CPR).

Our story, therefore, is about the building of three railways that would eventually become one. Each line stretched across isolated, unpopulated country—so empty of people that Harry Armstrong, who lived along the half-completed line out of Fort William, had to trudge fifteen miles (24 km) to work and back again each day. His nearest neighbour lived nine miles (14.5 km) away. Without any doctoring, he had to act as a midwife at the birth of his first child. Like everybody else, he fought off the mosquitoes and blackflies rising from the stinking, half-frozen swamps in clouds so thick they blotted out the sun.

This was the empty heart of Canada. The country was scarcely explored. There was no rail transportation to supply the railway builders. The contractors were forced to rely on steamers, flat boats, canoes, and barges to haul in supplies and construction materials.

At the end of the 1870s, when other contractors began to fill in the 181-mile (290-km) gap between the two useless lines of steel, every pound of goods had to come in over the lakes by canoe and portage because the end of steel was a good hundred miles (160 km) from Lake Superior. Steam shovels, horses, even locomotives and flatcars were hauled by sleigh in wintertime over frozen lakes, ice-sheathed granites, and snow-shrouded muskeg.

It was these muskegs—frozen masses of swamp and silt—that drove some railway contractors into bankruptcy. First, there were the notorious sinkholes—little lakes over which a thick crust of vegetable matter had formed and into which the line might tumble at any time. One, just north of Fort William, swallowed an entire train with a thousand feet (300 m) of track.

Sometimes new sinkholes would appear, even when the land seemed to be as solid as Gibraltar. When the railway builders tried to fill up the sinkholes with gravel, the frozen muskeg beneath would melt, and the entire foundation would heave and totter.

One giant swamp that thwarted the railway builders was the incredible Julius Muskeg, a vast bed of peat, six miles (9.6 km) across and of unknown depth. Here the naked trunks of dead trees protruded, their roots weaving a kind of blanket over a hidden jelly of mud and slime. Across these barriers, the railway builders built log mattresses, which were floated on top of the heaving bog. These contraptions of long interlaced timbers sometimes ran for a hundred feet (30 m).

Many of the lakes were equally treacherous. Their bottoms appeared solid, but actually consisted of more muskeg—muskeg so thick it swallowed up tons of earth and gravel, month after month.

One contractor who was defeated by the muskegs was Joseph Whitehead, mayor of Clinton, Ontario, and a Liberal member of parliament from 1867 to 1872. He was an enormous Yorkshire man with a great bald dome of a head, a vast beard, and a big, fleshy nose, who had been a railwayman since boyhood.

Whitehead had the subcontract to build a section of the railway near Rat Portage (present-day Kenora), but he saw his dreamed-of profits slowly pouring into Cross Lake, a notorious swamp. Alas, for him, it gobbled up 220,000 yards (201,000 m) of gravel at a cost of $80,000. And even then the line continued to sink into the morass.

It had seemed so easy to Whitehead! He thought he could simply carry his line of steel across a narrow expanse of water. Yet, ton after ton of sand and gravel vanished into that monstrous gulf. Every time he tried to build an embankment five or six feet (1.5 or 1.8 m) above the water, the lake would take a gulp and the entire mass would vanish beneath the waves. It bankrupted him.

After Whitehead's downfall, his section was taken over by a colourful Galway Irishman named Michael J. Haney, a lean, hard man with high cheekbones and a drooping moustache. Armstrong described him as "a rushing, devil-may-care chap who did things just as he chose without regard to authority." But the job almost did Haney in.

He risked his life many times. At one point he drained an entire lake and laid a mattress of timber across the mud bottom to carry the track. The rails were laid; the track looked firm; then, slowly, it began to sink.

His engineer refused to take a locomotive across this heaving mass. Haney announced he would do it himself. As he did, the log mattress sank deeper. The engine tilted wildly. Haney tried to back up but now the rails were at such an angle he could scarcely coax it up the incline, which was growing steeper by the minute. By sanding the rails for a better grip he was able to save himself, but only at the last minute.

Like the other contractors along the unfinished line, Haney faced the problem of alcoholism among his workers—"navvies," as they were called. There was a good reason for this. When they were not laying track across the soft porridge of the muskegs, they were blasting it through some of the hardest rock in the world—rock that rolled endlessly on, ridge after spiky ridge, like waves in a sullen ocean. That rock had to be blasted with nitroglycerine, the most unstable of explosives. Because every man who worked with explosives was in danger of his life, he drank to bolster his spirits.

Nobody seemed to care about safety regulations. Cans of nitroglycerine with fuses attached were strewn carelessly along the roadbed. They were carried about with such recklessness that the fluid itself splashed upon the rocks. Whole gangs were sometimes blown to bits in the explosions that followed.

If a container of nitroglycerine was shaken badly, it would explode. It couldn't be transported by wagons because the jarring along those trails would have caused disaster. The explosive had to be carried in ten-gallon (45-L) tins on men's backs.

This caused problems. Sometimes the packers would lay their tins down on a smooth rock and a few drops would be left behind from a leak. The engineers travelling up and down the line tried to avoid these telltale black specks, which could easily blow a man's leg off. Once, when a teamster took his horse to water at such a spot, the horse's iron shoe touched a pool of nitroglycerine. The resulting blast tore the shoe from his foot and drove it through his belly, killing him and stunning the teamster.

The number of men killed or maimed by such explosions was staggering. In one fifty-mile (80-km) stretch there were thirty graves, all the result of the careless handling of nitroglycerine. And yet the Irish navvies joked among themselves about the danger, often tripping gaily down a hill, each with a can of liquid explosive on his back, and making comments all the while:

"It's a warm day."

"That's so, but maybe ye'll be warmer before ye camp tonight."

"That's so. D'ye want any work taken to the Devil?"

"To hell, I guess."

"Take another train and keep a berth for me, man!"

"Is that yer coffin, ye're carrying, Pat?"

"Faith, ye're right; and the coroner's inquest to the bargain, Jim."

A woman who watched this scene wrote that, in spite of the jokes, "the wretched expression of these very men proved that they felt the bitterness of death to be in their chests."

There were terrible accidents. One young man, climbing a hill with a can of explosives, stumbled and fell. All they found of him was his foot in a tree a hundred yards (90 m) away. Another man's foot slipped as he handed a can of nitroglycerine to a driller. As a result, four men died and three more were maimed. One workman brushed past a rock where some explosive had been spilled. He lost his arm and his sight in an instant. At Prince Arthur's Landing at Lakehead, an entire nitroglycerine factory blew up in the night, hurling chunks of frozen earth for a quarter of a mile (0.4 km), and leaving a hole twenty feet (6 m) deep and fifty feet (15 m) across.

No wonder the navvies along the line turned to alcohol! As Haney himself recalled, "There was not an engineer, contractor, or traveller who were not hard drinkers. Practically every transaction was consummated with a glass."

The contractors tried—without success—to keep the camps dry, but the whisky peddlers had kegs of liquor concealed at points along the entire right of way. The profits were huge. A gallon (4.5 L) of alcohol, worth 50 cents in the eastern cities, could sell for 45 dollars on the line. Hidden out in the bush or on the islands that dotted the swampy lakes, the peddlers moved into the work camps in swift canoes of birchbark, then darted away at the approach of the law.

Haney made no attempt to stop this traffic—except when his men worked three round-the-clock shifts. At such times he would round up the whisky peddlers and get them to promise to stay away as long as the twenty-four-hour shift prevailed.

Generally this secret agreement worked. On one occasion, however, the presence of five hundred thirsty men was too much for the whisky peddlers. Haney came to work to find the whole camp roaring drunk. He moved quickly. There were four "whisky detectives" working on his section. Haney warned them that unless the peddlers were brought before him by noon, all four would be fired. That did it. The offenders were rounded up, fined a total of $3,600, and packed back to Winnipeg, with a warning that if they came back, they'd be jailed.

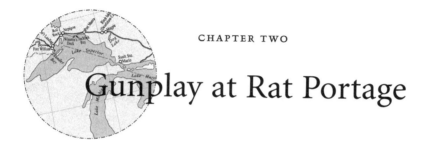

CHAPTER TWO

Gunplay at Rat Portage

By the time Michael Haney arrived on the scene at the end of the 1870s, the solemn, unknown land through which Harry Armstrong had trudged on his fifteen-mile (24-km) trek to the job site had come alive with thousands of navvies — Swedes, Norwegians, Finns and Icelanders, French Canadians and Prince Edward Islanders, Irish, Scots, English, Americans, and even Mennonites — all strung out over nearly five hundred miles (800 km) in clustered, hard-drinking communities.

The postmaster of Whitemouth, the railroad community halfway between Winnipeg and Rat Portage, described Christmas Eve in 1880: "The demon of strong drink made a bedlam of this place, fighting, stabbing, and breaking; some lay out freezing till life was almost extinct. The Post Office was besieged at the hours of crowded business by outrageous, bleeding, drunken, fighting men, mad with Forty-Rod, so that respectable people could not come in for their mail ... It is only a few days since in one of these frenzies a man had his jugular nearly severed by a man with a razor."

Because such communities only lasted a year or so, political organization was difficult. In July 1880, for instance, when End of Track moved beyond Gull River to Ignace, all the inhabitants had to move—stores, houses, boarding houses, a jewellery shop, a hotel, a telegraph office, a shoemaker, and a blacksmith shop.

The only permanent town along the half-built line, and by far the largest, was Rat Portage on Lake of the Woods. It called itself "the Future Saratoga of America"—a reference to that famous vacation spot in the eastern United States. It was nothing of the sort. We know it today as Kenora, and in its heyday it was the wildest community in Canada.

One newspaper correspondent summed it up in the summer of 1880 when he wrote: "For some time now the railway works in the vicinity of Rat Portage have been besieged by a lot of scoundrels whose only avocation seems to be gambling and trading in illicit whisky, and the state of degradation was, if anything, intensified by the appearance, in the wake of these blacklegs, of a number of the *demi-monde* with whom these numerous desperadoes held high carnival at all hours of the day or night."

One observer described the town as being "laid out in designs made by a colony of muskrats." Shanties and tents were built or pitched wherever the owners wanted and without any organization of streets or roadways. It had a floating population that sometimes reached as high as 3,000. The contractors of Section B on the railway ran the administration, built the jail, and organized the police. There was no real law.

In 1881, Manitoba's borders were extended and nobody was sure whether Rat Portage was in Manitoba or Ontario. Both provinces built jails and appointed magistrates and constables, and so did Ottawa. For a while it was more dangerous to be a policeman than a lawbreaker. Policemen began arresting each other until the jails were full of opposing lawmen.

Ontario constables were kidnapped and shipped to Winnipeg. The Manitoba jail was set on fire. Anybody who wished to could become a policeman. He was given free whisky and special pay because the job was so dangerous.

For a time some of the toughest characters in Rat Portage—with names like Black Jim Reddy of Montana, Charlie Bull-Pup, Boston O'Brien the Slugger, Mulligan the Hardest Case—were actually acting as policemen.

In 1883, both provinces called elections on the same day, and both premiers campaigned in Rat Portage. That election was certainly rigged: the premier of Manitoba actually got more votes than there were voters! The confusion didn't end until 1884, when the town was officially declared to be part of Ontario.

Rat Portage was the headquarters for the illegal liquor industry, with 800 gallons (3,600 L) pouring into town every month. The booze was hidden in oatmeal and bean sacks or disguised as barrels of coal oil. For every thirty residents, one was a whisky peddler. "Forty-Rod," so called because it was claimed it could drop a man at that distance, sold for the same price as champagne in Winnipeg. Illegal saloons operated on the islands that speck-led the Lake of the Woods.

Attempts at prohibition brought in gun-toting mobsters, corrupt offi-cials, and harassed police. One bloody incident, in the summer of 1880, involved two whisky traders named Dan Harrington and Jim Mitchell. It had all the elements of a western gun battle.

Harrington and Mitchell had worked for Joseph Whitehead but soon abandoned him for the more lucrative trade of liquor peddling. A warrant was issued for their arrest, but when the constable tried to serve it, the two beat him brutally. At Rat Portage the magistrate was in their pay. They sim-ply gave themselves up to him, were fined a total of $50, and got away. They headed east with fifty gallons (225 L) of whisky for a turbulent little com-munity named Hawk Lake, where the railroad navvies had just been paid.

The company's constable found Harrington and Mitchell in front of Millie Watson's tent at Hawk Lake. Mitchell fled into the woods, but Harrington announced he'd sell whisky in spite of the police. The constable took his gun from him and placed him under arrest.

Harrington asked for permission to go inside the tent and wash up. There a friend handed him a brace of loaded seven-shot revolvers. He cocked the weapons and emerged from the tent with both guns pointed at the constable. Alas for him, the policeman was a fast draw. Before Harrington could fire, he shot him through the heart.

Harrington dropped to the ground and tried to retrieve his guns. A sec-ond constable told Ross not to bother to fire again; the first bullet had taken effect.

"You're damned right it has taken effect," Harrington snarled, "but I'd sooner be shot than fined." Those were his last words.

Now Archbishop Taché of St. Boniface decided the workers needed a permanent chaplain. For that task he selected the best known of all the voyageur priests, Father Albert Lacombe, one of the nomadic Oblate Order, who had spent most of his adult life among the Cree and Blackfoot of the Far West.

In November 1880, Lacombe set out reluctantly for his new parish. A homely man whose long silver locks never seemed to be combed, Lacombe didn't want to be a railway chaplain. But he went where he was told.

Shocked by the language of the railroad navvies, Lacombe delivered an attack on blasphemy from his boxcar chapel as his first sermon.

"My God," he wrote in his diary, "have pity on this little village where so many crimes are committed every day." He soon realized he couldn't stop the evil, and so settled at last for prayer "to arrest the divine anger."

He moved up and down the line, covering thirty different camps, eating beans off tin plates in the mess halls, preaching sermons as he went, celebrating mass in the mornings, talking and smoking with the navvies in the evenings, and recording on every page of his little tattered notebook a list of the sins committed among his flock.

Ill with pleurisy, forced to travel the track in an open handcar in the bitterest weather, his ears ringing with obscene phrases he had never before heard, his eyes offended by spectacles he didn't believe possible, he could only cry out to his diary, "My God, I offer you my sufferings." He was as hard as frozen pemmican, toughened by years of prairie travel, but he almost met his match in the rock and muskeg country.

"Please, God, send me back to my missions," he wrote. But it was not until the final spike was driven that his prayers were answered. He made more friends than he knew, however. When it was learned that he was leaving at last, the workmen of Section B took up a large collection and presented him with a generous assortment of gifts: a horse, a buggy, a complete harness, a new saddle, a tent, and an entire camping outfit to make his days on the plains more comfortable. Perhaps, as he took his leave, he felt that his mission to the godless had not been entirely in vain.

CHAPTER THREE

The Armoured
Shores of Superior

IN 1881, JOHN A. MACDONALD'S GOVERNMENT GOT OUT OF THE RAILROAD
BUSINESS, AND THE NEWLY FORMED CANADIAN PACIFIC RAILWAY COMPANY
TOOK IT OVER.

In addition to completing the unfinished sections between Red River
and Lakehead, the CPR also contracted to build the line from Lakehead to
its eastern terminus at Lake Nipissing. There it would connect with an
already constructed line leading to Ottawa and the East.

The price of building the line north of Lake Superior was appalling. One
ninety-mile (144-km) section of rails ate up $10 million. One single mile
(1.6 km) of track was laid through solid rock at a cost of $700,000. By the
summer of 1884, close to fifteen thousand men and four thousand horses
were at work between Lake Nipissing and Thunder Bay. Every month the
company sent out a pay car with $1,100,000 in wages.

The amount of explosives needed to blast through the cliffs was staggering. Three dynamite factories, each capable of turning out a ton (900 kg)
a day, were built in the Caldwell-Jackfish area near the north shore of Lake
Superior. The bill for dynamite, nitroglycerine, and black powder came to
$7.5 million.

The new line would hug the armoured shores of Lake Superior.
Construction there would be heavy, but it would be easy to supply by lake
boats especially built for the purpose.

Supplies were shipped forward from Georgian Bay and distributed at
points a hundred miles (160 km) apart along the north shore of Superior.
Rough portage roads were blasted out between each delivery point to bring
provisions to the track-layers. Most of that transportation had to be done

208

in the winter when the lakes were frozen and the snow packed hard as cement. It took 300 dog teams to keep the railroad supplied.

The work went on winter and summer. Track had to be laid in all seasons—in snow five feet (1.5 m) deep and in temperatures that dropped to −40ºF (−40ºC). The drifts were often so high that nobody could find the centre line of the railroad. The rails were laid directly on top of the snow. Sometimes it was found, after the snow had melted, that the line as surveyed was in the wrong place.

William Cornelius Van Horne, the general manager of the railway, imported a new track-laying machine to speed up the work. This was really a train loaded with rails, ties, and track fastenings. High, open-top chutes with rollers spaced along the bottom were hung on either side. The ties and rails were then rolled along by manpower to the front, where they were manhandled onto the grade.

It was too expensive to cut through the hills and fill up the hollows with teams hauling rock and gravel away. Instead, Van Horne decided to build timber trestles over the valleys, gullies, and cliffs, and fill them in later when the trains themselves could carry the fill.

As always, the blasting of the Shield was done at the expense of men's lives. Although dynamite had replaced the more dangerous nitroglycerine, it too could be dangerous when carelessly handled. One man, for instance, who tried to pack a dynamite cartridge tighter by tamping it down with an iron crowbar was blown to pieces. A hotel proprietor from Port Arthur, out fishing, reached into the water and picked up a live discarded dynamite cap among the rocks. It blew off his hand. Once a rock from a blast tore through the roof of a cabin and killed a sleeping man.

The scenery, in the words of Superintendent John Egan, was "sublime in its very wildness … magnificently grand." He wrote that, "God's own handiwork stands out boldly every furlong you proceed. The ravines and streams are numerous and all is picturesqueness itself." For those who had time to look beyond the hardships, the dark rocks tinted with the bright accents of lily, rose, and buttercup or the sullen little lakes wearing their yellow garlands of spatterdock held a particularly Canadian beauty. But to the men on the job—throats choked with the dust of shattered rocks, ears ringing with dynamite blasts, arms aching from swinging sledges or carrying rails, skin smarting and itching from a hundred insect bites, nostrils assailed by a dozen stenches from horse manure to human sweat—the scenery was only a nuisance to be moved when it got in the way.

The summers were bad enough, with clouds of flies and mosquitoes tormenting everybody, but the winters were especially hard. In the flat light of December, the whole world took on a grey colour, and the cold wind blowing off the great frozen inland sea sliced through the thickest garments.

One railroad navvy gave this description of Christmas Day, 1883, at End of Track out of Port Arthur: "Somehow Christmas Day fell flat. Here and there a group were playing cards for ten-cent points. Some few melancholy-looking Englishmen were writing letters. I was smoking and cursing my stars for not being at home in the family group. I wondered how many men were in the same mood. Instead of having a good time, that Christmas afternoon was gloomy. Some of us turned it into Sunday and began darning socks and mitts. By and by a fair-haired boy from the old sod approached with a sigh: 'Where were you, old fellow, this time last year?'

"'Never mind,' I answered, 'Where were you?'"

The boy replied that he was driving his girl behind a spanking team to see his family. Then he blurted out the rest of the story. "It was an old tale. Someone drew a herring across his track, a fit of jealousy, etc., etc., which ended in his leaving home, and now he was sitting in the gloom beside a rough coon like me dressed only as a bushman or a railroader can dress and pouring into my ears a long love story."

The navvies lived in gloomy and airless bunkhouses that were little better than log dungeons. These were low-walled buildings, about sixty feet (18 m) long and thirty feet (9 m) wide, built of spruce logs, chinked with moss, and plastered with clay or lime.

Between sixty and eighty men were crammed into these hastily built buildings. They slept in lice-filled blankets on beds of hay in double-decker bunks. The ventilation was slight. A faint light entered from two small windows at either end—hardly enough to write or read by. At night steam rose from the wet clothes that hung over the central stove. In the summer the men burned straw and rags to drive off the maddening hordes of mosquitoes and blackflies, and this thickened the air. Baths were unknown. Men washed or laundered their clothes or not as they wished. There was little medical attention.

Van Horne believed in feeding his men well, but the menu was often monotonous and unhealthy because of the difficulties in transportation. The only real delicacy was fresh bread. Otherwise, the staples were salt pork, corned beef, molasses, beans, potatoes, oatmeal, and tea, with the occasional bit of frozen beef. The lack of fresh meat or vegetables and fruit made most men feel sluggish and weary. The conditions were so bad in those years that it was hard to get men to work in this situation, and the pay wasn't much of an incentive. Shovel men only got $1.50 for a ten-hour day and some as little as $1 a day. Anybody who tried to start a union was fired.

Things grew better in the winter of 1883–84. Wages rose to $1.75 for a shovel man and $2 a day for a rock man. But board was boosted to $4 a week, and so the net pay was about the same.

Men were paid only for the days on which they worked. If weather or sickness or delays kept them in the bunkhouses, they got nothing. Eight wet days a month could reduce a man's net pay, after board was deducted, to $4 a week. Besides that, he had to buy his clothing and gear at the company store at inflated prices and sometimes his meals and transportation enroute to the site.

He had no options because the company controlled his shelter and transport. If he complained, he could be fired. If he wanted to quit, he had to pay his board and room until the company could get him out to civilization—and then he had to pay his fare. Under such a system it was hard for anybody to save much money.

Yet these conditions were much better than those of the men who worked for themselves in small subcontracts, grading short strips of right of way with shovel and wheelbarrow or clearing the line of brush and stumps for fixed prices arrived at by hard bargaining.

This work might involve only two partners, or even a group of a dozen or more. There was one advantage—the men were their own bosses; they could work or not as they wanted. But this wasn't much of an advantage because most of them worked longer hours and under worse conditions than their fellow wage-earners and made no more money. The men who profited were the larger contractors who got the job done at a low cost.

The workmen here existed almost like animals in a cave. Harry Armstrong came upon one camp of French Canadians that he thought was the worst he had ever seen. They lived and slept in a windowless log hovel, lit by a candle made from a tin cup filled with grease and a rag as a wick. In one corner stood a cookstove, its smoke pouring out of a hole in the roof; in another corner, in the dim light, Armstrong could just make out a straw mattress occupied by an injured man waiting for a doctor.

One group lived during the winter in a kind of root cellar without windows. To enter they crawled through an opening in the bottom. There they lay most of the time, playing cards, but going out into the snow when the sun shone to do a little work, clearing the brush along the line.

There was no flooring, only a sea of black mud kept thawed by the heat of the stove. A few scattered poles lay across the mud over which the workmen were obliged to pick their way. If a man slipped off, he sank to his ankles in slime.

Armstrong hoped for something to eat. But all he got was some refuse from the table that had been scraped off after each meal. It was the best the French Canadians had to offer.

The Italian immigrants were even worse off. One group lived during the winter in a kind of root cellar without windows. To enter they crawled through an opening in the bottom. There they lay most of the time, playing cards, but going out into the snow when the sun shone to do a little work, clearing the brush along the line. Once a week they bought a sack of flour and a little tea on credit. By spring they had managed to clear half an acre (0.2 hectares). The proceeds had hardly paid for their winter's provisions and by then most were suffering badly from scurvy.

These hovels were in sharp contrast to the quarters of the major contractors, who lived in relative luxury. One man had a home complete with Brussels carpet and grand piano. Another had his own cow to dispense milk punches to his guests. And the contractors and senior engineers had their wives and children with them, thus escaping the loneliness of the bunkhouse.

Again, the navvies turned to alcohol to lighten their nights. The government had put through a special act, banning the sale of liquor along the line as far as Manitoba. But once again government agents fought a running battle with whisky peddlers.

In one section between Whitemouth River and Lake Wabigoon, some twenty-five hundred people managed to drink 800 gallons (3,600 L) of illegal spirits every month—at a cost of $15 a gallon. (In Toronto at that time the same whisky sold for as little as 50 cents.)

The whisky peddlers were clever in deceiving the police, even going so far as to get the railway foremen drunk. Often they seized control of the local police force and controlled the town through a vigilante committee. Violence was not unusual. On the Lake Superior line a company count revealed that there were 5,000 revolvers, 300 shotguns and rifles, and the same number of dirks and bowie knives in the possession of railway workers.

In Michipicoten (near the present town of Wawa), the vigilante gang that ran the town was actually headed by a former police chief, Charles Wallace. In October 1884, this gang attempted to shoot the local magistrate, who took refuge in a construction office, ducking bullets fired through the walls. A force of Toronto police was called to restore order. They holed up in a local boarding house and arrested seven men. But the boarding house became the target of hidden riflemen, who pumped bullets into it, grazing the arm of the cook and narrowly missing one of the boarders.

When the police poured out of the building with revolvers drawn, the unseen attackers fled. It was said that forty men, armed with repeating rifles, were on their way to rescue the prisoners, but the police maintained an all-night vigil, and there was no further trouble.

They destroyed 120 gallons (540 L) of rye whisky and seized a sailboat used in the trade. Then they laid plans to capture the four ringleaders of the terrorist gang, including Wallace.

With the help of spies, they descended upon a nearby Indian village where the culprits were supposed to be hiding. They flushed out the wanted men, but Wallace and his friends were too fast for them. A chase followed, but the hoodlums easily got away, apparently with the help of both the Indians and the townspeople.

No sooner had the big-city policemen left than Wallace and his three henchmen emerged and instituted a new reign of terror. Wallace was armed like a bandit, with four heavy revolvers, a bowie knife in his belt, and a Winchester repeating rifle on his shoulder. The gang boarded a lake steamer, pumped bullets into the crowd on the dock, and then left for Sault Ste. Marie. They weren't captured until the following February, after a gunfight in the snow in which one of the policemen was severely wounded. Wallace got eighteen months in prison, and by the time he got out of jail, the railway was finished, and the days of whisky peddlers were over forever.

CHAPTER FOUR

Treasure in the Rocks

WHEN THE CPR WAS BORN IN 1881, THE LINE BETWEEN FORT WILLIAM AND
SELKIRK WAS STILL NOT FINISHED. IN FACT THE LINE WAS SO BADLY PUT
TOGETHER, IT HAD TO BE REBUILT AND RELOCATED. BUT, BY 1882, THE GAPS IN
THE LINE BETWEEN WINNIPEG AND THUNDER BAY WERE FINALLY CLOSED.

But there was still no line of track between Thunder Bay and Lake
Nipissing. The contractors, supplied by boat, were strung out in sections of
varying lengths, depending on the ground. Indeed, some contracts were so
difficult that some only covered one mile (1.6 km) of line.

The Lake Superior line was divided into two sections. The difficult sec-
tion led east from Fort William to meet the easier section that ran west from
Lake Nipissing. At Lake Nipissing the new railway joined the Canada
Central Line out of Ottawa.

In the summer of 1881, an eighteen-year-old Scot, John McIntyre
Ferguson, arrived at Lake Nipissing. He was smart enough to buy 288 acres
(116.5 hectares) of land at $1 an acre and to lay out a townsite in the forest.
He built the first house in the region, and in ordering nails, asked the sup-
plier to ship them to the "north bay of Lake Nipissing." Thus the settlement
got its name. By 1884, North Bay was a thriving community. As for
Ferguson, he went on to become the wealthiest man in town and later its
mayor for four terms.

North Bay was the creation of the railway. Before its first buildings were
put up, the main institutions were located in railway cars shunted onto sidings. The early church services were held in these cars. The preacher, a giant
of a man named Silas Huntington, used an empty upended barrel as a pulpit and brooked no opposition from the rougher elements in his congregation. When two muscular navvies disagreed with one of his sermons,

Huntington left his barrel pulpit and started towards them, preaching as he went. As he drew opposite the intruders, he took one in each hand and dropped them out of the door, without pausing for breath or halting the flow of his sermon.

On another occasion, when Huntington's boxcar church was parked at a siding on a hillside, somebody accidentally released the brake. As Huntington was in the middle of his sermon, the car gave a jerk and slowly rolled downhill, gathering speed as it went. It ran down to the main line and off to the edge of the new town. But Huntington, without raising an eyebrow, continued his sermon. When he finished, the congregation sang "O God From Whom All Blessings Flow" and walked back without comment.

All the land between North Bay and Lake Superior was thought to be worthless wilderness. Many politicians had opposed the idea of building a railway over the bleak rocks and through the stunted forests of the Shield country. Why would any sane man want to run a line of steel through such a dreadful country? But John A. Macdonald insisted on an all-Canadian line.

The rails, moving westward from North Bay, cut through a barren realm, blackened by forest fires and empty of colour, save for the occasional dark reds and yellows that stained the rocks and glinted up through the roots of the dried grasses on the hillsides. These were actually the oxides of nickel and copper and the sulphides of copper and iron. But it needed a trained eye to detect the signs of treasure that lay concealed beneath the charred forest floor.

By the end of 1882, the Canada Central Railway reached Lake Nipissing. By the end of the following year, the first 100 miles (160 km) of the connecting CPR were completed. Early that year the crudest of roads, all stumps and mud, had reached the spot where Sudbury stands today. And there, as much by accident as by design, a temporary construction camp was established.

This was entirely a company town. Every boarding house, home, and store was built, owned, and operated by the CPR to keep the whisky peddlers at bay. Even the post office was on company land. And the company storekeeper, who later became Sudbury's first mayor, acted as postmaster.

On the outskirts of town, private merchants hovered about, hawking their goods from packs on their backs. It wasn't until 1884 that the most enterprising of these, a firm-jawed peddler named John Frawley, discovered that the CPR did not own all the land after all. The Jesuit priests had been on the spot for more than a decade and held title to it. Frawley leased a plot of land from the religious order for $3 a month, opened a men's furnishing store in a tent, and broke the company monopoly. By then a mining rush was in full swing, and Sudbury was on its way to becoming a permanent community.

A CPR blacksmith, Tom Flanagan, was the first to suspect there might be treasure hidden in the rocks. He picked up a piece of yellow bronze ore about three miles (4.8 km) from town and thought he had found gold. He was wrong. He had no idea he was standing not only on a rich copper mine but also on the largest nickel deposit in the world.

It would be nice to report that Flanagan became a millionaire as a result. Unfortunately, he did nothing about his find. But John Loughlin, a contractor cutting railway ties, was interested by the formations. He brought in three friends, Tom and William Murray, and Harry Abbott. In February 1884, they staked the land on what became the future Murray Mine of the International Nickel Company. It was to produce ore worth millions—but not for the original discoverers.

Some company employees became rich, however. One was a gaunt Hertfordshire man named Charles Francis Crean. He had been working on boats along the upper Ottawa, carrying supplies to construction camps. He arrived on the first work train into Sudbury on November 23 at a time when the settlement hadn't even been surveyed. The buildings were being thrown together and laid out with no thought for the future. The first log hospital turned out to be in the middle of what later became the junction of Logan and Elm Streets. The mud was so bad that a boy actually drowned in a hole in the road opposite the American Hotel.

On his arrival, Crean walked into the company store and saw a huge yellow nugget being used as a paperweight. The clerk thought the ore probably contained iron pyrites—fool's gold—but he gave Crean a piece of it. Crean sent it to a chemist friend in Toronto who told him it was an excellent sample of copper. In May 1884, Crean applied for a mining claim and staked what was to become famous as the Elsie Mine.

A month later, the observant Crean spotted some copper ore in the ballast along the tracks of the Sault Ste. Marie branch of the railroad. He checked back carefully to find where it came from and was able to stake that property. On this spot, another rich mine, the Worthington, was established. Later Crean discovered three other valuable properties, all of them steady producers.

A week after Crean staked his first claim, a timber prospector, Rinaldo McConnell, staked some further property which was to become the nucleus of the Canadian Copper Company's Sudbury operation—the forerunner of the International Nickel Company. It was copper, of course, that attracted the miners; nickel had few uses in those days.

Another prospective millionaire was a timekeeper named Thomas Frood, a one-time druggist and schoolteacher from southwestern Ontario. He acted on a trapper's hunch and discovered the property that became the most famous of all—the Frood Mine.

The story of northern Ontario mining—and, in particular, Sudbury—is a story of accident, coincidence, and sheer blind luck. The railway line was supposed to be located south of Lost Lake. The locating engineer decided to run it north. Sudbury wasn't even seen as a permanent community—just an unimportant spot on the map.

Thus, the politicians who had scoffed at the idea of a line running across the Shield were proved wrong. Alexander Mackenzie, when he was Leader of the Opposition, had said it was "one of the most foolish things that could be imagined." His colleague, Edward Blake, seconded that comment. Indeed, right to the moment of Sudbury's founding, some members of John A. Macdonald's cabinet, as well as a couple of the CPR's own directors, were opposed to the line across the Shield. It was only when the land began to yield up its treasure that the fuss about an all-Canadian line came to an end.

CHAPTER FIVE

Rebellion!

BY 1885, THE CANADIAN PACIFIC RAILWAY COMPANY WAS ON THE EDGE OF FINANCIAL COLLAPSE. NORTH OF LAKE SUPERIOR, VAN HORNE WAS DESPERATELY TRYING TO LINK UP THE GAPS BETWEEN THE ISOLATED STRETCHES OF STEEL. THESE GAPS TOTALLED 254 MILES (409 KM). UNTIL THEY WERE COMPLETED, THE CPR COULD NOT BEGIN ITS OPERATION AS A THROUGH ROAD AND START MAKING MONEY.

The government, pressed by its opponents, did not think it politically possible to guarantee any more loans to the CPR. Some kind of miracle would be needed to show how valuable a transcontinental railway would be to Canada. And in 1885, just as the company was foundering, the miracle occurred in the shape of Louis Riel.

In the Northwest, the railway had become a symbol of the passing of the Good Old Days. To the Indians, it was a new kind of boundary, solid as a wall. To the white settlers of northern Saskatchewan, it meant disappointment, because the CPR had refused to build the railway through the settled areas, preferring to drive the steel farther south where no settlements existed. To the farmers, the CPR spelled monopoly and grinding freight rates. To the Métis of the Red River and northern Saskatchewan, it stood for revolutionary social change.

The people of the Northwest were stirred up from Winnipeg to Edmonton. Whites, Indians, and Métis were all organizing. At the end of July 1884, the Crees of North Saskatchewan were welded into an Indian council by Big Bear, the most independent of the chiefs.

The Indians believed that the government had betrayed and deceived them, and they were right. Ottawa had promised to save them from starvation, but only one treaty spelled that out. Already their slim rations had been cut back as part of an official policy of saving money. It was plain that the politicians of the East had little understanding of conditions in the Northwest. Western newspapers supported the Indians, reporting that they were dying by the scores as the result of semi-starvation, resulting from the bad quality of food supplied by the government agencies.

The white settlers were angry too. The Manitoba Farmers' Union was threatening to pull out of Confederation, even to rebel. Other organizations were demanding that Ottawa change its attitude to the West. All these people wanted to run their own affairs, to reform the land laws, to control their own railways, to reduce the taxes on farm equipment imported from the United States, and to end the CPR monopoly.

The English, Scots, and the French-speaking Roman Catholic Métis had another grievance. In the North West Territories they wanted what the government had recognized and granted in Manitoba in 1870—a share in the aboriginal title to the land. They had been vainly petitioning Ottawa for this since 1873 but had been put off time after time.

A distinct community of Métis had been forming on the prairies as they struggled to maintain their identity. As the Moose Jaw *News* reported in April 1884, the Métis "have been driven by the inevitable back and aback, like their half-brothers, the red men of the continent ... What is their future?"

By the spring of 1884, protest meetings were becoming common at St. Laurent, the strongest and best established of the Métis communities, near Duck Lake on the South Saskatchewan River. In May 1884, one Métis wrote to Louis Riel (who had been exiled after the North West uprising in 1871) that the North West Territories "were like a volcanoe ready to erupt. The excitement is almost general. All minds are everywhere excited. Since the month of March last public meetings are everywhere frequently held ... French and English Half-breeds are now united ... On all sides people complain of injustice; they invoke equity, they desire to obtain our rights."

By then the united community on the forks of the Saskatchewan had decided Riel was the only man who could lead them—peacefully, it was hoped—in a campaign to force the government's hand. Fifteen years before, he had been a champion for his people in an uprising that turned him into a hero and laid the groundwork for the formation of a new province—Manitoba. Now the Métis leaders were determined to talk Riel into repeating that triumph. No one else had his magnetic personality, his sense of tactics, his eloquence, and, above all, his reputation.

In the spring of 1884, Gabriel Dumont, the most popular and respected man along the Saskatchewan, set off to see Riel with three other Métis delegates. Dumont, at forty-seven, was a swarthy, stocky man with bold shoulders and a handsome, kindly face. He had been chief of his people since the age of twenty-five, much beloved by all who knew him, including the Mounted Police.

Dumont and his followers arrived at Riel's small home in Montana on June 4, 1884. Riel was living in poverty. Canada, he believed, owed him both land and money as the result of the settlement made when Manitoba was created in 1871. He promised the delegation he would return to Canada to fight not only for his personal rights and those of his people but also for the white settlers and the Indians.

It was this decision that led to the bloody events of March 1885 that touched off the Saskatchewan Rebellion. The blood was spilled at Duck Lake on March 25 when, during a parley with Dumont and his men, the impatience of the police provoked a skirmish. The Métis won. Half an hour later, ten members of the mixed government force of police and volunteers lay dead. Thirteen more were wounded, two mortally. The Métis suffered only five casualties. The Saskatchewan Rebellion had begun.

Meanwhile, in Ottawa, John A. Macdonald had for some time been concerned about the situation in the Northwest—but not concerned enough to do anything about the Métis demands. He knew that some sort of outbreak was possible and could only wish that the CPR was completed. It wasn't. By the beginning of March, the number of gaps in the line had been reduced to four, but these still totalled eighty-six miles (138 km). Between these unconnected strips of track—much of it unballasted and laid hastily on top of the snow—was a frozen waste of forest, rock, and hummocky drifts, whipped up by the icy winds that shrieked in from the lake.

Macdonald was preparing a force to go out west to keep order, but how would they get there? William Van Horne knew how. He asked the prime minister to tell him when the government might expect to have the troops ready. Macdonald figured that it might be in the first or second week in March. Van Horne made an instant decision. He pledged he could get troops from Kingston or Quebec all the way to Saskatchewan in just ten days.

Van Horne could see how valuable the railway would be if a rebellion broke out in the prairies. The hard-pressed CPR could only benefit. How could the government refuse to aid a railway if it sped troops out west, took the Métis unaware, and crushed a rebellion? He immediately offered the Privy Council the services of his railway to move the troops. There was just one condition: he and not the army was to be in complete control of food and transport.

It sounded like a foolhardy promise. Could men, horses, artillery pieces, and military supplies be shuttled over the primitive roads that crossed this blizzard-swept land? The members of Macdonald's council refused to believe it.

"Has anyone got a better plan?" Macdonald asked. There was no answer. And so Van Horne was told to get ready to move a massive amount of men, animals, arms, and equipment over the Shield.

On March 23, the first suggestion of a coming rebellion appeared in the Ontario newspapers. The next day Van Horne had his plan in operation. He told his deputy, Harry Abbott, to get ready to move 400 men as far as End of Track at Dog Lake, west of Sudbury.

Joseph Caron, the minister of militia and defence, wasn't sure the plan would work. "How can men and horse cross Nepigon—answer immediately," he wired Van Horne. Van Horne replied that it could be done.

On March 25, Abbott reported that he was ready. John Ross, in charge of the western section of the unfinished line, was also ready and didn't expect there would be any delays. That same day the clash at Duck Lake took place. When that news burst upon the capital, the country was immediately mobilized. And Caron told Abbott that the first troops would be ready to move on March 28.

In Ottawa, George Stephen, the president of the company, wanted to quit. The CPR was out of money, and there was nothing more he could do. Only if Van Horne's gamble worked would the politicians and the public realize how valuable an asset a transcontinental line could be. It could bind the nation together in time of trouble. Perhaps then the government would be prepared to guarantee a loan to the faltering railway.

Southern Canada learned from its newspapers on March 27 that a bloody rebellion had broken out in the Northwest. Once the Indians learned of the Métis' victory at Duck Lake, they joined the rebellion. Prince Albert, Fort Carlton, Batoche, Fort Pitt, even perhaps Fort Qu'Appelle, Calgary, Edmonton, Moose Jaw, and Regina were all threatened.

A wave of anger, patriotism, and excitement washed over eastern Canada. The government had called out the only permanent force in all of Canada—two artillery batteries stationed at Quebec and Kingston. That same day several militia regiments were ordered to be ready to move immediately to the North West.

But how on earth would they get there, people asked. In Kingston, the *British Whig* pointed out that if the soldiers travelled through the United States they would have to be disarmed. They would have to wear civilian clothes as private citizens, with their rifles and artillery pieces boxed for separate shipment to Winnipeg.

There was a rumour, however, that this passage might be avoided by going over the partially completed Canadian Pacific Railway. That possibility was considered very remote. How could troops, baggage, guns, horses, and equipment be shuttled over those trackless gaps?

The newspaper pointed out that a man who had recently travelled through the country and was asked how long it would take to cover the unrailed section laughingly replied, "Oh, until July." Another railwayman reported that there was at least four feet (1.2 m) of snow along the track and that "there would be considerable trouble getting through."

Van Horne was determined to move 3,324 men from London, Toronto, Kingston, Ottawa, Montreal, Quebec, Halifax, and a dozen smaller centres to the Northwest. Indeed, he expected to have the first troops in Winnipeg no more than ten days after the news of the Duck Lake engagement.

Neither Harry Abbott nor John Ross was worried. After all, they had been moving hundreds of workmen over the gaps in the line all that winter. When Abbott learned that the first 800 troops would arrive March 28, he was ready to receive them.

CHAPTER SIX

Marching As to War

Now the news was out. The entire force was to be shipped west on the new railroad. A kind of frenzy seized the country. After all, the social life of the cities and towns revolved around the militia. Young officers were in demand at the winter sports that marked the era — the bobsled parties and skating fêtes and iceboat excursions and toboggan club outings.

The great social event of the year was the militia ball. And there were uniforms everywhere—at the opera house, at garrison theatricals, at afternoon teas. The tailors gave more attention to military fashions than to the civilian. The most popular weekend entertainment was watching the local militia parade through the streets or listening to a military band concert in the park.

Now, suddenly, these Saturday night soldiers were parading through the streets for the first time in earnest, for a country that had not yet fought a war of any kind. Never before had Canadians seen the kind of spectacular scenes that took place in every major town in the East during March and April—the cheers for Queen and country, the blare of martial music, the oceans of flapping banners, the young men in scarlet and green marching behind the colours, the main streets jammed with waving thousands, the roll of drums, the troop trains puffing through the small towns—the singing, the cheering, the weeping and the kissing, and the bitter goodbyes.

All this sound and spectacle, not to mention the military oratory that went with it, kept the country on an emotional binge for the better part of two weeks. This was true especially after April 2 when the news of the deaths of priests and civilians at Frog Lake at the hands of Big Bear's Indians filtered in to the cities.

The first units called out were the Queen's Own Rifles, the Royal Grenadiers, and the Infantry School of Toronto. The troops were required to be on parade by the morning of March 28. All that night, while the temperature hung around the freezing point, officers in hired carriages were rattling up and down the dark streets rousing their men. Long before dawn, the city was awake, thanks in part to the newly invented telephone, of which there were more than four hundred in the city.

Well before eight thirty on Saturday morning, West Market Street was jammed with people, while the entrance to the drill shed on Jarvis Street was "filled up to the throat." Everybody was on hand to see the unaccustomed sight of militia men being called out and paraded for active service. Many had learned of their muster only on their way to work and came to the station in civilian clothes. Most believed they would be shipped directly to the Northwest. But now they were told they would not be leaving until Monday, March 30.

In the early hours of Monday morning, men in uniform began to pour into Toronto from the outlying centres. The main streets were crowded with would-be soldiers, many of whom arrived by streetcar, one claiming that he wanted to give that luxury a fond goodbye before heading west.

At the drill shed, the crowd was so dense that the soldiers themselves had trouble making their way through. The supply system was in disarray. The men had to supply their own boots, socks, shirts, and underwear—even their own lunch. Few had any idea of what was needed. Some came with extra boots in their hands. All had packs bulging with pies, rolls, and cooked meat. Some had tin cups hanging at their belts. Most were armed with a revolver of some kind stuck into a pocket. One enterprising salesman squeezed his way into the shed and began selling boots to those who had not thought to bring a second pair.

At eleven, Colonel William Dillon Otter spoke to the men, urging them to stay away from all drink and to throw away any bottles that they might have hidden in their kits. The troops cheered and pounded their rifle butts on the wooden floor.

Outside, the scenes were chaotic. The *Globe* reported that never in the history of Toronto had there been such a jam of people on King Street. It looked as if every citizen who could walk or crawl had come from miles around to line the route of the march. The street was a living, moving mass of humanity. The rooftops and cornices were alive with people who had waited hours to see the troops. Hundreds paid for positions in the flag-decked windows overlooking King Street. Women and children fainted continually and had to be removed by the police. Their nerves had become unstrung at the thought of their husbands, fathers, brothers, and sons leaving for the frontier. Many were weeping.

Then, at eleven thirty, there came a cheer from the troops in the shed. The mob outside—more than ten thousand people—broke into an answering cry. The cheer moved like a wave along King Street, so loud that the band of the 10th Royal Grenadiers could not be heard from half a block away. The crush made it impossible to move.

Somebody spotted the first uniform—that of a member of the Governor-General's Body Guard on horseback, followed by Colonel Otter, marching on foot at the head of his men. A group of about five hundred civilians rushed ahead, clearing the way through the mass of spectators. And then could be seen the glittering brass of the band's instruments, the straight rows of fur caps, and the sharp outlines of rifles drifting above the craning heads.

Down the streets the young men came, as the crowd around them shouted themselves hoarse. Bouquets of flowers drifted from the windows above. Handkerchiefs fluttered. A thousand flags flapped in the breeze. Those who couldn't move along with the troops began to cry "Goodbye, goodbye!" as the musicians struck up "The Girl I Left Behind Me." That was the theme song of Canada that month.

The crowd had been pouring in an unending stream to the foot of York Street by the station—all kinds and conditions of people in carriages and hacks, express vans, on foot, or pushing baby carriages—and all hoping to catch one last glimpse of brother, son, father, or sweetheart. The crowd jammed the Esplanade from one end of the station to the other, swarming over the roofs of freight cars and perching in every window. It began to rain, the rain becoming a heavy sleet, but the people didn't move.

Crammed into the cars, the men leaned out of windows and waved at the throng pressed up against the train. The cars began to crawl forward. Arms appeared waving final greetings. These were answered from the windows by an assortment of fluttering handkerchiefs, toques, forage caps, sidearms, socks, and even underwear. Then the band of the Queen's Own struck up "Auld Lang Syne," and as the engine bell began to ring, the men joined in.

These scenes were repeated over and over again in the following days. Everywhere the crowds were afire with excitement. In Montreal, when the French-speaking 65th Battalion paraded to the station, the crush was so great that a vast double window burst out from a three-storey building, injuring twelve people. In Quebec, the 9th Voltigeurs attended mass in the basilica and then marched through a wild crowd escorted by the city's snowshoe clubs in uniform, carrying torches. Never before had any of these cities seen such intense excitement.

Only the Governor-General's Body Guard, the oldest cavalry regiment in Canada, left in quiet and secrecy because the authorities feared for the safety of the seventy horses among the press of the crowds. They were kept ready to move for several days with very little sleep. And when they finally left shortly after midnight on April 7, their colonel, George T. Denison, and his officers had not slept for three nights, but remained booted and spurred for all that time, ready to move on the instant.

The press was enthusiastic about the condition of the troops. The Ottawa *Citizen*, describing one company of the Governor-General's Foot Guards, wrote that "it is one of the finest bodies of men for rough and ready service ever brought together in the Dominion."

That was substantially true. The men from the farms and the cities were hard muscled, keen, and young enough to laugh at the kind of ordeal they would shortly face along the uncompleted route of the CPR. But they were also woefully under-trained and under-equipped. The York Rangers, huddled in the Toronto drill shed, looked more like sheep than soldiers. In Kingston, it was noticed that members of the Composite Midland Regiment were badly drilled. There were men in the 65th in Montreal who had never fired so much as a blank cartridge.

Few battalions left for the Northwest properly equipped. The belts and knapsacks of the Queen's Own had served in the Crimean War almost thirty years before. Their rifles were so old that they were mostly unreliable because of years of wear and tear. The clothing of the York Rangers was tattered and rotten, the knapsacks ill-fitting. Several of the Midland companies had no knapsacks at all and had to wrap their belongings in heavy paper. Others had no helmets. One outfit had no uniforms. Many of the 65th lacked trousers, tunics, and rifles. Even the crack Governor-General's Body Guard had not been issued satchels for their mounts; the men had been forced to wrap their personal belongings in blankets.

Until this moment, membership in the militia unit had been a social asset. Nobody had apparently ever considered the possibility that one day his unit would march off to war. The soldiers now had to depend on the generosity of the civilians. All the government was required to issue was a greatcoat, a tunic, trousers, and a rifle. Everything else was a soldier's own responsibility, and there was no provision made for wives and children left behind, although the civilians took up funds for the dependants.

The London town council supplied the volunteers with socks and underwear. A Montreal clothing firm gave the men of the 65th twenty-five dozen pairs of warm mittens. And, of course, there were bundles of bibles and second-hand books. At Almonte, a local storekeeper boarded a train with a more welcome gift—fifty packs of playing cards.

The trains sped off, two at a time, at staggered intervals, puffing through Carleton Place, Pembroke, North Bay, and Sudbury towards Dog Lake, where the real ordeal would begin. Van Horne insisted the officers be given first-class accommodation. He was determined that the image of the railway would be a good one. It was "important that the report of the officers as to the treatment of troops on our line should be favourable."

That's why the CPR was prepared to carry free any clothes or goods sent out to soldiers by friends or relatives. And Van Horne also made sure there would be mountains of food and gallons of hot, strong coffee along the way. He knew better than anybody what the troops were about to face. He couldn't protect them from the chill rides in open flat cars and sleighs, or for numbing treks across the glare ice, but he could make sure his army marched on a full stomach.

The Cruel Journey

As the cheering faded, the men from the cities, farms, and fishing villages of the East began to glimpse the rough face of the new Canada and to understand for the first time the real size of the country.

From North Bay the land stretched off to the horizon, barren and desolate, the spindly spruce rising in a ragged patchwork from the lifeless rock. The railway was completed for passenger traffic only as far as Biscotasing. Here the troops encountered the first of the CPR construction towns, a hard-drinking, backwoods village of log cabins. Just the day before the Queen's Own arrived, the police destroyed 500 gallons (2,250 L) of illicit whisky.

The first gap in the line began near Dog Lake, another construction camp not far from the site of present-day White River. Here the railway had prepared a marvellous dinner of beef, salmon, lobster, mackerel, potatoes, tomatoes, peas, beans, corn, peaches, currants, raisins, cranberries, fresh bread, cakes, pies, and all the tea and coffee they could drink. It was the last night of comfort that the soldiers would know for several days. An adventure they would remember for the rest of their lives was about to begin.

They were packed tightly in groups of eight in sleighs and set off behind teams of horses down the uncompleted right of way. At every unbridged ravine and unfilled cut, the sleighs had to leave the graded surface, sometimes for miles, and follow the "tote road." This roller-coaster path cut through the forests, ran over stumps, windfalls, and rocks, dipped up and down gorges, and wound through seemingly impassable stretches of tightly packed trees.

At some points the sleighs encountered seven-foot boulders. At others they pitched into holes as deep as graves. The occupants were flung over the dashboards and into the haunches of the horses. Spills and accidents were so frequent they were taken as normal. One sleigh overturned no fewer than thirteen times in the forty miles (64 km) between Dog Lake and End of Track at Birch Lake.

Men who had been frozen in the –20ºF (–29ºC) weather were hurled out and swallowed up in six feet (1.8 m) of powdery snow, often with all of their equipment. Caps, mitts, mufflers, sidearms, and other articles of luggage were lost in the white blanket through which the sleighs reared and tumbled. One man was completely buried under an avalanche of baggage. A friend of his was nearly smothered when a horse fell on top of him.

The sleighs carrying the troops westward ran into empty sleighs returning eastward for a second load. Chaos resulted. The detours were only wide enough to allow a single team to pass through without grazing the trees. If a horse got a foot or two (0.3 or 0.6 m) out of the track, the sleigh runners would lock onto a tree trunk, or, worse still, rise up on a stump, tilting occupants and baggage into the snow.

The trip was generally made by night, when the weather was cold enough to prevent the snow from turning into slush. The young soldiers crouched in the bottoms of the sleighs, wrapped in their greatcoats and covered with robes and blankets. But nothing could keep out the cold. To prevent themselves from freezing, officers and men would leap from the careering sleighs and trot alongside, trying to restore circulation. For some units, the cold was so intense that any man who left any part exposed, even for a few minutes, suffered frostbite.

At Magpie Point Camp—a halfway point along the unfinished right of way—the teams were changed. Here was more food. Many who arrived at Magpie thought that they had reached the end of their ordeal and were distressed when the bugle blew and they realized that it was only half over.

Scenes of confusion took place in the darkness. Men scrambled about seeking the sleighs to which they had been assigned. But the snow was dropping so thickly that friends could not recognize each other in the dark, with the horses whinnying and rearing, the Métis teamsters swearing, and the officers barking orders. The troops now realized that everything they owned was soaking wet and that they would have to endure four more hours of that bone-chilling journey.

Out of the yard the horses galloped along a route utterly unknown to them. They depended solely on their guides and their own instincts. Sometimes they tumbled, sleighs and all, over the high embankment, then righted themselves and plunged on. It took some nine hours to negotiate the gap between Dog Lake and Birch Lake. And at the end stood a lonely huddle of shacks which was swiftly named "Desolation Camp."

It certainly deserved its title. A fire had swept through the scrub timber, leaving the trees bleached a ghostly white. A cutting wind, rattling through these skeletal branches, added to the general feeling of despair. The only real shelter was a small, tattered tent, not nearly large enough for those who tried to crowd in. Some men had to remain there for hours, their drenched clothing freezing to their skin in temperatures that dropped as low as −35°F (−37°C).

The 10th Royal Grenadiers arrived at Desolation Camp at five one morning after a sleigh journey that had begun at eight the previous evening. Because the trains weren't there to take them on, they had to endure a wait of seventeen hours. There wasn't even a fire to greet them. Tumbling out of the sleighs like ghosts—for the falling snow had covered them completely—they tried to huddle in the tent. It was so crowded that nobody could lie down.

Some men tried to light fires outside in three feet (1 m) of snow, only to see the embers disappear into deep holes melted through the crust. Others rolled themselves in their blankets like mummies and tried to sleep, the falling snow forming over them.

Every regiment that passed through Desolation Camp had its own story of hardship. Some members of the Queen's Own arrived hysterical from the cold and had to be led on board the cars, uncomprehending and uncaring. Although the troops had very little sleep when they arrived, they couldn't sleep at Desolation Camp because that meant certain death from freezing. The last battalion to arrive from Halifax had to endure a freezing rain, which soaked their garments and turned their greatcoats into boards. When a man dropped in his tracks, a guard was ordered to rouse him by any means, pulling him to his feet, kicking him, and bringing him over to the fires to dry. There the men stood, shivering and half-conscious, until the flatcars arrived.

In these roofless cars—the same open gravel cars used by construction crews to fill the cuts—sleep was impossible. Rough boards had been placed along the sides to a height of about six feet (1.8 m) and were held in place by stakes and sockets. Wind and snow blew into the crevices between the planks. Rough benches ran lengthwise and here the men sat, each with his blankets, packed tightly together, or huddled lengthwise on the floor.

For the Governor-General's Body Guard, such a journey was complicated by the presence of horses. There were no platforms or gangways to take the animals off the train. The men were obliged to gather railway ties and build little inclined planes up which the horses could be led. The snow was generally three or four feet (0.9 or 1.2 m) deep. The ties were sheathed in ice. The makeshift ramps had to be covered with blankets so the animals wouldn't lose their footing. And all had to be watered and fed before the men themselves could rest.

Because the horses couldn't be moved by sleigh across the Dog Lake gap to Desolation Camp, the cavalry men rode or led their horses the entire distance. When the cavalry moved by train, the horses were placed in exactly the same kind of flatcars as the men. It took hours to unload them because all their hind shoes had to be removed to prevent injuries to men and steeds.

The artillery had its own problems. It wasn't easy to load the nine-pounder (4-kg) guns onto the flatcars. At one construction camp, four husky track-layers were assigned to the job. One ran a crowbar into the muzzle of a cannon to get purchase, an act that caused the major in charge to fly into a rage. He fired the men, called for twenty of his own soldiers to tie a rope around the breech and, with great difficulty, managed to get it hauled up an inclined platform and onto the car.

It was a relief, after that, to leave Desolation Camp behind, but the ordeal was by no means over. Three more gaps in the line lay ahead and the worst was yet to come.

CHAPTER EIGHT

End of the Line

FROM DESOLATION CAMP THE TRACK LED ON TO THE NEXT GAP AT PORT
MUNRO. HERE THE TIES HAD BEEN LAID DIRECTLY ON THE SNOW. IN SOME SEC-
TIONS WHERE A THAW SET IN, FOUR OR FIVE TIES IN SUCCESSION, SPIKED TO THE
RAILS, WOULD BE HELD OFF THE GROUND FOR SEVERAL INCHES.

One man said that the train's movement over those ties was like that of
a birchbark canoe. Trains were thrown off this section of the track daily, and
the rails were slowly being bent by the heavy passage. The trains rarely
exceeded five miles (8 km) an hour, and so the men faced the longest night
yet.

The Grenadiers, packed so closely together, took advantage of the mutu-
al body warmth. Unfortunately, the officers, who had more room in the
caboose, were in pitiful condition. One man's letter home describes what
some of them suffered on that section of the route: "At one end of the car,
lying on a stretcher on the floor was a poor fellow suffering from rheumatism and quite helpless with surgeon Ryerson patiently sitting at his head
where he had been trying all night, with little success, to snatch a little
sleep. The gallant colonel ... with elbows on knees, was sitting over the
stove looking thoughtfully into the embers with eyes that have not known
a wink of sleep for 50 hours. Then there was Major Dawson whose system
appeared to be rebelling against the regularity of life to which it had been
so long accustomed ... Captain Harston, with a face as red as a boiled
lobster sitting with arms folded on his knees [was] the very picture of incar-
nate discomfort."

On the map, Bandeville appeared as a town. But it actually consisted of
a single shack in the wilderness. Here the men were given sandwiches and
hot tea. Some were so stiff with cold they had to be lifted out of the cars.
Others were so bone-weary that the warmth of the shack was too much for

them after the cold of the journey. They dropped off into a sleep so deep it was impossible to wake them.

Now the men prepared for the next leg of the journey—seven chilling hours before End of Track at Port Munro was reached. Port Munro was a construction station and supply depot on the lakeshore, and here the troops were able to enjoy their first real sleep. In a deep, natural harbour, dominated by thousand-foot (300-m) crags, lay the schooner *Breck*. Two hundred troops slumbered aboard her, crowded together in the hold on mattresses composed of hay and dirt, and later of water. That leakage was caused by the weight of the human cargo grinding the vessel down through the ice. By the time the Halifax battalion arrived, the floor was afloat and pumps could not be worked because of the frost.

A second gap in the line, some twenty miles (32 km) long, began at Port Munro and continued to McKellar's Harbour, a small inlet near the mouth of the Little Pic River. There were not enough sleighs to carry more than the baggage, so the troops had to march across the glare ice of Lake Superior to the next piece of track. That journey took eight hours. They began in high spirits:

> *The volunteers are all fine boys and full of lots of fun*
> *But it's mighty little pay they get for carrying a gun;*
> *The Government has grown so lean and the CPR so fat*
> *Our extra pay we did not get—You can bet your boots on that!*

The Grenadiers, well fed and rested, moved out onto the ice at dawn on Easter Sunday—a long line of men with teams drawn up all around the bay. A black mountain towered above them, and the sun's first rays, red as blood, streamed down on the ice, lighting up the crags on the far side of the harbour. A bugle sounding the advance split the sharp morning air. When the men began to sing "Hold the Fort for We Are Coming," the echoes of their voices bounded across the rocks.

When the column of men moved out into the cold bosom of the lake, the joy did not last long. For the very sun that had greeted them that morning was to prove the worst of enemies. The glare on the ice was bad, even for those who had been issued sunglasses. These men came in with their faces scorched and blistered, sometimes almost beyond recognition. Others made eye-coverings, Indian-fashion, out of strips of birchbark with thin slits cut into them. But others were rendered painfully blind—a red haze blotting out all vision, as if the eyes had been sandpapered. Colonel Otter himself, at the head of his troops, was almost totally blind when End of Track was reached.

Buffeted by piercing winds on one side and blistered by the sun's glare on the other, the troops were strung out for seven miles (11.2 km) across the lake. Marching was all but impossible because the surface was glassy. Then, after ten miles (16 km), the texture changed. Deep cuts, broken blocks of ice, and rocks frozen into the surface began to tear at the feet of the men, especially those who had left home in light shoes. Some threw their kits away, piece by piece. Some collapsed in their tracks. Some became temporarily crazy. One man was ruptured. The baggage sleighs followed behind to pick up the casualties.

The track across the lake was only nine inches (23 cm) wide. If a man slipped off it, he would plunge into snow six to eight feet (1.8 to 2.4 m) deep. The men couldn't stop for a moment for fear of being frozen, even though the sun was burning the skin off their faces.

It was bad enough by day—but the conditions at night were fearful. The men crossed the lake like sleepwalkers in the blackness. The freezing weather, accompanied by a heavy snowstorm with a wild piercing wind, made the march a frightening undertaking. Any man who drifted away from the column knew he faced almost certain death. To prevent that, guards were assigned to ride around to head off the drifters and stragglers. Even the guide appointed to lead the troops lost his way, lengthening the ordeal by several hours.

The cavalry were even worse off. The infantry marched across the ice as far as McKellar's Harbour, where a short piece of line had been laid to Jackfish Bay. But because of the nuisance of loading and unloading horses for such a short distance, the Governor-General's Body Guard decided to ride or walk their steeds the full thirty-five miles (56 km) to Jackfish over the ice of the lake.

After about fifteen miles (24 km), the baggage sleighs turned off to the right to proceed to the track. The cavalry men halted for lunch, drew their horses up in line, adjusted the nosebags, and then, standing in the lee of their mounts, munched on chunks of frozen bread, washed down with lake water drawn from a hole chopped in the ice.

The remainder of the trip was another nightmare. Up to this point, the track had been marked by the passage of sleigh runners. But now the men on horses were on their own. For the next twenty miles (32 km), they faced a vast desert of ice, with snow and drifts everywhere, and no track of any kind. The surface was obscured by a crust under which two or three inches (5 or 7.5 cm) of water lay concealed. Above that crust there was about as much as a foot of light snow. This treacherous surface was broken by equally dangerous patches of glare ice. Through this chill morass, the horses, none of them with hind shoes, slipped, floundered, and struggled for mile after mile.

They were miles from shore in a wilderness of ice and snow-covered islands. It was clear a serious blizzard was about to descend upon them. Denison's idea was to move as swiftly as possible and get to land before the storm hit, but the ice was so bad the entire regiment came to a stop.

At the head of the column rode its commander, Lieutenant-Colonel George Taylor Denison III, a member of the most distinguished military family in Canada, an impressive figure—sabre straight, with bristling moustache and firm features.

Denison quickly realized he was leading his men into a trap. They were miles from shore in a wilderness of ice and snow-covered islands. It was clear a serious blizzard was about to descend upon them. Denison's idea was to move as swiftly as possible and get to land before the storm hit, but the ice was so bad the entire regiment came to a stop. Denison fanned his men out, seeking a route through the ice. When he found one, he rode on ahead with his adjutant, picking their way between the hummocks of land and ice. The first snowflakes were beginning to fall, but by good luck the blizzard held off until eight that evening, when the cavalry finally reached Jackfish.

The York Rangers had an equally uncomfortable adventure. They crossed the same gap in a driving storm of rain and sleet, trudging up to their knees in a gruel of snow and water, in gutters eight inches (20 cm) deep left by the blades of the cutters.

At McKellar's Harbour, the men were forced to wait six hours for the flatcars to come back for them. The temperature dropped, and their soaking wet clothes began to freeze on their backs. They built roaring fires and clustered around them, scorching in front and freezing behind, until the train finally arrived.

These long waits without shelter were among the cruellest experiences on the route to the Northwest. The Queen's Own, for example, endured three of these waits—two hours in a blinding sleet storm when a train broke down at Carleton Place, nine hours in the freezing cold at McKellar's Harbour, and four hours in driving sleet at Winston's Dock. Most of these waiting periods were spent standing up. It was simply too cold and too wet to sit down.

The next gap began at Jackfish Bay. The soldiers, badly sunburned and frostbitten, with their faces masses of blisters and their feet bruised and swollen, were billeted in shanties, freight houses, and empty transport cars. Here was more hot food—blackstrap molasses, pork, potatoes, tea, and hardtack. And then, for the lucky ones, a twenty-seven-mile (43-km) sleigh ride through the wet sleet to Winston's Dock. The rest faced a forced march through the heaped snow.

Now the bone-weary troops, gazing from the rims of the cutters and through the slats of the flatcars, began to see what Van Horne had faced. At Jackfish they could see the gaping mouth of one of the longest tunnels on the road, piercing a solid wall of rock, 150 feet (45-m) high, and stretching on for 500 feet (150 m). For nine miles (14.5 km) on end the roadbed had been blasted from the billion-year-old schists and granites of the Shield—chipped into the sheer surface of the dark cliffs or hacked right through the spiny ridges by means of deep cuts. In some places it seemed as if the whole side of a mountain had been ripped apart by dynamite and hurled into the deep, still waters of the lake.

The voyage between Winston's Dock and Nepigon was again made on rails that had been laid directly over the snow. Here the scenery grew grander. As the cars crawled along, the soldiers began to stand up in the seats to see sights they would never forget—the road torn out of the solid rock for mile after mile, skirting the very edge of the lake, from whose shores the mountains rose up directly. On some of the cars the soldiers produced song-books and began to sing.

Did any of them consider, during these brief moments of relaxation, the high cost of being Canadian? Did any of them pause to question the necessity of shipping them all off on a partly finished railroad on a bleak and friendless land? Did any of them measure the price to be paid in loss of national dignity against the easier passage through the United States? Did any of them think that it could have been accomplished just as quickly, and no more awkwardly and with a lot less physical suffering? But there's no evidence that anyone—soldier, general, politician, or journalist—ever seriously considered that alternative.

There was one final gap to come. For many it would be the most terrible of all. This was a short march over the ice of the lake between Nepigon and Red Rock. It was only ten miles (16 km), but it took some troops as long as six hours to do it.

The 10th Grenadiers started out in the evening into the darkness of the pines and hemlocks, along a trail so narrow that any attempt to move in columns of four had to be scrapped. It was almost impossible to stay on the track. And yet one misstep caused a man to be buried to his neck in deep snow.

They emerged from the woods and onto the ice of the lake—"the worst ice that ever mortal man encountered"—and were met by a pitiless, pelting rain that seemed to drive through the thickest clothing. The rain had softened the track made by the sleighs, covering it with a slush so deep that every step a man took brought him into six inches (15 cm) of icy porridge.

All attempts to preserve distance under such conditions had to be abandoned. The officers and men were forced to link arms to prevent tumbling. To move through the slush they had to raise their knees almost to their waists, as if marking time—a strenuous, exhausting effort because, in effect, they waded the entire distance.

As the rain increased, the lights of Red Rock, beckoning in the distance, winked out behind a wall of water. Now and then a man would tumble exhausted into the slush and lie unnoticed until somebody stumbled over him. One officer counted some forty men lying in the snow in this way, many of them face down, completely played out.

Some actually fell asleep as they marched. Others fell by the wayside and couldn't speak. A member of the York Rangers described one such case: "On the way across one of the boys of the 35th was so fagged out that he laid down on the sleigh and could not move an inch. Captain Thomson asked him to move to one side but not one inch would he stir, so he caught hold of him like bag and baggage, and tossed him to one side to let him pass."

By the time they reached Red Rock, the men were like zombies. They stood in ankle-deep ice water waiting for the trains, not knowing where they were. When the trains arrived, they tumbled into the cars and dropped in their tracks, lying on the floor, twisted on the seats all of a heap, sleeping where they fell.

One man, the son of a British general, crumpled up onto the floor in such a position that his head was under the seat "and no amount of shaking would wake him to improve his situation." There was tea ready for them all but, cold and wet as they were, many did not have the strength to drink it.

The ordeal was at an end. The track, as they well knew, now lay unbroken to their destination at Qu'Appelle. There would be no marching until the coulees of Saskatchewan were reached—time enough to reckon with Dumont's sharpshooters. For the moment, at least, they had no worries, and so, like men already dead, they slept.

CHAPTER NINE

The Eleventh Hour

THE NATIVE PEOPLES OF THE PLAINS MADE THEIR FINAL, FUTILE GESTURE AGAINST THE ONRUSHING TIDAL WAVE OF CIVILIZATION IN THE DEEP COULEES OF THE NORTH SASKATCHEWAN COUNTRY IN MAY AND JUNE. THE IMPETUOUS GABRIEL DUMONT, RESTRAINED ONLY BY A LEADER WHO HAD BECOME INCREASINGLY MYSTICAL AND IRRATIONAL, FINALLY BROKE AWAY AND MET THE MILITIA AT FISH CREEK. HERE THE YOUNG MEN WHO HAD ENDURED THE TRIALS OF THE CANADIAN SHIELD WERE LURED INTO A KIND OF BUFFALO POUND, WHERE DUMONT VOWED TO TREAT THEM EXACTLY AS HE HAD THE THUNDERING HERDS IN THE BRAVE DAYS BEFORE THE RAILWAY.

There his force of 130 Métis, armed for the most part with ancient shotguns and muzzle loaders, held back some 800 trained men under General Middleton, the bumbling and overcautious British Army regular. Then, on May 2 at Cut Knife Hill, Chief Poundmaker and 325 Cree followers emerged victorious against cannon, Gatling gun, and Colonel Otter's 540 troops.

But these were the last contortions of a dying culture. The Canadian government had 8,000 men in the field, transported and supplied by the new railway. The Indians had fewer than 1,000 under arms, and these were neither organized nor, in all cases, enthusiastic. Riel planned his campaign according to the almost daily spiritual visits he believed he received.

The more practical and pugnacious Dumont used his knowledge of the ground, his skill at swift manoeuvre and deception, and his experience in the organization of the great buffalo hunts to fend off superior forces. Perhaps if Riel had given him his head, he might have cut the main CPR line, derailed the trains, and harried the troops for months in a running guerrilla warfare. That would have stopped western settlement for years. But the outcome would have been the same.

In mid-May, Dumont fought his last battle at Batoche. It lasted for four days, until his ammunition ran out. It was remarkable, among other things, for the use of the first and only prairie warship. It also brought Riel's surrender and the flight of Dumont, who subsequently re-enacted the incidents of 1885 in Buffalo Bill's Wild West Show.

The rebellion had wrenched the gaze of settled Canada out to the prairie country and focused it on the railway. Every major newspaper had a war correspondent who travelled with the troops, reporting on their condition and the hardships they faced. But with these dispatches came something else—a new awareness of the land and of the railway's relation to it.

Thanks to Van Horne there were comments on the thoughtfulness and courtesy of their CPR attendants and amazement at the engineering marvels he had worked along the lakeshore. Week after week Canadians were treated to a continuing geography lesson about a land that some had scarcely considered part of the nation. Until 1885, it had been as a foreign country. Now their boys were fighting in it and for it, and soon anyone who wanted to see it could do so for the price of a railway ticket.

The CPR, meanwhile, was teetering on the edge of financial bankruptcy. But as Joseph Henry Pope, the minister of railways, told John A. Macdonald, if the railway went bankrupt, the government could not survive. The mood of the country was beginning to change. Because of the swift action of the railway, the government had a good chance of controlling the Saskatchewan Rebellion and preventing it from spreading.

Finally, after a long debate in Parliament—it lasted for the best part of a month—the bill to relieve the CPR with government loan guarantees was passed. It came on July 10, and not a moment too soon, for the company's credit had reached the breaking point. With a line across the Shield now complete and only a few dozen miles remaining to be filled in in the mountains, the railway was saved at the eleventh hour. It is doubtful if history records another instance of a national enterprise coming so close to ruin and surviving.

Before the end of the year, Riel was dead—hanged at Regina—and Canada was joined by a line of steel from sea to sea.

INDEX

About Fifth House

Fifth House Publishers, a Fitzhenry & Whiteside company, is a proudly western-Canadian press. Our publishing specialty is non-fiction as we believe that every community must possess a positive understanding of its worth and place if it is to remain vital and progressive. Fifth House is committed to "bringing the West to the rest" by publishing approximately twenty books a year about the land and people who make this region unique. Our books are selected for their quality, saleability, and contribution to the understanding of western-Canadian (and Canadian) history, culture, and environment.

Look for the following Fifth House titles at your local bookstore:

The Golden Trail: The Story of the Klondike Rush,
    Pierre Berton
Homemade Fun: Games & Pastimes of the Early Prairies,
    Faye Reineberg Holt
Monarchs of the Fields: The Story of the Combine Harvester,
    Faye Reineberg Holt
The Nor'Westers: The Fight for the Fur Trade,
    Marjorie Wilkins Campbell
Prairie Sentinel: The Story of the Canadian Grain Elevator,
    Brock V. Silversides
The Savage River: Seventy-one Days with Simon Fraser,
    Marjorie Wilkins Campbell
Settling In: First Homes on the Prairies,
    Faye Reineberg Holt
Threshing: The Early Years of Harvesting,
    Faye Reineberg Holt